Coastal management sourcebooks 2

Underwater archaeology and coastal management

In this series:

1. *Coping with beach erosion.*

UNDERWATER ARCHAEOLOGY AND COASTAL MANAGEMENT

Focus on Alexandria

Edited by
Mostafa Hassan Mostafa
Nicolas Grimal
Douglas Nakashima

UNESCO PUBLISHING

The designations employed and the presentation
of the material in this document do not imply the
expression of any opinion whatsoever on
the part of the UNESCO Secretariat concerning
the legal status of any country, territory, city
or area or of their authorities, or concerning the
delimitation of their frontiers or boundaries.
The ideas and opinions expressed are those of the
contributors to this report and do not necessarily
represent the views of the Organization.

Cover photos: Stéphane Compoint/CORBIS SYGMA
Cover design: Jean-Francis Chériez
Layout: Claude Vacheret

ISBN 92-3-103730-7

Published in 2000 by the United Nations Educational,
Scientific and Cultural Organization
7, place de Fontenoy, 75352 Paris 07 SP

Printed by Corlet, Imprimeur, S.A., 14110 Condé-sur-Noireau
N° d'Imprimeur : 44292 - Dépôt légal : avril 2000

Acknowledgements

The Alexandria project brings together a number of cooperating institutions in Egypt. Figuring among the key partners are the University of Alexandria, the Supreme Council of Antiquities (SCA) and the Governorate of Alexandria. Within UNESCO, it involves colleagues in the Cairo Office, and in the Divisions of Cultural Heritage, Water Sciences and Earth Sciences, who collaborate on the Coastal Regions and Small Islands platform.

With respect to the international workshop of which this publication is an outcome, particular recognition is due to the University for its lead role in the organization and hosting of the event, and special thanks are expressed to the workshop's Steering Committee, the University's Department of Oceanography of the Faculty of Sciences, and SCA's Department of Submarine Archaeology. The contribution and assistance of the following entities in Egypt are acknowledged: the Ministry of Tourism, the Egyptian Environmental Affairs Agency, the Italian Embassy in Cairo and Consulate in Alexandria, the French Consulate in Alexandria, the Institut Européen d'Archéologie Sous-marine of the Hilti Foundation, and the Association of Businessmen in Alexandria. Appreciation is also expressed to the Egyptian Permanent Delegation for their steady support.

This volume could not have been produced without the dedicated efforts of many individuals. Special acknowledgement is given to: S. Morcos, for the initial proposal to launch this endeavour, as well as for the constructive ideas and key illustrations that he contributed, and H. Awad, for his major role in preparing the workshop and forging links among people and institutions.

We are grateful to the Library of the Municipality of Rouen, the Regenstein Library of the University of Chicago and the École des Ponts in Paris, for providing photos of the Jondet maps included in Plates 1–3. J. Becton contributed to the scanning and editing of these images under the guidance of N. Tongring. The Supreme Council of Antiquities and the Marine Policy Center of the Woods Hole Oceanographic Institution supported these specific contributions.

Thanks are also due to: the Institut Français d'Archéologie Orientale and the Centre d'Études Alexandrines for their professional advice and assistance; S. Compoint/Corbis Sygma, for providing the underwater images appearing on the cover and in Part 2; and L. Ménanteau, CNRS researcher at the University of Nantes, France, for locating the NASA satellite image appearing on the inside front cover.

Preface

In recent decades, calls for interdisciplinary approaches to contemporary problems have been salient – and often central – in the conclusions of an ever-increasing number of conventions, agreements and workshops. Multi-sectoral from its birth a half-century ago, the United Nations Educational, Scientific and Cultural Organization launched, in 1996, an endeavour entitled Environment and Development in Coastal Regions and in Small Islands (CSI) to serve as a platform for developing intersectoral solutions to the dilemma facing coastal countries.

A poignant problem for societies, of late, is how to go about protecting one of humanity's most valued resources: the world's archaeological patrimony. One reservoir of such treasures – the coastal sea – has been increasingly explored in recent years. The submarine nature of this long-inaccessible reservoir, distinguishing it from the more easily surveyed and exploitable terrestrial heritage, presents unique problems necessitating special approaches. This need is all the more urgent in view of the impacts, on the coasts, of advanced development technology and in particular, the advent and easy availability of modern diving equipment.

The coastal waters of the Mediterranean constitute some of the planet's richest areas in terms of abundance in archaeological relics. In recent years, the city of Alexandria, Egypt, has captured public attention owing to the underwater discoveries of what are believed to be the remains of the Alexandria lighthouse and Cleopatra's palace. To further explore and develop techniques and strategies in pursuit of integrated approaches to coastal management, the University of Alexandria, the Supreme Council of Antiquities and UNESCO co-sponsored an intersectoral workshop in Alexandria (April 1997).

The present volume contains the edited papers from this workshop. It conveys the information, views and analyses of well-known experts from various disciplines who were asked to bring their knowledge and expertise to bear on the wide-ranging considerations at hand. As such, it provides much useful food for thought for coastal managers who are confronted with the task of finding an equitable balance between the preservation of underwater archaeological heritage and the pursuit of sustainable coastal development.

As the second contribution to the UNESCO series entitled *Coastal Management Sourcebooks*, this volume offers further insights into managing and developing coastal regions and small islands in environmentally sound, socially equitable and culturally appropriate ways.

DIRK G. TROOST
Chief, UNESCO-CSI

Table of Contents

Foreword

A lexandria – city of 2,000 years, city of Alexander the Great, Cleopatra, the Ptolomies, Romans, Copts, Arabs, as well as the disembarkment of Napoleon, defeat of the British, departure of King Farouk, nationalization of the Suez Canal, residence of cosmopolitans and the inspiration of artists and writers such as Durell, Kharat, Mostaki, Wanli ... Alexandria – city of the Seventh Wonder of the World, the Lighthouse, city of the Biblioteca Alexandrina, Pompey's Pillar, Roman Theater, Qait Bey Fortress ...

Founded by Alexander the Great in 330 BC, Alexandria extended to six kilometres along the seashore at the time of the Ptolomies and had shrunk to only three kilometres by the time Napoleon arrived in 1798.

In the nineteenth century the small city regained its role and became, under Mohamed Ali, the commercial harbour of Egypt. Mohamed Ali constructed the Mahmoudia Canal that supplied Alexandria with fresh water from the Nile. Abbas Pasha added the railway line between Cairo and Alexandria. Over the last two centuries, Alexandria's limits have expanded to enclose twenty-five kilometres of coastline.

The demographic development of Alexandria along the last two centuries is a phenomenon in itself. Upon the arrival of Napoleon in 1798, Alexandria had only 8,000 inhabitants. Since the time of Mohamed Ali, the city's population has increased by leaps and bounds – reaching 60,000 in 1840; 140,000 in 1848; 270,000 in 1874; 300,000 at the end of the nineteenth century; and today 4.5 million inhabitants crowd the city's streets.

In the last decade, Alexandria has witnessed three major archaeological events:

• The revival of the Alexandria Library, a UNESCO project that was launched by what is known as the Aswan Declaration, attested to by many sovereigns and heads of States, such as Presidents Mubarak and Mitterand. The library will be inaugurated in 2000.

• The investigation of the underwater artefacts in the Eastern Harbour of Alexandria, which started five years ago. Discovered were some three thousand pieces, of which about thirty have been lifted from the water. This area is considered to be one of the most fascinating underwater sites in the world. We are witnessing the uncovering of the monumental ancient Lighthouse of Alexandria.

• The Qabbari catacombs, accidentally found during the construction of a bridge which is to help solve the problem of congested cargo transport out of the harbour area to the Cairo-Alexandria highway. These catacombs are considered the largest of their kind in the Mediterranean region.

With these three important events, it has become obvious that Alexandria is in urgent need of master planning in order to guarantee the preservation of its cultural heritage and to assure, at the same time, its social and economic development.

In order to put Alexandria back on Egypt's cultural and tourist map, efforts are currently being applied towards the preservation of the newly discovered sites, be they underwater or above ground; however, the future trend should be towards achieving a master plan for the city with the twin objectives of preservation and development. This will mean that efforts henceforth can not be narrowly specialized or restricted to one discipline, but must be multi-sectoral. Viable solutions to the problems will require the collaboration of archaeologists, environmentalists, sociologists as well as specialists from a series of other fields of culture, education and the natural and social sciences.

FATHI SALEH
Former Ambassador Extra Plenipotentiary
Permanent Delegate of Egypt to UNESCO

Introduction
Alexandria in an evolving context

Today, with a disproportionately large percentage of the world's population crowded into the narrow strip of land that borders the sea, coastal regions have become arenas of intense competition. Port development competes with seafront housing projects, industrial pollution threatens artisanal fisheries, coastal wetlands are filled in for urban expansion, sand mining accelerates the erosion of tourist beaches and undermines seaside structures ..., these are but a sampling of the everyday conflicts which characterise coastal regions the world over. From this point of view, Alexandria is no exception. During recent decades its population has soared due to a steady rural exodus to this urban centre. Its tourist beaches, favoured destinations for Egyptians in summer, are threatened by the untreated wastewater generated by the ever-increasing urban populace. The pollution problem is further exacerbated by Alexandria's industrial sector, one of Egypt's largest.

But that which sets Alexandria apart from most other coastal cities, is not so much conflicts over contemporary uses of coastal resources, but rather conflicts between the city which is Alexandria today and the city, or more precisely cities, which Alexandria has been in the past. For through the centuries, Alexandria has been home to many illustrious peoples and cultures and they have all left their traces. As Alexandria struggles to renew its urban core, to resolve problems of traffic, to restore housing for a burgeoning population, to put some order into the urban sprawl ..., everywhere it is confronted and confounded by the archaeological remains of its remarkable past.

At the origin of the present volume is a seemingly banal attempt to deal with coastal erosion. The construction of a mere sea wall has triggered passionate debates over how best to manage Alexandria's cultural past in the face of contemporary urban and industrial realities.

CITIES OF ALEXANDRIA IN CONFLICT

Since its construction in the late 15th Century by a Mameluk sultan, the Qait Bey Citadel has guarded the outer arm of Alexandria's Eastern Harbour. Today, it has become an Egyptian landmark of national significance. Over the years, however, the waves of the Mediterranean Sea have continually gnawed at its northeastern perimeter and erosion has become an ever-present threat to the integrity of the site. In the early 1990s, the responsible national authority, the Supreme Council of Antiquities (SCA), decided that remedial measures must be taken to safeguard the Citadel.

Operations began in 1993 and some 180 cement blocks, each weighing several tons, were deposited on the sea floor along the vulnerable northeastern perimeter of the site. These efforts to protect the Citadel from the onslaught of the sea, however, had an unforeseen impact upon another archaeological site of significance. Hidden beneath the waves and partly buried under bottom sediments were the ruins of the Alexandria Lighthouse, one of the seven wonders of the Ancient World. Unwittingly, the cement sea wall was being raised on the vestiges of Alexandria's Pharos.

It was only by chance that a film crew shooting underwater footage discovered that the cement blocks were saving one heritage site at the expense of another. The alarm was rapidly raised and in response to a strong public outcry, the SCA eventually halted the dumping of blocks and launched an evaluation of the underwater site. For this undertaking, the SCA called upon the Institut Français d'Archéologie Orientale (IFAO) and in particular, the skills and knowledge of Dr. Jean-Yves Empereur, Director of the Centre d'Études Alexandrines (CEA).

This survey work underlined the perplexing nature of the present coastal management dilemma. Two important cultural heritage sites are situated side by side. The Qait Bey Citadel is threatened by encroaching coastal erosion. But remedial measures to protect the Citadel have proven detrimental to the adjacent underwater Pharos site. What can be done? Must one site be sacrificed in order to conserve the other? Or can a solution be found which conserves both sites?

INTEGRATED APPROACHES FOR MANAGING COMPLEX COASTAL PROBLEMS

The bio-physical and socio-cultural complexity of coastal environments have brought integrated and intersectoral approaches to managing coastal problems to the fore. Recognizing the multiple facets of the Citadel-Pharos dilemma, the University of Alexandria, the SCA and UNESCO jointly organized an intersectoral workshop on Submarine Archaeology and Coastal Management, which took place in Alexandria from 7–11 April 1997. A comprehensive understanding of the problem was of the essence. Archaeological experts shared their insights on current challenges and methodological innovations in the rapidly-evolving discipline of underwater heritage conservation. Geologists and oceanographers offered their understandings of ocean current patterns, sediment transport, erosion processes and their impacts on coastal archaeological sites. Coastal engineers provided expert advice on alternative measures for mitigating coastal erosion.

But this interdisciplinary array still only addressed part of the many-dimensioned problem. Alexandria's cultural heritage is menaced not only by erosion, but also by the city's heavily polluted coastal waters and the incessant pressures generated by a rapidly-growing metropolis. The dismal condition of coastal waters defaces the underwater archaeological sites, precluding their development for tourism. Furthermore, the heightened acidity of polluted waters augments their corrosive capacity, accelerating erosion of the largely calcareous coastline. Wastewater management must be part of any long-term solution and these and other interventions must be co-ordinated through a comprehensive urban planning

process. In other words, to develop a global understanding of the problem and set into place an integrated management strategy for Alexandria's natural and cultural heritage, one cannot do without an intersectoral group of experts, stakeholders and decision-makers.

BUILDING BLOCKS FOR AN ENVIRONMENTAL, SOCIAL AND CULTURAL MASTER PLAN FOR ALEXANDRIA

This volume brings together the contributions of twenty-seven experts from a wide range of disciplines and fields. While the juxtaposition of these seemingly disparate and unrelated themes and issues is unusual and even somewhat unsettling, recognition of the vital role that each of these contributions has to play is an essential first step towards an integrated and comprehensive solution for Alexandria. Today, Alexandria is rising to the challenge of weaving these multiple strands into a unified vision of the problem and its solutions.

The volume opens in Part 1 with two historical contributions that impress upon the reader the enduring significance of Alexandria as a strategic trade centre in the eastern Mediterranean. M. El-Abbadi provides a rich account of the military, political, economical and even meteorological dynamics that shaped Alexandria's destiny as 'the greatest emporium of the inhabited world'. To continue this saga, H. Tzalas guides the reader through a fascinating series of ancient plans and maps of the two ports of Alexandria. The nine maps reproduced in this volume extend over a period of 400 years.

From history, the theme shifts in Part 2 to archaeology or more specifically the history of underwater archaeological discoveries off Alexandria's shores. S. Morcos provides a personal and passionate account of early archaeological discoveries, including that of Bonaparte's fleet in Abu Qir Bay, Jondet's investigations of Alexandria's ancient Western Harbour, and Abul-Saadat's exceptional archaeological finds in the Eastern Harbour area. The intriguing life story of Kamel Abul-Saadat, Egypt's first and self-made underwater archaeologist, is revealed through the excellent investigative work of H. Halim. These early archaeological campaigns have opened the way for current investigations of the Pharos site under the direction of J.-Y. Empereur, who offers the reader an overview of discoveries made to date. Archaeological findings beneath the waters of Alexandria's Eastern Harbour are reported upon by F. Goddio.

Underwater archaeological sites present unique challenges for cultural heritage interpretation and conservation. Many countries around the Mediterranean basin are struggling to come to terms with this relatively new field. In Part 3, Alexandria's underwater archaeological discoveries are set in the context of the Mediterranean seascape. H. Frost stimulates the reader's imagination with her account of early predecessors to the Pharos lighthouse at Byblos and Ugarit, where stone anchors set at the lighthouse base and fires set on the roof, offered symbolic and material guidance to bring ships to safe anchor. Like Alexandria, other ancient ports have been the object of archaeological investigation. N. Bonacasa reports on findings at the port of Sabratha in Libya, and A. Simossi describes the configuration of the port of Thasos in Greece. D. Kazianis, while providing an inventory of underwater discoveries in Greece, offers insights into the threats posed to underwater cultural heritage by smugglers, fishing and harbour construction, as well as the role of conscientious individuals in reporting underwater discoveries. In a richly-illustrated contribution, E. Felici provides an important inventory of underwater sites along the Italian coast of the Tyrrhenian Sea, including detailed analyses of ancient harbour construction techniques.

Special techniques in archaeological research and conservation are presented in Parts 4 and 5. Remote-sensing is one valuable tool with growing application in archaeological investigation and conservation. F. El-Baz provides an overview of the current state-of-the-art with a focus upon applications in egyptology. H. Carr demonstrates the abilities of side-scan sonar for locating and imaging, with remarkable definition, submerged man-made objects. N. Tongring and N. Driscoll go on to propose how sonar remote-sensing can

be applied in Alexandria's harbours to help resolve some of its persistent archaeological mysteries. But the management of underwater cultural heritage requires not only an appreciation of the diverse nature of underwater sites, and of novel techniques for their discovery and interpretation. The conservation of artefacts found underwater (Part 5) necessitates the development of specialized techniques for *ex situ* preservation, as described by H. Wellman, and even more challenging procedures for *in situ* protection against vandals and pirates, as proposed by I. Negueruela. V. Sommella tackles the thorny, but inevitable challenge of managing the complex data sets generated by submarine archaeological research.

As underwater sites occur below the high tide mark, their legal status requires clarification in order to provide a sound basis for their protection from plundering. In Part 6, V. Négri provides the reader with an assessment of conventions and laws in the Mediterranean region, while L. Prott, from UNESCO's Cultural Heritage Division, examines international instruments that may be effectively brought to bear, in conjunction with national legislation, to protect Alexandria's offshore heritage.

In Part 7, the reader's attention is turned to environmental considerations that must figure in an integrated management plan for the coastal heritage sites of Alexandria. The problem of land-based sources of marine pollution and their impact on offshore archaeological sites is described by Y. Halim and F. Abou Shouk, as well as O. Aboul Dahab. A. El-Gindy assesses ocean current patterns in the Eastern Harbour and Qait Bey areas, and their impacts on the circulation of polluted waters. D. Aelbrecht, J.-M. Menon and E. Peltier present the results of a detailed modelling study of wave propagation and sedimentation in the Qait Bey area, under different wind and wave regimes, as well as with different dispositions of a hypothetical sea wall. Finally, A. Fanos and O. Frihy provide a review of coastal processes influencing shoreline change along Alexandria's shorefront.

The volume closes with the topic of integrated coastal and urban planning in

Part 8. I. El-Bastawissi argues the case for establishing a coastal management plan for Alexandria. V. Mastone presents the management policy established for underwater sites in the Boston (USA) area, from which some lessons learned can be applied to the Alexandria case. To conclude, M. Zaharan presents the existing urban Master Plan for Alexandria which grapples with the many challenging problems of population growth, pollution, housing, cultural heritage protection and tourism development.

STEPS FORWARD

United by their shared concern for the conservation of the Citadel and Pharos sites, the Workshop participants combined their diverse and distinct sets of knowledge, experience and expertise, and provided the Egyptian Authorities with a comprehensive set of recommendations. Currently being translated into action, these recommendations point the way towards a long-term and integrated solution to Alexandria's coastal problems (cf. p. 191).

To initiate and guide this process, several missions of international and national experts have been launched during the period 1997 to 1999. The SCA and UNESCO (in particular its Cairo Office, the Divisions of Cultural Heritage, of Earth Sciences and the Coasts and Small Islands platform) with the support of Électricité de France, jointly organized a mission of international experts from France, Germany and Italy in September 1997, to examine the Qait Bey Citadel site and consult with national experts from the University of Alexandria, the Governorate of Alexandria, the IFAO/CEA and other relevant bodies. The mission identified a course of action whereby measures can be taken to protect the Citadel from erosion, without impinging upon the Pharos underwater site. Actions are now underway to stabilize the Citadel and gradually remove the submerged breakwater that defaces the Pharos site.

In September 1998, a second mission of international experts from Australia and Turkey was sponsored by the SCA and UNESCO. Its mandate focused upon conservation and development options for the underwater archaeological sites of Alexandria. In consultation with relevant national experts and authorities, its was recommended to develop the Qait Bey, and eventually the Eastern Harbour sites as underwater museums and to consider their nomination for World Heritage Status. Water pollution, however, continued to be identified as a major obstacle to the realisation of these goals.

For this reason, UNESCO also drew its International Hydrological Programme (IHP) into the project. Co-operating once more with the SCA, experts missions focusing on the problem of wastewater management were sent to evaluate the situation in Alexandria in December 1998 and January–February 1999. Egyptian and Dutch experts collaborated in the formulation of recommendations that identify steps towards a comprehensive solution to this major problem. Continuing co-operation with The Netherlands has since led to a follow-up mission in November 1999 involving a social scientist and a water engineer, who will bring their findings before an international conference to be held in The Netherlands in 2000 to strengthen intersectoral approaches to water resources management.

As this book goes to print, progress continues to be made towards a strengthened dialogue amongst decision-makers, stakeholders and experts. While their viewpoints and understandings may differ, they nevertheless converge upon a common integrated solution that will allow the city of Alexandria today to live alongside and in accord with its illustrious past.

DOUGLAS NAKASHIMA
UNESCO-CSI

The greatest emporium in the inhabited world

MOSTAFA EL-ABBADI
University of Alexandria

Founded in 332–331 BC, Alexandria was primarily intended to be a new port for Egypt. Up to the time of Alexander the Great (Pella, 356 BC – Babylone, 323 BC), Egypt lacked permanent, suitable harbours on its northern coast, as those landing-places located at the mouth of some branches of the Delta (best known of which were the ones at Canopus and Pelusium) were of a temporary nature. They were at the mercy of the Nile flood and of its annual silt deposits, and every few years they had to be rebuilt where the silt had accumulated. The only permanent harbour that Egypt could boast of on the Mediterranean was the one on the island of Pharos, which had no direct access to the mainland.[1] Alexander, it is true, was no sailor, but he was an extremely shrewd leader who consulted with experts on practical matters with which he was not familiar. He therefore set up a committee to advise him on the choice of an appropriate site for his new city. Among his advisers were: Cleomenes of Naukratis, the prominent businessman and engineer; Deinokrates of Rhodes, the famous civic engineer; Numenius, the stone-mason and his brother Hyponomos.[2] With their expertise and thorough knowledge of the geographical layout as well as of the climatic and marine conditions (namely the western and northern winds and the west-to-east sea current), they wisely chose a site west of the Delta. The obvious suggestion was made, furthermore, to build a causeway (later on known as the Heptastadium) to connect the island of Pharos with the mainland at Rakotis. In this way, two harbours were created at the same time, the main *Portus Magnus* to the east of the

causeway, and that of *Eunostos* to the west. Within the latter, close to the Heptastadium, a structure known as the *Kibotos* (box) was carved out. Reaching south to lake Mariout through a navigable canal, it functioned as a lock to connect the open sea with the lake. In its turn, the lake was connected to the Nile by canals. In this way, an extra harbour was established on the lake-side of Alexandria.[3] Through this complex system of harbours and canals, maritime shipping at Alexandria was linked to the inland waterways of Egypt, thereby greatly increasing the possibilities of transport and trade.

During Alexander's lifetime, several developments took place which confirmed the function of Alexandria as a trade centre. From the very beginning, Alexander instructed his finance minister, Cleomenes of Naukratis, to transfer to it the emporium (trade-centre) of Canopus (present-day Abu Qir).[4] Cleomenes took full advantage of his important position and established a monopoly of international trade in grain throughout the Mediterranean with Alexandria as his base. In addition, he provided the city with a mint as early as 326 BC. Thus the position of Alexandria as an international trading centre was assured.[5] Under the Ptolemies, the city's commercial significance advanced by leaps and bounds and foreign merchants and businessmen began to frequent it in increasing numbers. A papyrus, dated

---

[1] *Hecateus of Abdera, apud Diod.I.31; Eratosthenes, apud Strabo 17.1.19.*
[2] *According to Ps. Call. it was on the advice of Hyponomos that a network of channels and drains running into the sea were constructed. 'Such canals are called Hyponomos after him.'*
[3] *Strabo, 17.1.7.*
[4] *Ps. Arist. Oec. II.33 c.*
[5] M. El-Abbadi, *'Cleomenes'*, Bull. Fac. of Arts, *Alexandria 17 (1964) 65–85 (in Arabic).*

October 258 BC, has preserved a *prostagma* (royal ordinance) of Ptolemy II Philadelphus (308–246 BC, Reign 285–246) establishing control on foreign currency entering the country, which ordained that 'all foreign merchants were required to exchange their gold and silver for new Ptolemaic silver coins, in order to make their purchases in Alexandria and the rest of the country.' Furthermore, in the same document, we find a certain Demetrios, who was in charge of the Alexandrian mint, complaining of the difficulties the mint faced to cope with the exchanges required.[6] It is obvious that the amount of foreign gold and silver brought in exceeded the capacity of the Alexandria mint. This situation reflects the great foreign demand on the supplies of the markets in Alexandria and Egypt around the middle of the third century BC.

During the following (second) century BC, the Ptolemaic dynasty gradually grew weaker and increasingly came under the sway of Rome. Paradoxically, this political development reflected favourably on business life in Alexandria. Names of Alexandrian merchants were found in inscriptions from different parts of the Mediterranean; a fact which testifies to the wide range of their trading activities which took them as far as the northern coast of the Black Sea.[7] Yet their trade had to follow lines favoured by Rome and this can be traced in two different areas: the eastern Mediterranean and the Red Sea.

In the eastern Mediterranean, the island of Rhodes had developed during the fourth and third centuries BC into a powerful commercial state, due to its position at the crossroads of the principal sea routes in that area. It continued to maintain, with Alexandria, strong ties of friendship and mutual commercial interest both under Cleomenes of Naukratis, whose offices in Rhodes played a vital role in the operation of his trade network,[8] as well as under the early Ptolemies in the third century BC.[9] However, this situation changed drastically with the sudden rise of Rome as the dominant Mediterranean power, after her victory over Hannibal in the west in 202 BC. It was then that Rome adopted a policy of expansion and supremacy over the East. In application of this new policy, Rome

looked upon the prosperity of independent Rhodes with disfavour, but not wishing to resort to the use of force against that powerful distant island, Rome launched a policy of economic blockades by inducing other countries to switch their routes and agencies from Rhodes to the nearby poor island of Delos. Under Roman pressure, Alexandrian merchants were accordingly forced to move their depots and agencies and there is ample evidence from the second century BC to testify to the close trade connections between Alexandria and Delos. Significant in this respect is a dedicatory inscription which was set up in Delos by 'the chiefs of the union of Alexandrian merchants.'[10]

A further development occurred in the direction of the Red Sea and the Indian Ocean. With the growing awareness in Rome of the possibilities of an oriental and southern trade in incense, spices, aromatics, precious stones (and later on in silk), Roman businessmen sought to invest more in this line of commerce via Alexandria. Consequently, as accumulating evidence demonstrate, more capital was pumped into its market.

A papyrus[11] of the middle of the second century BC informs us that there was in Alexandria, an international company for the importation of aromata from the 'incense-bearing land', an area south of the Red Sea known in ancient Egypt as Punt (present day Somaliland). It is a maritime loan contract in which twelve names have partially survived representing the different parties to the agreement: a creditor, a banker, five debtors and five guarantors. Among these twelve

---

[6] *P. Cairo Zenon 59021. cf. Cl. Preaux,* Économie Royale des Lagides, *271, n.2.*
[7] *Rev. Et. Gr. 52 (1939) p. 483 no. 235 from Callatis (NW of the Black Sea); B.C.H.5 (1881) p. 461, 1 (Delos); Durrbach, Choix Ins. Delos 108 (127–116 BC). Also cf. P. Roussel, Delos Colonie Athenienne (Paris 1916), pp. 92–3.*
[8] *[Demosthenes] 56. 7 ff.*
[9] *Diod. 20.81,4 ; cf. F. W. Walbank,* Hellenistic World, *Harvard U. Press (1981) p. 101. It was the Rhodians who in 304 BC glorified Ptolemy I as a Saviour God, Soter, Diod. 20.100,4; Paus. 1.8.6. On Amphorae of Rhodes found in Egypt, cf. C.C. Edgar,* Annales des Services. *22 (1922) 6.*
[10] *Durrbach, Choix, 108 (127–116 BC).*
[11] *Sammelbuch 7169.*

persons, we find at least seven different civic affiliations, from Rome, Carthage, Messalia (= Massalia), Elea, Thessalonica and Macedonia. The others bear regular Greek names. It is significant that the one Roman, whose name is Gnaeus, was the banker through whose bank the transaction was managed. Interest in the importation of 'precious stones, frankincense and other magnificent objects' is reported in an inscription dated 130 BC.[12]

Other inscriptions from Delos of the second half of the second century BC, illustrate that Romans and Italians were already firmly established in Alexandria and not in small numbers. In one example, a dedication was made by 'Italians at Alexandria' (Alexandreae Italicei).[13] In another we find Roman ship owners and merchants expressing, in a votive dedication to Apollo, their gratitude on the occasion of the recapture of Alexandria by King Ptolemy Euergetes II (127 BC).[14]

This class of Romans and Italians was not confined to Alexandria, as we find evidence of their presence as far south as the island of Philae (near Aswan). A small group of Latin inscriptions lately discovered on that island attest to this fact.[15] Four names have survived:

a) Gaius Acutius (written in Latin and Greek), who proudly adds 'hoc venit primus' ('came here first')
b) M(arcus) Claudius Varus
c) Sp(urius) Varaeus N(umeri) f(ilius)
d) M(arcus) Ti..trius N(umeri) f(ilius) / Graicanus /Nucrinus
(The first three visitors wrote down the date of their visit according to the Roman calendar [= 26 August 116 BC].

No further information is given about their persons or the purpose of their visit. The fact that Ptolemy VIII had died only a couple of months earlier on 28 June 116 BC, may lead one to suspect a political connection. But the period of less than two months does not allow enough time for the Senate to have reacted, followed by a journey from Rome to Alexandria and from thence up the Nile to Philae. There is no indication whatsoever to suggest that these persons had any specific political or military assignment of any sort. It is more probable, like the other examples above, that they were on a business trip to Egypt, like

'the residents from Italy' in about 59 BC who, according to Diodorus, seem to have been engaged in business transactions.[16]

The date 116 BC of these Latin inscriptions is of special interest because it coincides with an event of global significance, namely the discovery of the monsoon winds in the Indian Ocean by Alexandrian navigators. The story of the discovery was reported by Poseidonius (c.130–51 BC) and later recorded by Strabo (2.33. 4–5). We are told that a shipwrecked Indian sailor was discovered, half-dead, by coast guards on the Red Sea, and was brought to the King. To gain favour, the Indian promised to guide any of the King's navigators on a voyage to India. Eudoxus of Cyzicus, an adventurous Greek seaman employed by Ptolemy VIII for navigation up the Nile, was appointed to that mission. Poseidonius reports two direct journeys to India. The first in 118 BC, guided by the Indian sailor, proved successful when Eudoxus returned with a cargo of aromatics and precious stones. The second, under the sole guidance of Eudoxus, occurred in 116 BC, just after the death of Ptolemy VIII and during the reign of Cleopatra III, his wife and queen.

Our main source for this story is Strabo who is very sceptical about it. He goes so far as to accuse Poesidonius of either inventing it wholly himself or of being over-credulous in accepting it on hearsay. He is particularly suspicious of the role played by the Indian sailor. Nevertheless, modern scholarship has considered the facts of Eudoxus' two voyages seriously.[17] They fit in well with the

[12] Dittenberger, O.G.I.S. 132.
[13] Durrbach, Choix, 107.
[14] Op. cit. 105–6.
[15] A. Roccati, Nuove epigrafi grechi e latine da file, Homage Vermaseren III., pp. 988–96, esp. 994 ff. nos. 5–6 = Année Épigraphique (1977) 838–9; and Supplementum Epigraphicum Graecum, 28, no. 1485.
[16] Diod.1.83, 8–9; for this interpretation of the text see E. van't Dack, 'Les relations entre l'Égypte Ptolemaïque et l'Italie', Egypt and the Hellenistic World, Studia Hellenistica 27 (Louvain 1983) 383–406, esp. 393–6.
[17] J. Thiel, Eudoxus of Cyzucus (Groningen 1966) passim, W. Otto & H. Bengtson, Zur Geschichte des Niederganges des Ptolemäerreiches (München 1938) 1–22.

conditions then prevailing in the Indian Ocean, where Alexandrian merchants controlled sea-borne trade in the Red Sea, Nabataeans and South Arabians controlled overland caravan trade across Arabia. Indian and South Arabian merchants kept strict and complete control of commerce in the Indian Ocean. This delicate balance was maintained and jealously guarded throughout the third and second centuries BC by the South Arabians whose country profited and prospered as the main entrepot centre for the north-south trade. It was in Eudaemon Arabia (Arabia Felix) that Alexandrian merchants could barter their wares with their Indian counterparts as well as purchase equally precious South Arabian goods. This commercial set up is reflected in a statement by Diodorus about the 'prosperous islands near Eudaemon Arabia which were visited by sailors from every port and especially from Potana, the city which Alexander founded on the Indus river.'[18] A more direct description of the situation is found in the late but important text known as 'The Periplus of the Erythraean Sea' by an unknown author. In it we read that 'Eudaemon Arabia (Aden, is meant here) was once before a fully-fledged city, when vessels from India did not go to Egypt and those of Egypt did not dare sail to places further on, but came only this far.'[19] Any attempts by Alexandrian ships to sail beyond Eudaemon Arabia were strongly discouraged; if they did sail, it was by laboriously hugging the coasts and in the words of Periplus, 'sailing round the bays'.[20]

This was the situation until Roman financiers entered the Alexandrian money market towards the middle of the 2nd century BC as demonstrated earlier. The ensuing rise of demand for oriental and southern goods in the Mediterranean markets, whetted the appetite of Alexandrian merchants to increase their share in the north-south trade. They realized that their only chance lay in bypassing the Arabian ports and in breaking directly across the ocean to the rich Indian market. Ptolemy VIII, friend of Rome as was his wife after him, demonstrated personal interest and involvement in the project which indicated the great hopes all parties in Alexandria attached to the success of the venture. The expertise of an Indian pilot with a thorough knowledge of

the secret of the Monsoon winds, would therefore have been very much in demand.

The discovery of the monsoon winds and their use in navigation by Alexandrian sailors, had a very marked effect on the Egyptian scene.[21] Not long after Eudoxus, a new important office was created for the first time in the Egyptian administration, that of 'commander of the Red and Indian Seas', very probably under Ptolemy XII, nicknamed Auletes (80–51 BC).[22] The creation of such an office implies that the utilization of the monsoons led to a marked increase in the regular commercial transactions with India. It is also perhaps not entirely irrelevant that in 55 BC, the Senate decided to send Gabinius at the head of a Roman army to restore Auletes to his throne and remain in Alexandria for the protection of the king against possible future revolts.[23] We can easily detect behind this drastic step, considerable Roman assets at risk in the case of sudden undesirable internal changes in Alexandria. This should warn us against accepting at face value Strabo's often quoted remark that it was only under 'the diligent Roman administration that Egypt's commerce with India and Troglodyte was increased to so great an extent. In earlier times, not so many as twenty vessels would have dared to traverse the Red Sea far enough to get a peep outside the straits (Bab-el-Mandab), but at the present time, even large fleets are dispatched as far as India and the extremities of Aethiopia, from which the most valuable cargoes are brought to Egypt and thence sent forth again to other regions.'[24] This is clearly an overstatement, intended as a

---

[18] Diod. 3.47.9.

[19] L. Casson, ed. The Periplus Maris Erythraei (Princeton 1989) 26. lines 26–32.

[20] Op. cit. 57; also see editor's introd. & comm. p. 71–2.

[21] I hereby ignore the seemingly fictitious character of Hippalus, who was assumed by Periplus (57) to have been a later discoverer of the monsoons; the same assumption was made by Pliny, H.N. 6.26 ; and Cl. Ptol., Geogr. 4.7.41.

[22] Sammelbuch, 8036, Coptos (variously dated 110/109 BC or 74/3 BC; and no. 2264 (78 BC); Inscriptions Philae, 52 (62 BC) {as n. 15}.

[23] Caesar, BC. 3. 110.

[24] Strabo, 17.1.13.

compliment to the new Roman administration, considering that Aelius Gallus, the prefect of Egypt, was Strabo's personal friend at whose house he stayed as a guest for five years (25–20 BC). Strabo's statement stands in sharp contrast to the earlier data of the above mentioned inscriptions and to the more matter-of-fact statement of the later author of the Periplus (c. 40 AD), who rightly perceived that the great change in the modes of navigation and the vast expansion of trade were the direct result of the discovery of the Monsoon winds, at least half a century before Augustus conquered Egypt. Strabo himself witnessed the flourishing state of Alexandria only five years after the Roman conquest, and very shrewdly observed the active trade that went through its several harbours. He says, 'Among the happy advantages of the city, the greatest is the fact that this is the only place in all Aegypt which is by nature well situated with reference to both things, both to commerce by sea, on account of the good

harbours, and to commerce by land, because the river easily conveys and brings together everything into a place so situated, the greatest emporium in the inhabited world.'[25] Admittedly, Egypt's Indian trade continued to flourish more and more in Roman times as the result of other drastic developments. For it is apparent that the same Roman economic interests that had urged Ptolemaic oriental trade to establish direct sea connections with India by circumnavigating Eudaemon Arabia, continued to motivate Augustus' foreign policy in that region. Soon after the annexation of Egypt, the Emperor Augustus (Rome 63 BC – Nole 14 AD) in 26 BC commissioned his prefect in Egypt, Aelius Gallus, to invade southern Arabia by land.[26] This land onslaught caused considerable damage to the Sabaeans as far as Ma'ereb, but did not entirely cripple the commercial activity of the Arabian ports on the ocean. Not satisfied with this result, in AD 1 Augustus launched another devastating attack – this time by sea – which resulted, in the words of Periplus,'in sacking Eudaemon Arabia' which declined into, 'a mere village after having been a fully fledged city (polis)'.[27] Now that Eudaemon Arabia (Aden) was out of action, Alexandrian sailors of the Roman period experienced unrivalled dominance of the sea route to India.

*Figure 1.
Egyptian-Indian
trade routes in
Hellenistic and
Roman times.*

[25] ibid.
[26] Strabo, 16.4.23–4.
[27] Periplus, 26; Pliny, H.N. 6.32, 160 &
12.30,55; Also cf. H. MacAdam, 'Strabo, Pliny and
Ptolemy of Alexandria', in: Arabie Pre-Islamique
(Strasbourg 1989) 289–320.

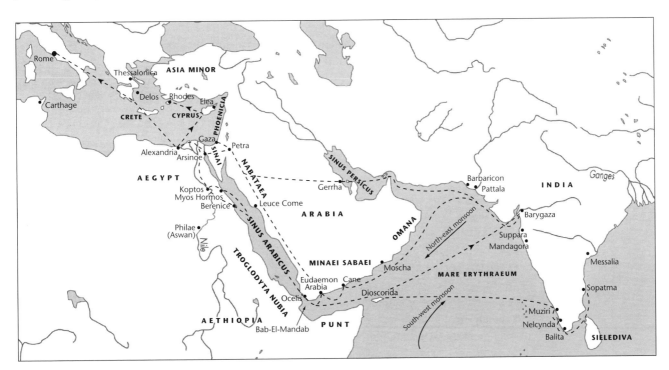

The two ports of Alexandria
Plans and maps from the 14th century to the time of Mohamed Ali

HARRY E. TZALAS
Hellenic Institute for the Preservation
of Nautical Tradition, Athens

Early history of the ports of Alexandria

When referring to the ports of Alexandria we should bear in mind that one or more prehistoric havens existed on Pharos island[1] before the time of Alexander the Great. Râ-Kedet, or Rhakotis as the Greeks called it, was a port known in Homeric times and had maritime contacts with the Phoenicians, the Cretans and the Aegeans. Future underwater research, as well as new evidence from excavations on the mainland, may prove that this port was more important than is usually thought.

It is at this ideal location on the sea lane between East and West that Alexander decided to establish his new capital in 332–331 BC, 'συνδεσμω τινι της ολης γης', as a connecting point of all the earth. The ambitious project carried out by Dinocrates comprised the connection of the island of Pharos to the mainland with a seven-*stadium* [1 stadium ≈ 186 m] dike, the *Heptastadion*, resulting in the creation of two ports. The Eastern, or *Megas Limin*, later called the Old Port, and the Western, or *Eunostos*, the 'Port of Safe Return'. The choice of two ports – which were inter-communicating in antiquity – depending on weather conditions and wind direction, was beneficial and added to the safety of anchorage or berthing.

A monumental lighthouse, the very first structure of this type, attaining a colossal height of over 100 m, was erected at the eastern end of the island of Pharos. It became for many centuries the landmark for Alexandria and its ports.[2] The Pharos remained standing, although in a derelict condition, until the 14th century when it was destroyed by a tremendous earthquake. Some hundred years later, on its site and using its remains, the fortress of Qait Bey was erected.[3] That fortress continued to be called Pharos by travellers of medieval and later times; the smaller fortification at the other end of the Eastern Port on the tip of ancient Cape Lochias was known as the Pharillon. Old maps, plans and charts refer to these names, although sometimes there is a confusion between the two.

The commercial importance of Alexandria and its ports is obvious; one has only to look at an ancient map of the then known world. It stands at a crucial location, linking the three continents on which Alexander was forming his Empire. The ports of Alexandria could also communicate with the rest of Egypt

---

[1] Jondet, G. *Les Ports Antiques de Pharos.* Bulletin de la Société d'Archéologie d'Alexandrie *13. Alexandria (1910) and Les Ports submergés de l'ancienne île de Pharos.* Mémoire de la Société Sultanieh de Géographie d'Égypte. *Institut Français d'Archéologie Orientale du Caire, Cairo (1916).*

[2] *The underwater archaeological survey of the Centre d'Études Alexandrines in the vicinity of the Qait Bey fortress, now in progress under the direction of Dr J.-Y. Empereur, has confirmed beyond any reasonable doubt the location of the Pharos.*

[3] *Circa 1480 is usually given as the date for the construction of Qait Bey fortress, but since the view of Alexandria in the Codex Urbinate of 1472 shows the fortress, it can be assumed that its construction started at the beginning of the 1470s or in the late 1460s.*

through the Nile canal[4]. Besides controlling the Mediterranean trade, Alexandria became an important transhipment centre, since goods arriving from the Far East via the Red Sea could be carried forward by caravan and fluvial transport to Alexandria. From there, cargoes were loaded onto merchantmen destined for the markets of the West.

The ports of Alexandria flourished during the Hellenistic and the Roman periods up to the last decade of the 4th century AD. Notwithstanding the supremacy of Rome and later of Constantinople, Alexandria remained a major trade centre. Certainly the city suffered greatly, as did its ports, from the continual uprisings of the Alexandrians against their Roman rulers. Troubles started with the war of Caesar when the Egyptian fleet was set on fire, damaging the port and numerous buildings, among which, the famous Library. But destruction was even greater in the centuries to follow under Trajan (98 AD), Caracalla (215 AD), Claudius (269 AD), Aurelian (273 AD), and Diocletian (295-296 AD), to mention only the most severe. In fact the decline of the city began with its sacking by Caracalla.

At the end of the reign of the Lagides, as Diodorus states[5], Alexandria had a population of 300,000 citizens. If we bear in mind that only the Greeks were considered to be citizens, then with the addition of the local populations of Jews, Levantines and a multitude of slaves, its population can well be estimated at one million souls, making Alexandria the largest city in the world.

But social unrest was not the only cause of the gradual decline of Alexandria. Natural disasters during the 3rd and 4th centuries AD greatly affected the city and its port installations, as terrible earthquakes often followed by tidal waves and a lowering of the sea level, devastated the region.

During the period that follows, called Late Roman, Christian or Byzantine, Alexandria maintained its relative importance, and its ports received a large number of trading vessels as well as warships. Not a period of peace, the city at the end of the 4th and the beginning of the 5th century was torn by religious dissidence of such violence that buildings were destroyed. Blood often flowed in the streets of Alexandria.

Although greatly exaggerated, the report of Amr Ibn el Ass to the Caliph after taking Alexandria in 641 leaves no doubt that the city was magnificent, extensive, with impressive buildings. It is probably then that the land on both sides of the Heptastadium dike started silting up and two distinct ports were formed.

Under the rule of the Ommeyads of Damascus in 658, and of the Abbasides after 750, Alexandria, although gradually losing its importance, was still a trade centre and the second city of Egypt after Fostat. The shrinking of the city is however obvious and we know that, in response, Ahmed Ibn Touloum decided in 875 to reduce the walled periphery. (The reign of the Fatimides started in 969 AD.)

During the two centuries of the Crusades[6], the ports of Alexandria were often attacked by Christian fleets. The Normans attacked in 1153 and 1155, and Amary, the Latin King of Jerusalem, took the city in 1165, holding it for only 75 days. The Normans landed again at Pharos in 1174. The ports of Alexandria were quite busy during the reign of the Touloumides and the Ayyoubides of Salah-el-Din (868–1171) and retained some of their importance as trading centres, but also as naval bases.

We know that, during the crusades and notwithstanding repeated papal interdictions, trade between the Islamic World and the Christian States continued and Alexandria had its share in the traffic.

There are reports from Christian spies of the 13th and 14th centuries giving information on the fortifications of the town and its ports.[7] They confirmed that the fortifications were strong and that attack would be difficult. In

---

[4] The Kadiga or Kadig of the Arab period.
[5] Diodorus Siculus, Biblioteca Historica XVII, 52, 2. Loeb Classical Library, Vol. 12 (1933–63).
[6] 1095 to 1291.
[7] La Devise des Chemins de Babilone and Rélation d'Orient de Hayton. cf. Étienne Combes. Alexandrie au Moyen Age, Le sac de la ville par Pierre Ier de Lusignan en 1365. Cahiers d'Alexandrie. Alexandria (1964).

fact, the Sultan Baybars, aware of the danger that such attacks presented, had the walls repaired in 1265. That is when Alexandria became a base for the Arab fleet that threatened the Byzantines in the Eastern Mediterranean. In the *Chanson de Roland*[8], Alexandria is mentioned as the base for the Islamic fleet '... de venir le secourir à Saragosse. A Alexandrie où il y a un port sur la mer il a disposé toute sa flotte ...'.

The year 1365 is marked by a catastrophe: the fleet of the Latin King of Cyprus, Pierre I of Lusignan, anchored off Alexandria, attacked and pillaged the town and withdrew after setting the town on fire.[9] A few years later, a disastrous earthquake brought down the remains of the Pharos and transformed the morphology of the coastline by land subsidence and raising the sea level.

Under the Circassian Mameluks (1382–1517) Qait Bey built the fortress[10] that bears his name and which could, at the same time, protect both ports, the Western, which was exclusively reserved to Islamic vessels, and the Old Eastern Port, which was open only to Christian ships.

Figure 1. View of Alexandria in the 15th century, annexed with others to the Codex Urbinate in the Vatican Library; i.e., Codex Latinus de Tolomeo. The Codex was drafted for Ugo Comminelli de Maceriis in 1472.

Plans and maps of Alexandria

In spite of the fact that the Mediterranean Sea at that time was infested with pirate ships – Christian and Islamic – and that the plague of piracy continued until the end of the 19th century, there is a gradual increase in the number of Christian travellers calling at Alexandria on board European vessels. From the middle of the 14th century, the visits of these travellers are documented by their travel diaries, which provide valuable information on the trade and the movement in the ports.

Most of these travellers were pilgrims, merchants, diplomats and scientists, and have left valuable observations as well as a number of maps, plans and illustrations of Alexandria and its ports.

Prior to the view of Alexandria that is depicted in the Codex Urbinate made for Ugo Comminelli in 1472[11] (Fig. 1), all the earlier representations were schematic and do not provide reliable information on the appearance of the town and of its ports.[12]

So the plan of Comminelli is, as far as we know, the very first panoramic depiction we have of the town and its ports. It should however be stressed that all the early plans, although extremely useful for the understanding of the medieval topography of the town, were often much influenced by the artist's imagination. It was also customary to copy previous plans and maps, with additions.

[8] *Étienne Combes*, supra cit.
[9] *Étienne Combes*, supra cit.
[10] *Built probably between 1470 and 1480.*
[11] *Codice Urbinate 277, Biblioteca Vaticana, cf. Gaston Jondet,* Atlas Historique de la Ville et des Ports d'Alexandrie, *pl. I. Société Sultanieh de Géographie d'Égypte, Cairo (1921).*
[12] *The ancient panoramas of Alexandria are very scarce; only the following views are attributable to Alexandria: the sarcophagos of Julius Philosyrius from Ostia, 3rd–4th c. AD, cf. Ch. Picard,* Bulletin de Correspondance Hellénique, *76 (1952), p. 92, fig. 14; a mosaic of the 5th–6th c. AD from Sepphoris; cf.* Biblical Archaeological Review, *vol. 18, no. 6 (1992); and another from Jerash of ca. 530 AD; cf. Ch. Picard,* Bulletin de Correspondance Hellénique, *76. (1952); and perhaps a representation made of* opus sectile *from Kenchreai, near Corinth, 4th c. AD; cf. L. Ibrahim,* Kenchreai Eastern Port of Corinth, *vol. VII, Leiden (1972).*

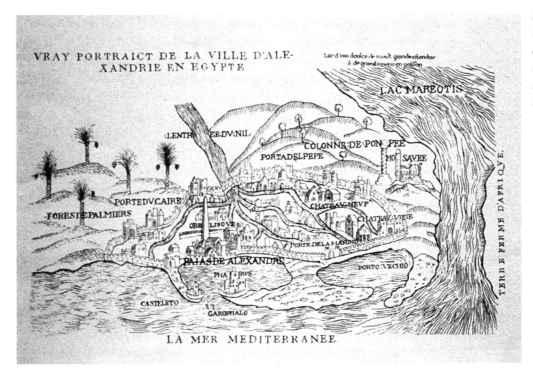

Figure 2. 'Vray portraict de la ville d'Alexandrie en Egypte', 1548. By Pierre Belon du Mans.

There are some 70 plans and charts showing Alexandria and its ports from the mid-14th to the mid-19th century. Most of these early maps are distorted and exaggerated. Some are the result of earlier works by persons who had never set foot on Alexandria's soil. In spite of their inaccuracies, these maps and plans, supplemented by the narratives of travellers, are precious documents that deserve close investigation. They are valuable for the study of Alexandria's old ports and can contribute to a better understanding of its medieval and post-medieval topography and importance.

[13] One in the Vatican Library (Codice Urbinate 277), the other in the Bibliothèque Nationale, Paris.
[14] Pierre Belon du Mans, Les Observations de plusieures singlularitez et choses mémorables, trouvées en Égypte. Paris (1554) and Institut Français d'Archéologie Orientale du Caire. Cairo (1970). Plan in: G. Jondet, supra cit., pl. II.
[15] Abraham Ortelius, Theatrum orbis terrarum, tabulis aliquot novis vitaque auctoris illustratum, Antwerp (1570). In: G. Jondet, Atlas Historique. supra cit., pl. III.
[16] Alexandria. Braun & Hogenburg (1573), British Library Maps, C.7. d.i. (i) No. 56. In: J. Janssoni, Civitates orbis terrarum, Amsterdam (1657). In: G. Jondet, supra cit. pl. V.

We know of two variations of the plan of Alexandria made in 1472 for Ugo Comminelli de Maceriis.[13] Both show the two ports with few differences in the depiction. It should be noted, however, that the fortress at the eastern extremity of the Pharos is differently represented on each of the versions both of which show the newly built Qait Bey fortress. It is also worth noting that a multitude of rocks practically block the entrance to the Eastern Port and that the Pharillon had not yet been built. There is also a strange elongated island with houses in the port itself. The Eunostos has two rocks at its entrance with a tower on a third. The two ports are separated by what is depicted as an isthmus. The city walls and the gates are most impressive.

The 1548 plan by Pierre Belon du Mans[14] (Fig. 2) is the very first 'real portrait of Alexandria', as its title says. The two ports are well delimited. The Western Port is called 'Porto Vechio'; the Eastern Port, with its two facing forts – the 'Pharus' and the 'Casteleto' – is called the Garophalo. This plan has often been copied with minor changes.

The Atlas of Abraham Ortelli[15] of 1570 contains a map of Egypt with a more detailed plan of the wider region of Alexandria showing the town with its two ports.

Figure 3. 'Ancienne Veue d'Alexandrie'. Variation of the Braun-Hogenburg plan from an unidentified French book.

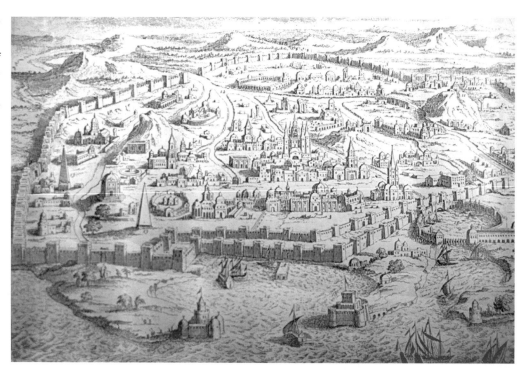

Braun-Hogenburg's map of 1573[16] is the first grand panorama of Alexandria, depicting the city with its extended walls and impressive buildings. We can reasonably suppose that most of these buildings are the result of the artist's imagination.[17] The two ports on this map are interesting notwithstanding the errors and confusions – Pharillon is called Pharus; Qait Bey, Garophalo – which certainly indicates errors in the copying of an earlier map. The Western Port, exclusively allocated to Islamic vessels, shows in fact two such oared ships manoeuvering; the inner part of this port comprises an enclosed area, an arsenal, surrounded by fortified walls and a closed entrance.[18] Vessels of the western type are shown in the Eastern Port. The presence of a variety of eastern and western ships, seventeen in all, of all sizes, makes this plan an interesting document for the study of various types of sea craft of that period. The tower on the top of Kom el Nadoura hill marked as 'Castelle noue' or new castle, is also depicted. This was the lookout and the semaphore tower that regulated the traffic in both ports. It remained in use until the middle of the 20th century.

Braun-Hogenburg's plan is included in the famous Atlas of Jansson.[19] It seems that this work has been the preferred source and, as a result, repeatedly copied, with small or major changes, in the illustrations of various books and atlases. We have counted seven versions used to illustrate Dutch, English,

Figure 4. 'Plan de la ville d'Alexandrie', 1585. By H. von Bretten.

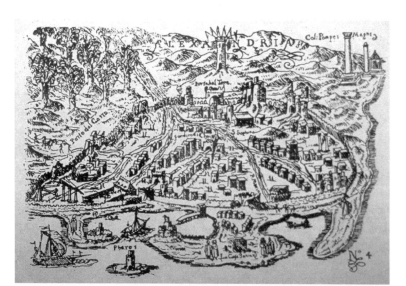

---

[17] *This panorama is a combination of buildings and ruins existing at the time it was drawn and ancient constructions known to have existed in antiquity rendered as imagined by the artist with additions by the successive copyists. See variation in G. Jondet,* supra cit.*, pl. VII.*

[18] *The closed inner port is an invention of the artist in his attempt to represent the ancient port of Kibotos.*

[19] *See note 17.*

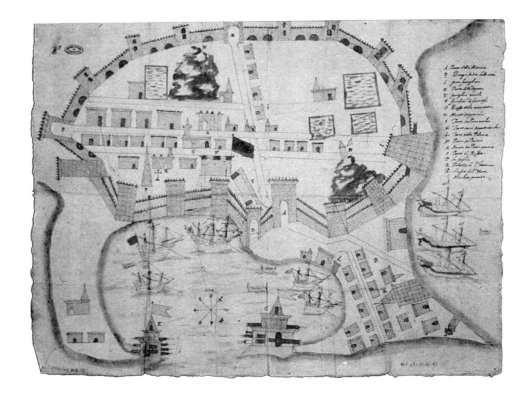

Figure 5. Plan of Alexandria. From the Archivo General de Simancas.

1

ALEXANDRIA IN EARLY TIMES: HISTORICAL PERSPECTIVES

German, French (Fig. 3) and Latin books. It is interesting to see the different types of ships that are shown on these plans as well as the differences introduced by the artists in depicting known monuments, as the Qait Bey fortress, the Pharillon, the Obelisks, the Column of Diocletian.[20]

Heberer von Bretten's plan[21] (Fig. 4), drawn in 1585, shows both ports with a panorama of Alexandria. There is a ship in the Western Port, one approaching the Eastern Port and a third doubling Cape Lochias. Three fortresses are depicted: one is on an islet at the entrance to the Eastern Port, marked Pharos, and the other two are Qait Bey and the Pharillon. The 'Porta Marina' leads to the Eunostos; a wooden wharf is

shown south of Qait Bey. This small jetty is in fact repeatedly depicted on nearly all maps up to the end of the 19th century.

The map attached to the documents E1102-36 and E1103-34 of the Archivo General de Simancas[22] (Fig. 5), made before 1605 by a spy working for the King of the Two Sicilies, is an extremely interesting document. Unpublished to-date, it is presented for the first time. This plan accompanies manuscripts composed of letters exchanged between the Marqués de Santa Cruz and the King proposing the organization of an attack on Alexandria by an armada composed of ships from Christian states aiming at looting the cargo of the 'Caravana', the Turkish fleet, and taking some 2,000 slaves. This attack was never carried out. The importance of this plan lies in the fact that it was made not by an author concerned with the illustration of his book, as so often was the case, but by a spy – perhaps an architect, or an officer in disguise – who was solely concerned with drawing what he saw without any exaggeration, enhancement or embellishment. The plan was to be used for a landing operation or, if necessary, for a bombardment of the town from the ships of the invading armada, so it had to be clear and accurate. The ports are

---

[20] Known as Pompey's pillar.

[21] Voyage en Égypte de M. von Bretten, 1585–1586. Institut Français d'Archéologie Orientale du Caire (1976).

[22] A detailed study and translation from Spanish to French of the manuscripts E1102-36 and E1103-34 of the Archivo General de Simanca has been presented by the author as an appendix to his Mémoire Le Tombeau d'Alexandre le Grand, la légende et les faits historiques at the École des Hautes Études en Sciences Sociales, Paris, and is expected to be published in 1999.

shown with the batteries of the two fortresses closing the entrance of the Eastern Port. Qait Bey fort called 'gran fariglion' and the fort on Cape Lochias marked 'fariglion piccolo' are well drawn. The walls are also carefully shown. There are landmarks for recognition: eventual targets to be gunned, and others, as churches and the 'Fondica de francesi', to be avoided. Three Islamic galleys are shown at anchor, stern to shore, in the Eunostos, while five three-masted and two-masted vessels, as well as three rowing tenders, are anchored in the Eastern Port. Kom el Nadura, marked as 'Monte de guardia', is correctly portrayed.

The text of the missives with the report on the proposed operation gives a good description of the situation of the city and port fortifications. These are described as weak. The main target of the proposed attack was the 'Caravana', the fleet that once a year loaded in Alexandria the wheat to be transported to Constantinople.

The 1665 plan of De Monconys[23] is rather sketchy and shows very basic characteristics of the city, its two ports with the fortresses and the jetty in the vicinity of the 'Porte de la Marine' or 'Porta della Dogana' which must have certainly been adjacent to the customs house. We know that there was taxation of the different goods that were loaded and unloaded in the port.

Figure 6. Panoramic view of Alexandria. By V. Barkij.

In 1687, the French engineer Razaud[24] drew two charts of the ports that can be considered scientific. In 1699, two French pilots, Christian Melchien[25] and Antoine Massy[26], drew two different charts of the two ports giving detailed soundings of the area. It seems that the French had a particular and continued interest in the cartography of the ports of Alexandria during the 17th, 18th and 19th centuries, as is shown by the '*plan et élévations de la rade d'Alexandrie*' made by Marquese de la Garde[27] in 1713. Other charts made by French cartographers[28] followed. This is not surprising, since most of the visitors were French (Table I).

In 1731, the Russian monk Vassili Barkij[29] drew a bird's eye panoramic view of Alexandria and its ports giving important eye-witness details (Fig. 6). The two ports are represented extending on both sides of the old Heptastadion where a densely built new agglomeration has been formed. A large three-masted warship can be seen at anchor in the Eunostos, while a smaller lateen sailing-vessel is manoeuvering. There are also three dinghies and three rowing tenders. In the Eastern Port, a smaller three-mast merchantman is at anchor, while a three-masted lateen sailing vessel is manoeuvering. There are another six different sailing craft entering or leaving port and, along the wharf, six smaller craft are moving. The proportions of the Qait Bey fort relative to the Pharillon on Cape Lochias opposite are well respected.

That same year, the French scholar Bonamy[30] visited Alexandria and drew a map of the city in a first attempt to show how Alexandria was in antiquity and, more precisely, at the time of Strabo.

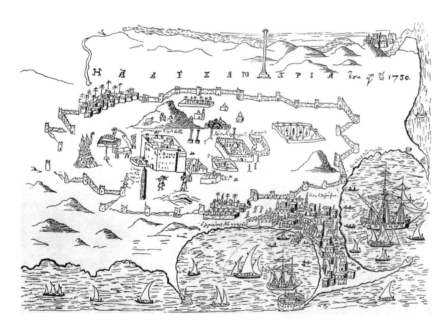

[23] Journal des Voyages de M. de Monconys. *Lyon (1665). In: G. Jondet, supra cit., pl. VI.*
[24] *In: G. Jondet, supra cit., pl. VIII.*
[25] *In: G. Jondet, supra cit., pl. IX.*
[26] *In: G. Jondet, supra cit., pl. X.*
[27] *In: G. Jondet, supra cit., pl. XI.*
[28] *Reference is made to plans and charts reproduced in G. Jondet,* Atlas Historique.
[29] *Voyage de Basile Grigorovitch-Barski-Plaka-Alba, 1723–1747, aux Lieux Saints etc., St. Petersbourg (1778). In: Oleg V. Volkoff,* Voyageurs russes en Égypte. *Institut Français d'Archéologie Orientale du Caire, Cairo (1972), and* La pérégrination de Vassili Barkij. *Société Orthodoxe de Palestine. N. Barzoukov, St. Petersbourg (1885–87).*
[30] *Bonamy,* Description de la ville d'Alexandrie, telle qu'elle étoit au temps de Strabon. *Paris (1731).*

In 1738, the Danish Captain Frederick Norden[31] drew a reliable plan of the 'New Port of Alexandria' with methodical soundings and a general view of the old and the new town with the two ports (Fig. 7).

Both plans were used by the Russian Archemandrite Constandios[32] who visited Alexandria at the end of the 18th century and wrote a book on Ancient and Modern Alexandria in 1803. On these plans, the notes were transliterated into Russian.

Richard Pococke illustrates his *Description of the East*[33] with a plan drawn in 1743. It shows both of Alexandria's ports with soundings and a detailed description of the topography.

The 'Plan d'Alexandrie' of Bourguignon d'Anville[34], drawn in 1766, was used by Bonaparte during his landing at Alexandria in 1798. Soundings are meticulously recorded. A detail worth noting is the rock called 'le Diamant' precisely shown at the north-east tip of Qait Bey. This islet, noted also on other plans and drawings, which could be seen just rising above water level, has today disappeared into the sea. This dramatic change cannot be attributed to a gradual rise in the level of the Mediterranean Sea but must be due to a geological disturbance. Such phenomena periodically occur in the area.

Savary's plan of 1785[35] is mainly based on the work of d'Anville.

In 1795, Allezard drew two charts of the ports, one of which is shown in Figure 8.[36] Pharos and Pharillon are schematically drawn

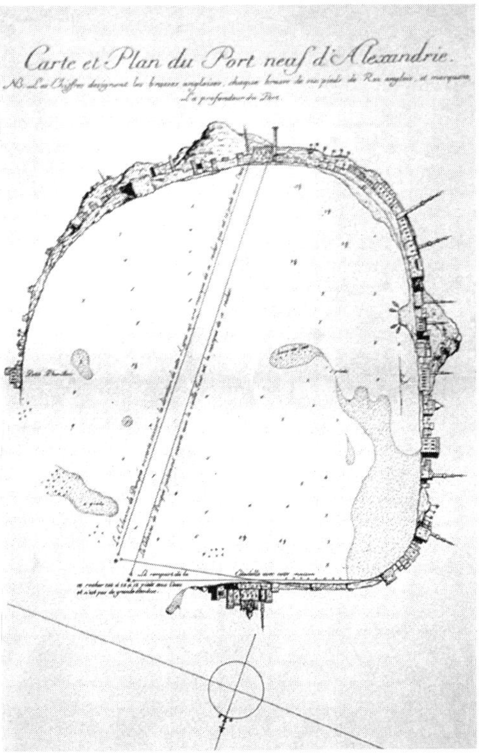

Figure 7.
F. L. Norden's chart of the New Port of Alexandria, 1738.

and the location of the wharf is noted on one of the plans with the mention 'caricator'. That jetty must have existed since medieval times, and until the end of the 19th century was the usual landing and embarkation pier for passengers as well as being the loading and unloading point of the Eastern Port. Large vessels that could not approach in the shallows, remained safely at anchor while their goods and passengers where transhipped on tenders or barges.

Table I. The number of travel writers visiting Alexandria from the mid-7th century to the end of the 18th century, by nationality.

[31] Frederick Norden, Travels in Egypt and Nubia. *London (1757).*

[32] Archémandrite Constandios, Ancient Alexandria *(in Russian and Greek). Moscow (1803).*

[33] Richard Pococke, A Description of the East. *vol. I. Observations on Egypt (1743), plan in G. Jondet, supra cit., pl. XIV.*

[34] J.-B. Bourguignon d'Anville, Mémoire sur l'Égypte ancienne et moderne. *Paris (1766), plan in G. Jondet, supra cit., pl. XV.*

[35] Claude E. Savary, Lettres sur l'Égypte. *Paris (1785) and Paris (1798), plan in G. Jondet, supra cit., pl. XVI.*

[36] In: Nouveau recueil des plans des ports et rades de la Méditerranée par les meilleurs auteurs. *A Gènes, chez Yves Granier, Imprimeur (1838). pl. 65 and 65a. British Library Maps C. 27.b.5 pl. 65-9540352 and C. 27.c.19 pl. 65-9540352.*

TRAVELLERS-AUTHORS VISITING ALEXANDRIA

CENTURY	UNKNOWN	FRENCH	ITALIAN	GERMAN	ENGLISH	DUTCH	SWISS	POLISH	CZECH	SPANISH	SCOTTISH	DANISH	RUSSIAN	AUSTRIAN	LITHUANIAN	TOTAL
VII	1	1														**2**
VIII																**0**
IX		1														**1**
X-XIII																**0**
XIV		2	3	2	1											**8**
XV		2	3	1	1	1										**8**
XVI		9	7	3	1	1		1					1	1		**24**
XVII	2	16	4	3	6	1	1		1	1	1		1	1	1	**39**
XVIII		23	7		5							1	1			**37**
	3	**54**	**24**	**9**	**14**	**3**	**1**	**1**	**1**	**1**	**1**	**1**	**3**	**2**	**1**	**119**

Figure 8.
'Alexandrie,
Barbarie', 1795.
Chart by Allezard.

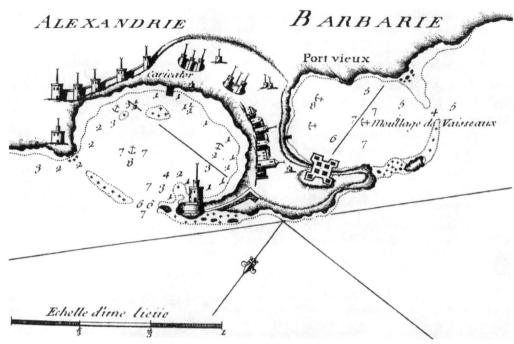

The French Expedition of Bonaparte comprised no less than 122 artists and scholars in various fields who produced the well known monumental work *Description de l'Égypte*.[37] Our knowledge of Alexandria, as of the rest of Egypt, greatly benefited from this detailed and profusely illustrated description of sites and monuments.

The mapping of the ports reveals the increased naval traffic, and the multitude of cartographic documents that follow the French and English presence in Alexandria after 1800 denotes the gradual rise of Alexandria as a commercial centre. Some good charts were made by Captain Thomas Walsh in 1802[38], George Viscount Valentia in 1806[39], as well as by other map-makers.

In the 1830s, Alexandria started developing as a modern city and the importance of its Western Port gradually increased. Maritime traffic boomed. An ever increasing number of vessels unloaded in the Western Port – which Mohamed Ali had opened to ships of all flags – the necessary materials, specialized technicians and labourers for the grandiose urbanization projects of the Khedive. There was a need for proper charts for the navigation in the often treacherous shallows of the Western Port, and British and French captains competed in the production of modern charts. Still today, the charts of the British Admiralty and of the

French Department of Charts are based on these early plans.

The charts of Captain W. H. Smyth in 1833–1843[40], le Capitaine Le Saulnier de Vauhello in 1834[41], Lieutenant-Colonel E. Napier in 1841[42], of the Spanish Admiralty in 1857[43] (based on the work of Masell) and the 'Nouveau projet des travaux du Port' by Linant de Bellefonds[44] in 1869 are only a few of the modern attempts at charting the port of Alexandria and its approaches.

In 1870, the Frenchmen Malaval and Jondet[45] completed a scholarly work *Le Port d'Alexandrie* that included methodical

[37] Description de l'Égypte. *19 vols., Paris (1809–1824);* Monuments of Egypt. *The Napoleonic edition, Princeton (1987) and* Description de l'Égypte. Réimpression des planches des vols. I à IV. *Bibliothèque de l'Image (1993). Plans reproduced in G. Jondet , supra cit., pls. XVII, XVIII, XIX, XX, XXI, XXII, XXIII.*
[38] *G. Jondet, supra cit., pl. XXVII.*
[39] *G. Jondet, supra cit., pl. XXVIII.*
[40] *G. Jondet, supra cit., pl. XXXI.*
[41] *G. Jondet, supra cit., pl. XXXII.*
[42] *G. Jondet, supra cit., pl. XXXIII.*
[43] Plano del Puerto de Alejandría levantado en 1857 bajo la dirección del Commander A. L. Mansell. *Madrid (1869).*
[44] In: *G. Jondet, supra cit., pl. XLI.*
[45] *Malaval et Jondet,* Port d'Alexandrie. *Cairo (1912).*

soundings of the Eastern Port. Gaston Jondet[46], in 1898 and 1911–1915, surveyed the underwater area around the island of Pharos and its ancient submerged ports. Also to be acknowledged is the great importance of the work *Survey of Egypt* and Gaston Jondet's monumental publication *Atlas Historique de la Ville et des Ports d'Alexandrie*[47] which assembles all the plans and maps of Alexandria known to have existed at that time.

During the second half of the 19th century, however, there is also an attempt at cartography related to the topography of Ancient Alexandria and its ports. Archaelogists and historians of the 19th and 20th centuries are greatly indebted to Mahmoud Bey el Falaki who, in 1865–66, drafted two maps of Alexandria and its surroundings (Fig. 9) and, in 1872, published his *Mémoire sur l'Antique Alexandrie, ses Faubourgs et Environs*.[48] Although 130 years have elapsed, many scholars continue to draw upon El Falaki's work.

We can conclude that the maps and plans of Alexandria are closely related to the use of its ports. Since the great majority of western travellers, and merchants in particular, arrived in Alexandria by ship, their presence in the town denoted the traffic in its ports, particularly the Eastern Port which was reserved for Christian vessels.

The activity of Alexandria's ports

An exhaustive study of the commercial activities of the port of Alexandria from the beginning of the Islamic period to modern times has never been attempted. A multitude of data exists and can be found in the diaries of travellers. Such a study would provide a beneficial addition to our knowledge of seafaring and trade in the Mediterranean.

There are indications that allow us to reasonably suppose that the ports of Alexandria never stopped being active, in contrast with numerous other ancient harbours which, in the late antiquity and the Middle Ages, were abandoned. Of the three ancient ports of Piraeus, only Kantharos retained some maritime activity during the Middle Ages, while the renowned Zea and Mounichia were totally forgotten.

There was certainly a gradual decline of Alexandria, starting in late-Roman times and

[46] See note 1.
[47] *Fifty-four plans and charts from 1472 to 1920 with accompanying texts are reproduced in the* Atlas Historique *of Gaston Jondet.*
[48] *Mahmoud Bey el Falaki,* Mémoire sur l'Antique Alexandrie, ses faubourgs et environs. Copenhague (1872) *and in: G. Jondet, supra cit., pls. XXXVI, XXXVII and XXXVIII.*

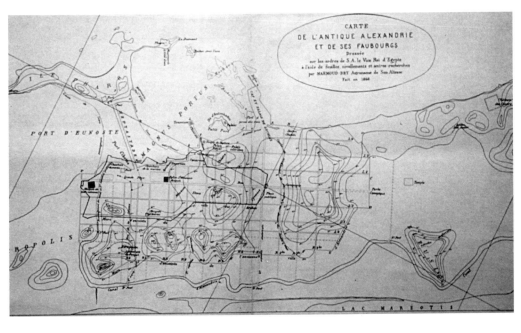

Figure 9. 'Carte de l'Antique Alexandrie et de ses Faubourgs'. By Mahmoud Bey el Falaki.

culminating in the 15th century when the new sea route via the Cape of Good Hope delivered a serious blow to Alexandria's maritime activities. Nevertheless, the traffic of its ports, although greatly diminished, never ceased.

In accordance with Ashtor[49], we may note that, even at its nadir, the Christian vessels continued to use the port of Alexandria. In 1400, twelve vessels were registered as calling at its port: 1 Venetian, 6 Genoese, 2 Catalan, 1 Florentine, 1 Neapolitan, 2 Anconan. In 1401, there were 21 calls, 9 in 1402, 9 the following year, 13 in 1404; in 1405, the number increased to 23; twenty-two years later, in 1427, the number was 12, and in 1435, there were 14 entries (Table II).

It is our belief that the presence of authors of travel accounts provides a good indication of the activity of a port. Accordingly a list has been compiled showing the numbers of such authors who visited Alexandria, arriving or leaving by ship (Table I). There are, of course, limitations as regards this list. The main period of interest is the time between the fall of Alexandria to Amr Ibn el Ass and the arrival of the Bonaparte Expedition.

During the 7th century, two authors briefly mentioned Alexandria, but only one did so during the 9th century. After a gap between the 10th and 13th centuries, there were eight travel accounts for the 14th century, another eight for the following hundred years. During the 16th century, the number increased to twenty-four and, for the 17th century, there is the impressive number of thirty-nine. For the 18th century, there are thirty-seven travel accounts (Table I).

Taking into consideration the fact that we limit this list to European authors, we must assume that it refers to only a very small percentage of those travellers who visited Alexandria. These travel accounts shed light on the traffic of the ports where the coming and going of ships must have been continual.

An indication of trading activity in the ports is provided by the installation of the *fondiques* for the Christians in the centre of the walled town, for the accommodation of travellers and the deposition of their merchandise, as well as the presence of consular authorities for European states and of a customs service.

We may assume that the above-mentioned figures include only a portion of the number of western ships that entered the port of Alexandria, and we may suppose that the number of Islamic vessels coming from the East and from North African ports, calling at the Western Port, was also important.

The revival of the port of Alexandria started between 1818 and 1824. An important factor was the reopening of the Nile canal which, as in ancient times, allowed communication between Alexandria and the towns of the Nile Delta, Cairo and Upper Egypt.

Some figures are worth noting[50]: in 1816, 296 merchant vessels flying the Austrian, English, French, Swedish or Sardinian flag, called at the port of Alexandria. In 1822, this number had more than tripled. There were 900 calls of vessels flying the flags just mentioned, plus others flying the Spanish, Danish, Russian or Dutch flag and 28 ships of unidentified registry. The total annual number increased to 1,012 and 1,290 calls in 1823 and 1824, respectively.[50]

Further research is necessary. It is hoped that studies will be undertaken by the new generation of students at the University of Alexandria, to shed light on the unbroken chain of over two millennia of maritime activity of the most prestigious port of the Mediterranean region.

Table II. The number of Christian vessels registered as calling at Alexandria from 1400 to 1435 AD (L. Ashtor).

	Venice	France	Genoa	Sicily	Catalunia	Florence	Greece	Crete	Cyprus	Malta	Naples	Raguza	Ancona	Rhodes
1400	1		6		2	1					1		2	
1401	3	2	7	2	6			1						
1402	4				2		1	1	1					
1403	3	2			2			1						1
1404	2	3	3	1	1	1			1			1		
1405	1		6	4	8					1				2
1427	3		3	2	1			1	2					
1435	5		3		1			3						1

[49] L. Ashtor, Levant Trade.
[50] Miège, J. L. La Navigation Européenne à Alexandrie 1815–1865. Revue de l'Occident Musulman et de la Méditerranée, 46, 1987–4.

Early discoveries of submarine archaeological sites in Alexandria

SELIM A. MORCOS
Former Professor of Oceanography
University of Alexandria
Former Senior Programme Specialist
UNESCO

The eventful history of ancient Alexandria has left a variety of archaeological remains, some standing on the surface, some buried under the surface or displayed in Alexandria's Graeco-Roman Museum and in other museums of the world. These monuments and buildings were in many instances products of the creative mixture of major civilizations that has characterized the city during its long history. Although immensely valuable, these remains represent only a small fraction of the heritage of a city that occupied such a prominent place in the ancient world.

Yet anyone who is familiar with the circumstances in which the city of Alexandria developed, and with the geography, topography and geological history of the region, will realize that the story of the archaeological exploration of the Alexandrian metropolis is not over. New chapters remain to be written on the basis, too, of the archaeological discoveries being made nearby under the sea. Since the coastal region where Alexandria is situated has subsided since ancient times, many features of the old city and the nearby town of Abu Qir have been lost to the sea.

Archaeologists of Alexandria were aware early enough that a significant part of the ancient city was lost under the sea, but no serious attempt was made by them to explore what lay beneath the sea surface. This is understood in light of the rich unexplored heritage on land and of the primitive state of the tools available for exploring the

underwater environment before World War II. The task was left to haphazard discovery and, in some fortunate cases, to those pioneers who were driven by a great deal of scientific curiosity and enthusiasm.

Furthermore, the history of Alexandria is closely linked to the maritime activity in the Mediterranean and is associated with its impact on trade, politics and economics, as well as its influence on blending the peoples and cultures of the coastal Mediterranean.

At least three major old ports had successively served the maritime transport activity in the region of Alexandria. One of them is probably the oldest documented natural harbour: that at Canopus (near the present Abu Qir) on the eastern side of Alexandria. The second is the ancient harbour of Pharos, discovered below the waters of the present Western Harbour by Jondet between 1911 and 1915. The third is the Eastern Harbour of Alexandria (The Great Harbour) created by Alexander the Great in 332 BC.

Canopus and Abu Qir

The town of Abu Qir lies 22 km east of Alexandria, situated on an ancient site once occupied by three towns: Canopus, Heraclium and Menouthis. The best known of these was Canopus, which stood at the mouth of the Canopic, or westernmost, distributary of the Nile Delta. This was one of the seven distributaries that flowed before the 9th century AD carrying the waters of the Nile to the Mediterranean. Of these seven distributaries, five have since dried up, leaving only the present two branches: Damietta and Rachid.

The significance of Canopus and the Canopic Branch of the Nile in the foreign trade of Egypt is well documented. Before its disappearance, the Canopic distributary was navigable. It received its waters from the Rachid Branch near Menouf and flowed to its mouth on the Mediterranean near the present Madhia, where Lake Edku opens to the sea. Of the seven branches of the Nile, the Canopic Branch was the only one open to navigation by foreign ships. The Greek traveller Herodotus visited Egypt in the 5th century BC and sailed the Canopic Branch up to Necoratis, which he described as the only port authorized to handle the foreign trade of Egypt, and recorded the fact that foreign sailors arriving at other branches were directed to proceed to the Canopic Branch. This branch was frequented by other visitors and writers, such as Strabo, the Greek traveller and geographer. Ptolemy the geographer, who lived in Egypt, described it as the 'Great River', or the 'Great Spirit'. Alexander the Great used the Canopic Branch to reach the site of Alexandria, after navigating the Pelusiac Branch south to Memphis then the Canopic Branch north to Canopus.

The Canopic distributary continued to be the major channel for trade in and out of Egypt, until the 9th century AD, when it ceased to be navigable. What was certainly the oldest port in the country, and perhaps one of the oldest natural harbours in the world, prospered at the mouth of the distributary. Archaeologists disagree as to the exact locations of Canopus, Menouthis and Heraclium, but they agree that these three towns lay in the vicinity of Abu Qir Bay.[1, 2, 3]

Canopus and the surrounding communities constituted a major commercial and religious centre at the time of the arrival of Alexander the Great. From here, he sailed across Lake Mareotis to the town of Rhakotis (the site of Alexandria). A strong rivalry developed between Alexandria and Canopus which ultimately led the rich merchants as well as the markets to move to the new city. Subsequently, Alexandria's prosperity flowed back in the direction of Canopus and Menouthis, nearby. The area prospered, linked to the metropolis by a navigation canal which carried throngs of visitors bound for its temples or in search of entertainment.

It was not long before a number of temples arose, including the Temple of Aphrodite at Abu Qir Point and the Temple of Osiris or Serapis – the remains of which are believed to be among the ruins of Canopus. The first-named of these temples became celebrated for its reputed power to protect seamen from the perils of the sea, while the second acquired fame for its curative powers and thus attracted many pilgrims.

Abu Qir's submarine remains

Breccia[4] gave an account of the excavations which he undertook in the Abu Qir area, referring in several passages to the archaeological remains extending from the shore and disappearing under the waves. He described a number of pools or baths and alluded to the submerged remnants of a massive building that he believed to have had a connection with one of the temples.

Despite this long history of exploration and the wealth of temples, churches and other edifices that have come to light, it appears that the antiquities uncovered to date represent only a small portion of the total. Many of Abu Qir's monuments suffered heavily during the various religious conflicts of the past and, among those surviving, there has been extensive plunder. Some have been used as quarries, providing cut stone for new construction. Considering what has happened to the shoreline of Alexandria, however, it is clear that the whole story of Abu Qir has not yet been told – that the waters are bound to contain innumerable relics, probably in a much better state of preservation than would have been possible if they had been left exposed on the surface, within the reach of irresponsible people.

In 1859, Larouse, an engineer in the Suez Canal Company, discovered that the ancient Canopic distributary extended for a distance of 8 km into the bay below the sea surface.

[1] Favre, J. (1918). Canopus, Menouthis, Aboukir. Société de Publications Égyptiennes, Alexandrie.
[2] El Faham, I. M. (1958). Abu Qir. Cairo (in Arabic).
[3] Habashi, L. and Shoukri, M. (1960). Abu Qir. Alexandria (in Arabic).
[4] Breccia, E. (1914). Alexandrea ad AEgyptum. Municipalité d'Alexandrie, Alexandria, and Istituto Italiano, Bergamo. 319 pp.

This feature, now appearing on hydrographic charts, probably explains the reference in the writings of Pliny to an island at the mouth of the Canopic distributary. Omar Toussoun[5] has argued that this may be a reference to Nelson Island, which lies 11 km out to sea. This discovery and other supporting observations point to the subsidence of the mouth of the Canopic Branch and the surrounding land, and to the consequent disappearance, into the sea, of a significant part of the old buildings of the Abu Qir region. It also explains the difficulty and controversy in identifying the geographical positions of the three main towns of the region.

In the early 1930s, Captain Cull, flying from the British Royal Air Force base at Abu Qir, observed below the waters of the bay a large area of the sea bed covered by remains and statuary. He communicated his observations to Prince Omar Toussoun who, with the assistance of local fishermen, identified two neighbouring areas covered by old remains, including 30 to 40 columns and the foundation of a destroyed building. The Prince's engineers surveyed the area which was located 1,800 m inside the Bay to the east of Borg El-Ramlah.

On 5 May 1933, Omar Toussoun, accompanied by Professors Breccia and Adriani of the Graeco-Roman Museum, watched the Prince's divers who were able to locate a number of marble and red-granite columns in an area of about 5 m deep and to raise some statuary remains, including a larger-than-life head of Alexander the Great made of white marble. The statue, which shows the effect of sea water, is on display in the Graeco-Roman Museum. Toussoun and his engineers explored the Bay of Abu Qir in the summer of 1933 and identified several locations of archaeological importance, which were described in his paper and map presented to the Archaeological Society of Alexandria.[5]

Since 1933, no serious attempt has been made to explore the archaeological wealth of Abu Qir Bay. Kamel Abul-Saadat, diver and archaeologist, made a few attempts, but with little success owing to lack of funds and support at that time. These attempts were reported in the press.

The Battle of the Nile and Bonaparte's fleet

Under Abu Qir Bay's calm waters reposes part of the fleet that carried Napoleon to Egypt. In one of history's most famous naval engagements, the British naval units commanded by Admiral Nelson sank most of Napoleon's flotilla on 1 August 1798. The Battle of the Nile, as it became known, was a crucial turning point in the struggle between Britain and France during the 18th century. Because Napoleon's flagship, *L'Orient*, is thought to have carried the pay of the fleet and army personnel transported to Egypt, location and recovery of the ship would be an attractive salvage operation. Substantial archaeological and other technical benefits would accrue from such an effort – which would also stimulate the tourist industry. Since the battle was well described, the remains of the fleet should not be difficult to locate, inspect and salvage.[6] Some have maintained that something of the shipwrecks can be seen and that their mastheads are visible under water on windless days with a calm sea. In collaboration with the local fishermen, Kamel Abul-Saadat succeeded, in 1965, in identifying three sites of wrecks. Later, he led excavation missions of four divers. Sami Dessouki's report in *Al Ahram* of 19 August 1977 noted that a silver coin bearing the legend 'Ferdinand V, King of Naples', as well as the date '1798' had been recovered.

The institutional support came later when the French lawyer and diver Jacques Dumas obtained the endorsement of the Musée de la Marine in Paris and the French Embassy in Cairo, before receiving the permission of the Egyptian authorities in 1983, to dive and salvage.

[5] Toussoun, O. (1934). Les ruines sous-marines de la Baie d'Abukir. Bulletin de la Société Archéologique d'Alexandrie, 29: 342–354, Pl. XIII–IX, Alexandria.
[6] Morcos, S. A. (1985). Submarine archaeology and its future potential: Alexandria casebook. Chapter 19, pp. 195–212, in: Managing the Ocean. (J. G. Richardson, ed.). Lomond Pub., Inc., Maryland, USA. And: Morcos, S. A. (1993). Alexandria studies in memoriam Daoud Abdu Daoad. Bulletin de la Société Archéologique d'Aléxandrie, 45:199–216. Alexandria.

In June 1983, the French minesweeper, *Vinh Long*, working in close collaboration with the Egyptian Navy, found the site of the disaster of *L'Orient*, 8 km from shore in Abu Qir Bay. The wreckage was strewn over a distance of 150 m, with guns and anchors scattered about. In the autumn, Dumas, working with Abul-Saadat and other Egyptian divers, detected the sites of the 74-gun *Le Guerrier* and the 4-gun frigate *L' Artémise*.

In September 1983, Abul-Saadat and the team of divers were busy salvaging larger items from the sea bottom in Abu Qir Bay. In addition, the group was operating a suction pump with a vacuum-cleaner-like hose along the seafloor, which created an 'air lift' drawing the muddy water covering the wreckage. Dumas spent much of his time with a sieve on board ship, examining and recording the smaller artefacts recovered. So far, no one has recovered the hoard of gold, silver and jewels said to have been seized by Napoleon from the Knights of Malta. A treasure of everyday objects has been found, however – buttons, buckles, wine bottles and kitchen spoons, all preserved in the silt deposited by the Nile nearby. Besides large objects, such as cannons and anchors, a miniature world of the things needed in daily life (coins, cups, pots, pistols and swords) were slowly adding to a reconstruction of living in the late-18th century.

By June 1984, a concerted attempt to search for the French fleet began aboard the small French ship, *Bon Pasteur*, with a 12-man team of French and Egyptian divers concentrating on *L'Orient*. Kamel Abul-Saadat died on 22 June 1984, in the place he loved most: the waters of Alexandria. The encouraging start to the season was marred by the sudden death of this gallant and committed diver and archaeologist.

In the 1984 season, the divers from the Egyptian Navy and the Société Francaise d'Archéologie Sous-Marine (SOFRAS) salvaged many artefacts not only of military or navigational interest, but also items from daily life, which were displayed in a temporary exhibition in Qait Bey Fort in the Eastern Harbour.[7]

The silver coins found there faithfully identify the era. Some bear Louis XV's profile, some, that of Louis XVI, and others carry the 'Union et Force' slogan of the French Revolution and

the dates An II, An IV or An V. Among the most interesting objects recovered from the sea bed were the bits of lead type in Arabic and Latin characters. Napoleon had acquired his Arabic-language press from the Vatican, 'borrowed' by his chief scientist, Gaspard Monge (the mathematician and inventor of descriptive geometry). Bonaparte's declarations to the Egyptian population were disseminated via this Arabic press, the first to be used in Egypt.

Before the start of the 1985 season, Jacques Dumas died on 22 March 1985, while lecturing in Agadir, Morocco. The expedition continued under a new leader, but the initial plan for an ambitious project was scaled down or put on hold after the sudden death of Maître Dumas. These plans included the Egyptian project of building a museum in Abu Qir to house the recovered objects, and of maintaining two laboratories, one for the treatment of metallic finds and the other, of non-metallic finds, which were offered by the public utility Électricité de France. A pledge of support also came from the Institut Français de Recherche pour l'Exploitation de la Mer (IFREMER) and the Regional Council of Provence-Alpes-Côte d'Azur, since *L'Orient* had been built in Toulon (whence Napoleon's fleet had sailed to Egypt) about two centuries earlier.[6]

The ancient harbour of Alexandria

This ancient harbour was brought to the attention of the world by Gaston Jondet, the Chief Engineer of the Department of Ports and Lighthouses, when he discovered massive maritime structures below the sea, during his work on improving and expanding the Western Harbour of Alexandria. His studies from 1911 to 1915 revealed in great detail, the nature of these structures, their distribution, mode of construction, and functions, as well as the topography of the terrain. He gave a preliminary account of his findings in a lecture to the Archaeological Society of Alexandria,

[7] Dumas, J. (1985). *Sous la mer, les canons de Bonaparte.* Geo *(French edition), April 1985, 74:76–88, Paris.*

which was published in the Bulletin of the Society in 1912.[8] His detailed study appeared in 1916 as 'Memoires présentés à l'Institut Égyptien'.[9] This was followed by his historic atlas of the city and harbours of Alexandria, published in Cairo in 1921 by the Geographic Society.[10] Because of the difficult access to these rare publications, I am giving here a summary of Jondet's main findings.

His 1916 study covered three regions: the Ancient Great Western Harbour, Anfouchy Bay, and the western part of Pharos Island at Qait Bey. Of these, we shall discuss only his main discovery of the old Western Harbour. Plates 1, 2 and 3 (see colour fold-out) are reduced copies of the final versions of the large-scale maps by Jondet.[9, 10] Plate 2 shows the modern great breakwater (constructed in 1870–1879) extending from the Lighthouse of Ras El-Tin to the west just south of the Abu Bakar Rock. This solid submerged rock was considered by Jondet as the cornerstone of the Great Ancient Western Harbour. He described the submerged ruins of large structures forming the ancient great breakwater, extending 2,360 m from Abu Bakar Rock to the western edge of Anfouchy Bay, at a depth of 4.5 m, and a distance of 300 m north of the coastline, thus protecting the harbour from the prevailing N and NW winds.

To the west of Ras El-Tin, where the modern breakwater starts, Jondet observed a gap of 200 m free of submerged structures, which he designated as the Entrance of the Ancient Harbour. From the west of the entrance to the Abu Bakar Rock, a distance of 800 m, extends a pier of solid and robust structures which can be observed by standing on the modern breakwater. The ancient harbour is closed to the west by a double pier, 200 m long, which connects with the ancient great breakwater, thus surrounding the rock of Abu Bakar from the west and north, which represented a formidable defence for the ancient harbour.

Most of Jondet's research was carried out between 1911 and 1913, but in 1915 he discovered a line of external submerged ruins, 200 m to the north and parallel to the ancient great breakwater. This interrupted line of structures forms the external breakwater, extending from north of Abu Bakar Rock to

the east at a depth of 6.5 to 8.5 m below the sea surface. The water body between the two breakwaters forms the external basin of the harbour which communicates with the Great Western Harbour by a passage north of Abu Bakar Rock.

Among many details, Jondet described two small harbours: the Harbour Master's private harbour, for him and his staff, which lies east of the entrance of the Ancient Harbour close to the present Ras El-Tin lighthouse. The harbour of commerce, which catered for the trade of Pharos Island, is located about 200 m from the eastern end of the ancient great breakwater.

The immense size of the harbour is amazing, as is the gigantic scale of the structures. The ancient harbour covers 60 hectares; the artificial structures surrounding the harbour are more than 4 km long. Adding the 1.6 km of the Pharos coastline brings the total circumference of the harbour to about 6 km. The width of the harbour varies between 200 and 400 m. These dimensions were almost doubled after the addition of the external basin when the external breakwater was discovered in 1915.

It is not only that the colossal scale of the ancient harbour dwarfs many of our present harbours, but that its layout and the skillful use of the configuration of the sea bottom equals the works of modern harbour engineers.

The bathymetric chart in Plate 2 reveals that the ancient builders constructed the great break water along the crest of a submerged ridge which rises to within 4 m of the surface. Behind this ridge is an elongated depression extending from east to west. Their ability to use a natural depression to create a major artificial harbour that can accommodate a large fleet attests, according to Jondet, to a technical ability and genius of great power to be able to build such a magnificent port.

[8] Jondet, G. (1912). Les ports antiques de Pharos. Bulletin de la Société Archéologique d'Alexandrie, 14:252–266, Alexandria.
[9] Jondet, G. (1916). Les ports submergés de l'ancienne île de Pharos. Mémoires présentés à l'Institut Égyptien, IX:101 pp, planches I–IV, Cairo.
[10] Jondet, G. (1921). Atlas Historique de la Ville et des Ports d'Alexandrie. Mémoires présentés à la Société Sultanieh de Géographie, II. XVII pp, 13 pp, Planches I–L IV, Cairo.

Mode of construction

The mode of construction of various submerged elements was discussed by Jondet. He gave a detailed description of the perfectly preserved 160 m landing quay, which lies at about 1.30 m depth to the east of the entrance of the Ancient Harbour and inside the present harbour. Jondet described and gave details of a cross-section and surface view showing the material used in the construction, after the demolition of part of the pier by one of his helmet-and-hose divers; he noted that the blocks and the quarry stones were obtained from the nearby Mex quarry. At the northern end of the landing quay, there is a breakwater extending 130 m to the west, where it limits the entrance to the ancient harbour. The breakwater, at 2 m below the sea surface, has a different structure. It consists of two parallel walls of about 2 m thickness, with a distance of 8 m between them filled with sand, bringing the total thickness of the pier to about 12.5 m.

Jondet distinguished several sections of the ancient great breakwater; starting from the west, he found the remains of a thick wall at a depth of 4.50 m north of Abu Bakar Rock. This part of the breakwater is 500 m long and was built on the slopes of Abu Bakar. It was perfectly visible at certain points on calm days at a depth of 1.70 m.

Towards the east, the breakwater has no foundations, except at isolated points where the builder doubled the walls to reinforce the resistance to the violent sea. Between the two walls, a large distance, of 40–60 m, was filled by large material to form a robust structure (Fig. 1). This was the general situation in the eastern part; in the central section, however, the ruins were greatly scattered. It took hard work and many attempts at sounding to prove the continuity of the breakwater in this 600-m section. It was by laborious and difficult dredging that Jondet was

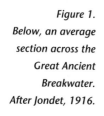

able to find the foundations of the breakwater in this section, and to observe that the remains were placed on a line extending between the two extremities of the breakwater. The relative position of the remains indicates the existence of the two identical walls already found in the eastern section.

The eastern section of the breakwater, extending north of Ras El-Tin to Anfouchy Bay, is the best preserved. The breakwater consists of two parallel sea walls of 8 and 12 m across at the top and a well pronounced external slope augments the thickness at the base. This massive structure is composed of natural blocks of very large dimensions, roughly cut and assembled; the spaces were filled by small quarry stones (Fig. 2). The upper surface of the external sea-wall has a slope of 3 to 4 cm/m towards the sea. Jondet observed along its median line a trench void of masonry. It is one metre wide and its depth is almost half the height of the sea-wall. Jondet surmised that this trench was used to erect defence works.

The sea walls appeared in fractured pieces of different lengths, 10 to 30 m, separated by variable intervals, 0.5 to 2 m. In most cases, the fractured surfaces indicate precise cuts, so that it is possible, according to Jondet, to fit the consecutive parts together. He theorized that the sea wall was fractured as a result of uneven sinking or a small shift in the sea bottom.

Figure 1.
Below, an average section across the Great Ancient Breakwater. After Jondet, 1916.

Figure 2.
Above, upper surface view of the Great Ancient Breakwater. After Jondet, 1916.

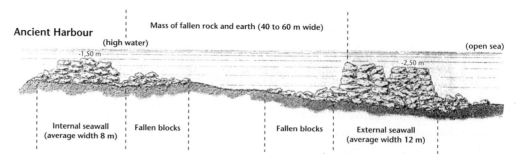

Ancient Harbour

Mass of fallen rock and earth (40 to 60 m wide)

(high water)

(open sea)

-1,50 m

-2,50 m

Internal seawall (average width 8 m)

Fallen blocks

Fallen blocks

External seawall (average width 12 m)

Excitement and scientific debate

Jondet's discovery aroused considerable interest at the time because of the massive size of the submerged masonry and the fact that this was one of the first discoveries in submarine archaeology. The excitement was reflected in scientific journals and the public reaction. The discovery was also highly unexpected. With the exception of a reference by Homer[11] to a port on the Island of Pharos, there were no indications of the existence of this harbour anywhere in antiquity's written record. Jondet was honoured in 1918, when the Geographic Society of Paris selected his 1916 monograph in the Bulletin de l'Institut Égyptien as the winner of the Jules Girard Prize.

Opinions differed regarding the origin of the discovered structures. Some specialists surmised that the breakwaters had been built to protect the coastline in the region of Alexandria[12] during the Graeco-Roman period, whereas others agreed with Jondet that the ruins were those of a seaport dating from Pharaonic times. Jondet attributed this ancient harbour to Ramses II or Ramses III, after comparing the architecture of the submerged structures with the building in the Late Kingdom when large blocks of stones were likewise used in the temples of Karnak and Thebes. Other scholars[13] traced the origin of the ancient harbour to the Old Kingdom, referring to the similarity of the linear pattern of architecture to that of the pyramids in Giza, in addition to many historical arguments. These researchers were suggesting, in fact, that the Alexandria underwater structures were the remains of the oldest known man-made harbour.

Weill[14] argued in a paper published in 1919 in the Bulletin de l'Institut Français d'Archéologie Orientale in Cairo, that the ancient harbour was not built by the Egyptians but by a rich sea power, with a strong fleet and expertise in building maritime works. He maintained that ancient Egypt had fluvial ports such as Peluse, Tanis and Canopus, and that the Egyptian fleet was familiar with the navigational routes and coasts of the Eastern Mediterranean. However, Egypt was not in need of sea ports on the Mediterranean, because of the excellent waterways that provided an established link to the interior of the country. Of course, this did not apply to the Red Sea where Egypt had seaports and maritime activity. Weill attributed the construction of the ancient harbour of Alexandria to the people of Crete who were known for their peaceful sea trade with their Mediterranean neighbours during the Minoan civilization which preceded that of ancient Greece. This theory was supported by several scholars, including Sir Arthur Evans who discovered the palace of King Minos of Knossos in Crete. Although these scholars differed in many details, they did agree that this harbour could not have been built without the co-operation of the reigning pharaoh, possibly Sensuret II (XII dynasty) around 2000 BC.

Jondet revisited

Reading Jondet's monograph is an interesting exercise. He worked with full energy over several years to comprehend fully what he believed to be the ancient harbour of Pharos or the Port of the Pharaoh. This was not his primary job in the service of the Government of Egypt as Director of Ports and Lighthouses. However, he managed to find the time and resources to accomplish his goal. His monograph covered many details and discussed many aspects of a variety of disciplines, such as engineering, cartography, geology, geography, history and classical studies. He gave a fascinating description of a perfect harbour built by a competent harbour engineer very attentive to many details. The perfection is so striking that one wonders whether Jondet had been influenced by his profession as a harbour engineer or by his fascination with the discovered harbour.

---

[11] Homer. Odyssey, Book IV.
[12] Thuile, H. (1922). Commentaires sur l'Atlas de Jondet. Bulletin de la Société Géographique, XI. Cairo.
[13] El-Fakharany, F. (1963). The Old Harbour of Alexandria. Public Lecture Series, University of Alexandria, 1962–63, 38 pp, Alexandria (in Arabic).
[14] Weill, R. (1919). Les Ports Antéhelleniques de la Côte d'Alexandrie et l'Empire Crétois. Bulletin de l'Institut Français d'Archéologie Orientale, 16:37 pp. Cairo.

The methodology used by Jondet was not described in detail. However, it is not difficult to give a brief account of his methods from the information available at various places in his text. He used the naked eye to observe shallow structures when the sea was calm and the water was transparent. He used a glass device (*lunette d'eau*), commonly used in maritime construction to peer below the surface. Once a structure was found, a tachometer was used to survey the depths and elevations, which were plotted on a topographic chart covering more than 4 km showing the exact positions of the submerged structures.

In certain cases, Jondet employed divers to examine the better preserved submerged structures, which were also the better protected from the violent sea, as those found to the south-west of Ras El-Tin. The divers carefully cleared these structures of the sand and vegetation covering them, to scrupulously draw a sketch of the side section. In other cases, Jondet asked his divers to demolish part of the submerged elements so as to be able to study their material and mode of construction. One should remember however that those divers were using the classical heavy diving suit supplied with air by a hose, the scaphander or the helmet-and-hose method which restricted their movement and made work very cumbersome.

Jondet maintained that the principal structures were measured with the best possible precision expected under the conditions prevailing during his research. He stressed, however, that he was not making a typical archaeological excavation, which would require dredging instruments and a team of equipped divers, which were not available to him.

In addition to the above-mentioned topographic studies showing the distribution of submerged structures, Jondet conducted a bathymetric survey showing the depth of the sea floor west of Pharos where most of the submerged structures were found. In fact, Jondet was able to show the complementarity of the distribution of these elements and the bottom relief, by describing the condition of navigability and access to the port of Pharos, as well as the depths of anchorage in what he designated as the mooring grounds.

The work of Jondet was single-handed, based mainly on his own observations and interpretations. It was not team work in which his conclusions were reached through discussion and consultation. He did, however, show his discovery to his contemporary scholars. As an example, Forster[15] thanked Jondet 'for taking me to see his fascinating discovery, the Prehistoric Harbour, and for placing at my disposal his unrivalled collection of Maps and Views'.

Jondet's work, appreciated though it is, should not be the final word in respect of this important discovery. In fact, it is quite amazing that this fascinating harbour has not been investigated since its discovery more than 80 years ago. It is recommended that the University of Alexandria, the Supreme Council of Antiquities, the Navy, the harbour authorities and other institutions of learning in Alexandria join forces and launch an interdisciplinary research programme to re-investigate what lies in their backwaters. The expected results will be far-reaching in shaping our views on this unique harbour and its place in history.

The Eastern Harbour

When Alexander the Great reached the site of the present Alexandria in the year 332 BC, the ancient great Western Harbour had already disappeared under water. The eye of the Macedonian leader was caught by an Egyptian fishing village along the Mediterranean coast known as Raqoda or Rhakotis – just opposite of which lay the small island of Pharos. Alexander ordered his engineers to draw up plans for a city with a great harbour that would include the village and the island within its boundaries (Fig. 3).

Alexander's engineers linked the island to the mainland by a narrow causeway that they named *Heptastadion* because it was seven stadia long (about 1,300 m). This causeway divided the waters of Alexandria into two parts, the Eastern Great Harbour and Western Harbour or Eunostos. The Eastern Harbour was the main port, and the city's palaces, gardens and government buildings were built around it;

---

[15] *Forster, E. M. (1938).* Alexandria: a History and a Guide. *Whitehead Morris Ltd., Alexandria. 218 pp. (First edition, 1922).*

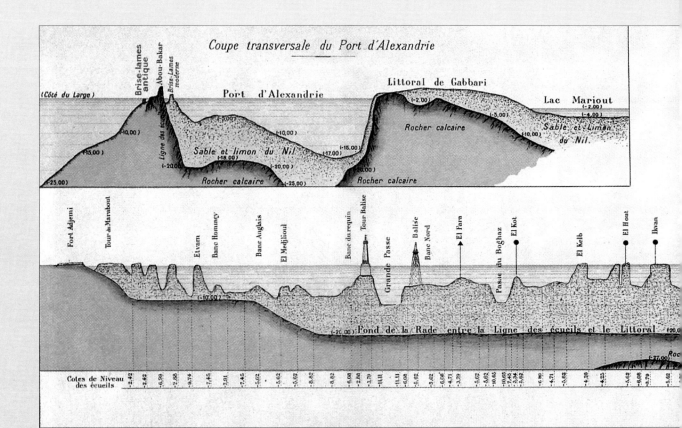

Coupe transversale du Port d'Alexandrie

Plate 3.
Vertical section of limestone 'reefs'
enclosing the roads (greater port area)
of Alexandria.
After Jondet, 1916; Coll. University of
Chicago and École des Ponts, Paris.
Photo edited by J. Becton
Source: N. Tongring

Plate 4.
Original drawing by Kamel Abul-Saadat,
showing the positions of his discoveries
inside and outside the Eastern Harbour.

Plate 1.
Map showing maritime structures found
around ancient Pharos Island.
Coll. University of Chicago, and École
des Ponts, Paris.
Photo edited by J. Becton
Source: N. Tongring

Plate 2.
The submerged Ancient Harbour of
Alexandria (Pharos Island) based on
research between 1911 and 1915.
After Jondet, 1921; Coll. Bibliothèque
municipal de Rouen.
Photo: D.Tragin/C. Lancien.

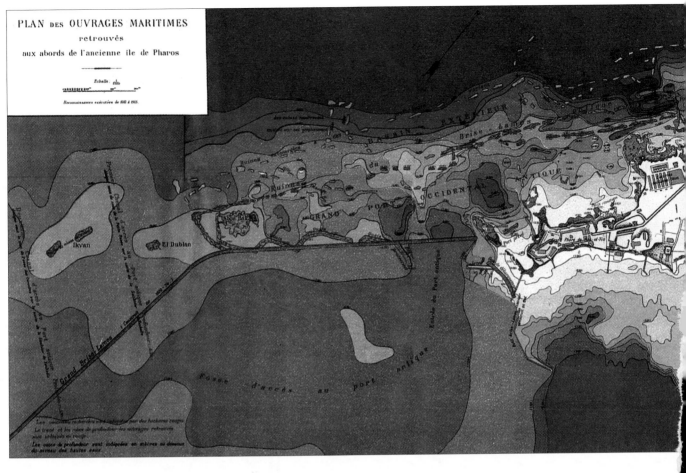

PLAN DES OUVRAGES MARITIMES
retrouvés
aux abords de l'ancienne île de Pharos

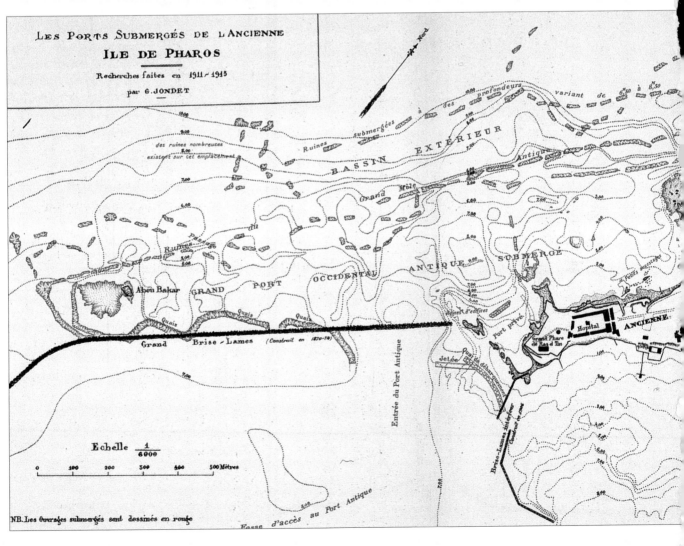

LES PORTS SUBMERGÉS DE L'ANCIENNE
ILE DE PHAROS

Recherches faites en 1911-1915
par G. JONDET

Echelle $\frac{1}{6000}$

NB. Les Ouvrages submergés sont dessinés en rouge

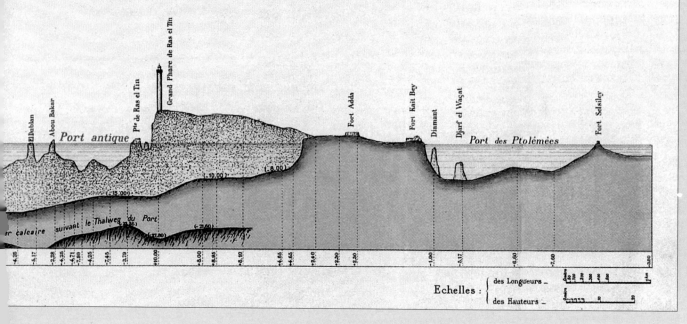

Profil en long des écueils fermant la Rade d'Alexandrie

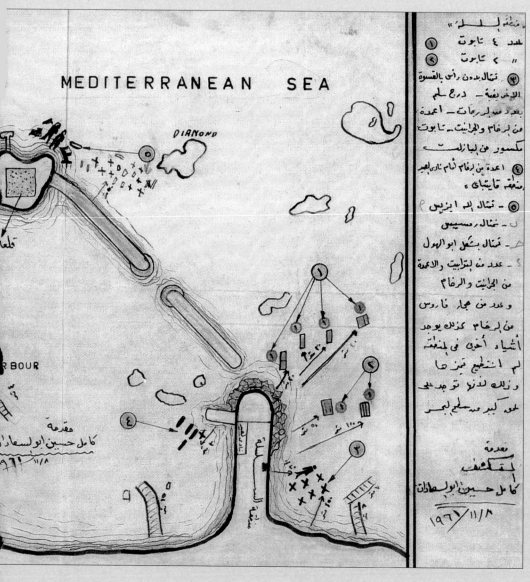

MEDITERRANEAN SEA

DIAMOND

HARBOUR

it handled the more important naval and commercial vessels. These were guided into port by the celebrated Alexandria lighthouse which stood on what is now the site of the Qait Bey Fort. Over the years, owing to a number of factors, the Eastern Harbour gradually declined as a seaport while the importance of the Western Harbour grew: it is the latter that has become the major port of contemporary Alexandria. As the *Heptastadion* became progressively silted up, it lost its original configuration, and Pharos Island became part of the mainland city of Alexandria.

Perhaps the most picturesque description of the Eastern Harbour as it was during the period of Alexandria's prosperity under the Ptolemaic kings is one left by Strabo, a geographer of the 1st century BC. According to Strabo[16], 'On entering the great port, the island and lighthouse of Pharos lie to the right while on the left are seen a cluster of rocks and Cape Lochias, on whose summit a palace stands. As the ship approaches the shore, the palaces behind Cape Lochias astonish one because of the number of dwellings they contain, the variety of constructions, and the extent of their gardens…'

The most important feature of the Eastern Harbour was that it was protected from the east and from the west. To the east, stood Cape Lochias, most of which has been lost to the sea and of which only the El-Silsila promontory remains. To the west, lay the *Heptastadion* and the eastern tip of Pharos Island, upon which the lighthouse of

Alexandria once stood and where Qait Bey Fort now stands. A sea wall extending from Cape Lochias protected the harbour's entrance from the north wind and sea currents.

In the middle of the harbour and towards the south-west, facing the area between the present-day Al-Raml Station and the El-Silsila promontory, lay Antirrhodos Island – probably named after the island of Rhodes. On this isle and on Cape Lochias along the eastern shore of the harbour stood the royal palace, all of which presumably has been submerged beneath the sea as a result of geological subsidence. At the south-eastern corner of the harbour, where Cape Lochias met the shore, there was a small inner marina reserved for the use of the royal household, known as the Royal Port. At a point near today's Al-Raml Station, a tongue of land jutted into the middle of the Eastern Harbour. At the edge of this promontory, Marcus Antonius built the Timonium as a place of meditation and seclusion from the world.

Subsidence and sedimentation

Ever since its foundation, Alexandria has been affected by the two natural processes of siltation and geological subsidence. These

[16] *Strabo.* Geography. *XVII.*

Figure 3. Positions of harbour installations of Ancient Alexandria superimposed on a chart of the present-day city.

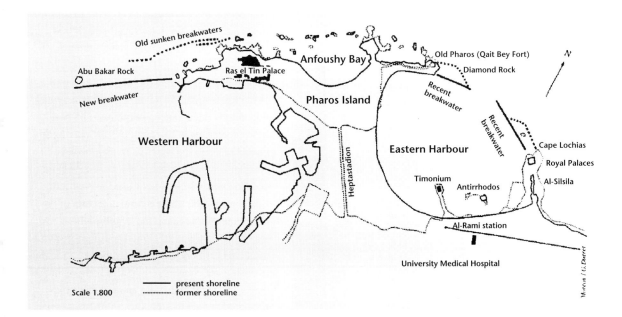

processes have brought extensive changes to the local topography, resulting in the loss of many of the city's ancient monuments. There has been also the accumulation of material from successive periods.

The most striking evidence of the geological subsidence is what happened to Cape Lochias, at the eastern end of the Eastern Harbour, and Antirrhodos Island, at its centre, as well as the submergence of the many structures once standing on the shores of this harbour and its islands. For example, at the time that Gorringe transported one of the two obelisks of the Caesareum Temple in Alexandria (Cleopatra's Needle) to be erected in New York's Central Park in 1879, he reported that there were several columns standing under the waters of the Eastern Harbour. He noted that they were visible on a clear day and that they constituted an obstacle preventing ships from reaching the point ashore where the obelisks stood, whereas we know that, in Roman times, vessels could sail right to the shore. Breccia, a former curator of the Graeco-Roman Museum, maintained that the general outline of Antirrhodos Island and the monuments could be seen on a clear day under the waters of the Eastern Harbour.

There is no doubt that the configuration of the Eastern Harbour is now markedly different from what it was. All that remains of Cape Lochias today is the El-Silsila promontory and, while the entrance to the harbour was very narrow in the past, in the course of time it became so wide that a major breakwater had to be built to protect the piers.

Figure 4. Colossal statue of Goddess Isis from the third century BC (red granite, 7 m long, 25 tons), shown here beside a statue of a man (120 cm long) on the grounds of Pompey's Pillar (Koum El-Shoukafa), before being moved in the late 1980s to its present site in the gardens of the Maritime Museum. Photo: S. Morcos.

Archaeological finds in the Eastern Harbour

In October 1962, a group of navy divers succeeded in raising a massive statue weighing approximately 25 tons from a depth of 8 m behind Qait Bey Fort outside the Eastern Harbour. After examining it and removing the seaweed with which it was covered, Dr. Henry Riad (then Curator of the Graeco-Roman Museum) decided that the object was a statue of the Goddess Isis dating from the 3rd century BC (Fig. 4). The news media were quick to announce the find abroad, and the great size and antiquity of the discovery stirred interest around the world.

In a letter received in reply to a question I had put, Dr. Riad stated, 'I remember that in 1961 Mr Kamel Abu Al-Saadat [Kamel Abul-Saadat], a local amateur diver, came to the Museum and showed me some fragments of antique pottery which he had found under the water. He also indicated two sites where there were similar pieces lying amid great piles of blocks of stone of various shapes.'

'The first of these two sites was in the vicinity of Al-Silsila, a long strip of land constituting the eastern flank of the Eastern Harbour. This area had once been known as Cape Lochias (the royal palaces stood there in Ptolemaic times) and proved to contain oblong sarcophagi, statues and building fragments.'

'The second site was in the vicinity of Fort Quaitbay [Qait Bey Fort] at the Eastern Harbour's western edge. (The fort occupies the place where the lighthouse once stood). Different types of statuary and fragments of crowns and entire buildings lay submerged at this site outside the harbour.'

'In 1962, frogmen from the Egyptian navy had begun to bring up such antiquities. The best time of year for such operations is September-October, when the sea is calm and the water clear. A red granite statue of a man in standing position was successfully raised from the Al-Silsila area. The statue's head and parts of its legs were missing, and the length of the surviving part was 120 cm. The figure wore a toga-like garment, draped over the left shoulder, exposing the chest, the right arm hanging at the side. (The right hand held an unidentifiable object.) The fact that the back of the statue was flat indicated that it had been placed against the wall of a building. The artefact dated from Roman times and was still in good condition – even though it had been immersed in salt water for more than 1,500 years.'

'The frogmen also retrieved a large statue, broken into two parts, from the sea bed at the fort, and also made of red granite. It lacked parts of its legs but was seven meters long and weighed roughly 25 tons. The monument represented a woman standing with her left foot forwards and her arms at her side. The eye sockets were empty, but unquestionably they once held appropriately coloured stones (as was usual in ancient Egyptian art), and traces of the sacred snake were visible on her forehead. The statue had a supporting column at its back. All this shows that the sculptor had been heavily influenced by the cannons of ancient Egyptian art.'

'The lady wore, however, a Greek gown with a knot tied between her breasts; in Graeco-Roman times, this knot was associated with, specifically, the Goddess Isis. This deity was also depicted with plaited hair hanging in symmetrical strands down both sides of her head. It is thus very likely that this statue does indeed represent Isis and that it dates from the third century BC'.[17]

Kamel Abul-Saadat's contribution

In 1964, I gave a lecture to the Archaeological Society of Alexandria on the submarine archaeological discoveries in the Mediterranean Sea.[18] At the end of my talk, Kamel Abul-Saadat presented himself. I gradually came to know him as a model citizen who was let down by his society. He gave me copies of his letters to the authorities and the press at that time (1963–1964), which describe his state of mind at this time in his life, as presented by Miss Hala Halim in the present volume.[19] He lacked recognition of his work as well as the moral and material support to pursue his research. Believing in the potential of submarine archaeology in Alexandria, and in his capability, I embarked on three fronts: to speak in his favour to the scientific community and authorities; write to the leading submarine

archaelogists abroad and to UNESCO; and encourage him to write on, and make illustrations and maps of, his findings.

In summer 1965, I met in London Miss Joan du Plat Taylor, Professor of Archaeology at London University and Miss Honor Frost to raise interest in and support for the exploration of the potential of underwater archaeology in Alexandria. My letters to the specialists and concerned organizations received a good response and encouragement.

In his letter of 29 December 1966[20], S. Abdul Hak, Head of Museum and Monuments Division, UNESCO, replied, 'We are in agreement with your suggestion ... that action will be developed and expanded more especially in submarine archaeology, under the Participation Programme in the activities of Member States'. He added that, 'the Delegation of the United Arab Republic to the General Conference presented a request for assistance ... to organize an international expert meeting in Alexandria during next biennium 1967–1968, to study the problem of submarine archaeology in the Mediterranean and the problem raised by the ancient submerged harbour of Alexandria.'

'Now we are studying this request carefully and will make a favorable recommendation. However, we need supplementary information on the problems involved', he concluded.

I responded to his request for more information in February 1967, but the outbreak of the 1967 War put the matter on hold. It was not until autumn 1968, when the UNESCO mission, composed of Ms. Honor Frost, from London, and Vladimir Nesteroff, the geologist, from the University of Paris, finally came. During six dives in October-November 1968, Frost and

---

[17] See also: Riad, H. (1964). Récentes Découvertes à Alexandrie. Conférence de la Société Archéologique d'Alexandrie, 7 pp., Alexandria.

[18] Morcos, S. A. (1968). Submarine Archaeological Discoveries in the Mediterranean Sea, Archaeological and Historical Studies, Alexandria Archaeological Society, I:39 pp., Alexandria (in Arabic).

[19] Halim, H. (in this volume). Recuperating an Alexandrian pioneer in submarine archaeology: Kamel Abul-Saadat.

[20] Abdul Hak, S., UNESCO (personal communication). Letter of 29 December 1966.

Abul-Saadat examined the salient finds in an area of some 180 sq. m with direct measurement. In her report to UNESCO, Frost[21] confirmed what we have believed all along[17, 22], that the ruins described are not only of great historic importance; they were also likely to arouse popular, international interest because they represent a part of Pharos, the Seventh Wonder of the Ancient World. The UNESCO mission came at a difficult time for Egypt: the aftermath of the 1967 War. I recall a meeting at my home with Frost, Abul-Saadat, Dr. Zaki Iskander, Director, and Amir Abul-Wafa, Engineer, of the Antiquity Department, to discuss the mission's work, future plans and recommendations to UNESCO. We soon realized the depth of the problem in such a gloomy and discouraging situation. In fact, the coastal area of Alexandria had become a military zone, out of bounds for diving and archaeological exploration. Only Abul-Saadat, because he had the confidence of the military, was occasionally allowed to dive, sometimes at great risk to his life. For more than ten years, activities ceased, but correspondence continued between myself in UNESCO, Paris, Abul-Saadat, in Alexandria, Honor Frost and Sami Dessouki, in London. The latter was *Al-Ahram*'s correspondent who had covered Abul-Saadat's discoveries in the 1960s, now editor and consultant with 'Lloyd's List' known for its wide interest in marine affairs. The objective was to raise interest in launching an international initiative to explore and salvage the Pharos. The three of them visited me in UNESCO, to drum up support for the project. Abul-Saadat's visit to Paris was his only travel to Europe.

In her letter of May 1984[23], Honor Frost described that period: 'It has been the deepest disappointment for me to have been unable to help survey the area. It would have been easy', she continued, 'to raise international support for such a project, from both the archaeological world and the press.'

The field work came to a halt, but Abul-Saadat, with my encouragement, set to the task of recording his findings. One should realize that he had not the background nor the capability of Omar Toussoun or Gaston Jondet who managed to publish their findings

in a scholarly way. However, he managed, with some assistance, to come up with some interesting maps of the Eastern Harbour with the approximate locations of his findings. One of them is worth publishing here (see Plate 4). In addition, Kamel Abul-Saadat made me a list of 18 items scattered on the sea floor between Qait Bey Fort and Diamond Rock, a distance of 130 m. Starting from the position of the Isis statue, which was salvaged from the bottom, he gave a sketch showing the approximate distance between each item and the next. He further drew sketches of each item. These items appear also among the 22 items reported to UNESCO by Frost[21], and the 19 items described in detail by her, later.[24] In 1969, she wrote, giving credit to Abul-Saadat, 'Our object in November 1968 was not to search the site for new finds, but rather to examine the site for those already reported by Mr. Kamel Abu El-Saadat [Kamel Abul-Saadat], and to assess their importance in relation to possible excavation. Nevertheless, the crown of Isis Hathor is an important addition to what was already known.'

The charts of Abul-Saadat (and eventually those of Honor Frost in her report to UNESCO) are now overtaken by the present more precise work of Jean-Yves Empereur and his group since 1994, as well as the more recent work of Franck Goddio. However, the drawings made by Abul-Saadat, upon my advice, are of special interest, since they represent some of the objects found by him since 1961. Figure 5 is an unpublished drawing by Abul-Saadat of a colossal statue 7 m tall. Frost[24] gave a description of a female pillar-statue and a male pillar-statue, not counting the female pillar-statue of 'Isis' already raised in 1962. Empereur[25], again in 1994, found the trunk of

[21] Frost, H. (unpublished manuscript). Report and recommendations on the submerged architecture and statues at the site of the ancient Pharos, Fort Kait Bay, Alexandria. UNESCO Report, 1969. Paris. 10 pp.
[22] Morcos, S. A. (1965). Sunken Civilizations, the Story of Submarine Archaeological Discoveries. Cairo, Dar-el-Maaref. 162 pp. (in Arabic).
[23] Frost, H. (personal communication). Letter of 16 May 1984.
[24] Frost, H. (1977). The Pharos site, Alexandria, Egypt. Nautical Archaeology, 41:126–130.

a colossal statue of a man 4.50 m from the neck to the knees. This statue (Fig. 6), which was raised in 1995, compared favorably in size with the statue of Isis, which measures 7 m from the top of the head to the knees. Empereur also confirmed the presence of four large square bases (plinths), each 2.30 m high, which brings the height of the statue to approximately 13 m. Empereur believes the four bases indicate two Ptolemaic royal couples, since their form belongs to that of the Hellenistic era. Three of the statues have been found. Only the fourth is missing, which may suggest that it was buried under the modern cement blocks which were recently dumped in the area to protect Qait Bey Fort. The drawing by Abul-Saadat (Fig. 5) may, in a complete form, represent the huge male statue brought up in 1995 (Fig. 6), before its feet were lost under the cement blocks. Professor Jean-Yves Empereur supports this interpretation[26]. However, Abul-Saadat presented that to me as a female statue. He found it in 1961, but not during the visit of Frost in 1968. According to Abul-Saadat, it

[25] Empereur, J.-Y. (1995). Alexandrie (Égypte), les fouilles sous-marines. Bulletin de Correspondance Hellénique, 119:756–760. Athens.
[26] Empereur, J.-Y. (pers. comm.). Meeting in Centre d'Études Alexandrines (CEA), August 1997.

might have been covered by sand. Was this the missing fourth statue (of a male) which appeared to Abul-Saadat as a female statue in the turbid waters of the Eastern Harbour? Furthermore, the theory of the two royal couples will exclude the identification of the female statue hauled up in 1962 as being that of the Goddess Isis. This is an old question, since the discovery of the statue. Riad[17] in a lecture in YMCA, Alexandria in October 1964, raised the same question 'Is there a controversy about the statue: Does it really represent Isis? or can it be a Queen represented in the form of Isis? This is possible ...'. Advancing a number of arguments that the statue is Egyptian, he maintained that the statue is that of Isis 'until proof to the contrary' emerges.

Finally, I wish to conclude by quoting the tribute of Honor Frost to Kamel Abul-Saadat, who '... found colossal statuary, possibly from the original Pharos, one of the Seven Wonders of the Ancient World. In addition M. Kamel Saadat found the remains of submerged buildings that may represent the lost palace of Alexander and the Ptolemy (supposedly the final resting place of the glass sarcophagus containing the body of Alexander the Great). Thus, he has presented archaeologists with the potential locations of two of the most sensational sites in the Mediterranean.'

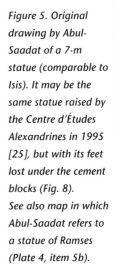

Figure 5. Original drawing by Abul-Saadat of a 7-m statue (comparable to Isis). It may be the same statue raised by the Centre d'Études Alexandrines in 1995 [25], but with its feet lost under the cement blocks (Fig. 8). See also map in which Abul-Saadat refers to a statue of Ramses (Plate 4, item 5b).

Figure 6. Colossal statue of a Ptolemy represented as a pharaoh (in Aswan granite); the trunk was found in 1994 [25] and raised in 1995; the head was found later. Here, it is shown at an exhibition "La Gloire d'Alexandrie" at the Petit Palais in Paris, May-July 1998. Photo: S. Morcos.

Kamel Abul-Saadat: a pioneer in Alexandrian underwater archaeology

HALA HALIM

The underwater archaeological work done by Kamel Hussein Abul-Saadat (1933–1984), the late Alexandrian diver, is in many respects singular. Abul-Saadat's investigations of submerged sites were a self-motivated, self-financed, single-handed endeavour. Amateur though it was, this endeavour is all the more significant for having taken place at a time when the authorities had neither the equipment, the expertise nor even the interest to deal with underwater archaeology. This brief sketch of Abul-Saadat's contribution is, therefore, also a reading in the socio-cultural and political factors that dictated the parameters of what could and what could not be done in the period when Abul-Saadat did most of his work – from the 1960s to the early 1980s (he died in 1984). Given that most of the sites Abul-Saadat discovered and explored have been, since then, scientifically surveyed, and in some cases excavated, this paper also attempts to set his work in the context of subsequent campaigns.[1]

Nothing about Abul-Saadat's background and education would have indicated his later passion for underwater archaeology. Born in 1933 to Alexandrian parents, Abul-Saadat spent the early years of his life in Cairo where his father held a clerical post in parliament. When his parents divorced, he moved back to Alexandria with his mother who later remarried. He eventually dropped out of school before obtaining his high-school certificate and started working with a customs depot company in the Alexandria harbour, where he was to remain for the rest of his life – apart from a period in the 1950s when he worked in the south of Sudan.[2]

From a very early stage, Abul-Saadat's hobbies were diving and spear-fishing and it was out of these hobbies that his fascination with submerged antiquities developed. It was while fishing in Silsila in 1960 that he came across sherds of pottery that reminded him of pieces he had seen at the Graeco-Roman Museum, as he explains in an interview with *La Réforme Illustrée du Dimanche* (28 May, 1961). And 'from that day', he says, 'my friends would go fishing while I made for the sea-bed which I combed from Ibrahimia to Chatby, and if by chance I came across a fish, well then I'd catch it'.[3]

In Alexandrian homes where there is a diver in the family, salt-encrusted amphorae and sherds of pottery are not uncommon. Few refrain from appropriating whatever portable pieces they find and fewer still go as far as reporting their finds to the antiquities authorities, as Abul-Saadat did. Nor is this standard behaviour for a man who lived just above the poverty line. His spear-fishing

[1] I would like to express my deep gratitude to Kamel Abul-Saadat's half-sister and half-brother Leila and Ezzat Mohamed Sadeq, who were most generous with their time and recollections, and put at my disposal Abul-Saadat's papers, including his correspondence and press clippings about his work. Many thanks are also due to Ms Honor Frost and Professor Selim Morcos for the moral support I received from both and all the material they furnished me with. I am also grateful to Mr Ibrahim Darwish, head of the Underwater Archaeology Department of the Supreme Council of Antiquities (SCA), for allowing me to consult the SCA's files on Abul-Saadat. Both Mr Sameh Ramses of the SCA and Captain Mohsen El-Gohari, a friend of Abul-Saadat's, offered valuable insights. A version of this article was published in the Al-Ahram Weekly *(1–7, 1997), issue no. 323, Features page.*
[2] Sadeq, Ezzat M. Pers. interviews. March 1997.
[3] See report by Sami Dessouki, Al-Ahram, *22 May 1961.*

equipment was hand-made, as his half-brother Ezzat Mohamed Sadeq explains; as for his diving equipment, he was dependent on discards from foreign friends.[4]

By May 1961, Abul-Saadat had identified two distinct submerged sites and amassed enough observations on statues and masonry there to decide to alert the antiquities authorities. To the east of Silsila – or Cape Lochias in antiquity, site of the Ptolemaic Royal Quarter – he had found, among other things, 'a staircase with eight steps, less than one metre wide, with marble columns scattered around it. The staircase led to what looked like a large sarcophagus. I also saw a life-size Roman statue of red granite. It was headless and lay on its side. Nearby, there was what resembled a cylindrical chair.'[5] It was in Silsila, too, that Abul-Saadat found a gold coin with a Latin inscription on one side and the face of a woman, identified as Penelope, on the other.[6] To the north-east of Qait Bey Fort – the Pharos site where the lighthouse and the shrine of Isis Pharia once stood – he had found 2 headless sphinxes, marble columns and a colossal female statue broken in two, and further on, a jumbled heap of columns.[7] When in 1961 Abul-Saadat went to meet the director of the Graeco-Roman Museum in Alexandria, Dr Henry Riad, he took along the gold coin and several sherds of pottery with which he hoped to endorse his statements and his plea that something be done about these sites.[8]

The gold coin was initially thought to be Byzantine, but given that the Graeco-Roman Museum had no numismatist at the time, the coin, Dr. Youssef El-Gheriani recalls, was eventually delivered to the Egyptian Museum in Cairo. Finally, El-Gheriani adds, the coin was pronounced a fake. It is not known whether the possibility that the coin was an ancient fake was entertained, but Mrs. Mary Morcos, who later came to know Abul-Saadat, recounts that the piece was returned to him and that he eventually traded it in for some decent diving equipment.

The colossal female statue, the so-called Isis which Abul-Saadat had found off Qait Bey Fort, was raised in 1962. The tardiness and many other circumstances surrounding the raising of the statue are an indication of the authorities' attitudes towards underwater archaeology and the social and political context at the time. The question of a proper underwater archaeological survey of the sites seems not to have come up. Granted, the antiquities department did not have any experts to undertake such a survey – eventually, it was the Navy frogmen who were called upon to survey the sites and raise the statue. But the question that needs to be asked is why the antiquities department lacked the motivation, at that stage, to call upon foreign expertise.

Indeed, the *Progrès Égyptien* of 5 March 1962 reports that 'On the 19th of May the frogmen from the Navy discovered, again at Qait Bey, a six-metre [sic] female statue [...] The news was reported all over the world. An American expert in such matters, Peter Thorkmorton [sic], currently in Greece, sent to the concerned authorities a detailed report on the subject, expressing his readiness to help raise the submerged antiquities for a thousand dollars per month. September and October passed, and the said antiquities were still lying on the sea-bed.'

That nothing came out of Peter Throckmorton's offer is not surprising. In the straitened economic conditions of Egypt in the 1960s, archaeology – particularly underwater archaeology – ranked far below other concerns on the agenda of national priorities, an agenda which privileged military spending and industrialization. Furthermore,

---

[4] According to Professor and Mrs. Morcos. Personal interviews. October 1996 and April 1997. In a letter to Frost (dated 12 July 1980; written in French), Abul-Saadat speaks of his Italian journalist and filmmaker friend 'Mr Bruno Vailati ... a friend of mine since childhood. As you probably know, he's from Alexandria like me. Besides, it's he who taught me diving. And it's he who always sent me from Italy all the diving equipment that I needed.' See note [24]
[5] Al-Ahram, 22 May 1961.
[6] Interview with Abul-Saadat in La Réforme Illustrée du Dimanche, *28 May 1961; reproduction of the coin accompanying the article.*
[7] La Réforme Illustrée du Dimanche, 28 May 1961.
[8] El-Gheriani, Youssef. Personal interview. March 1997. At the time, Mr. El-Gheriani was working at the Graeco-Roman Museum which he later came to head.

in the years to come, from about 1967 to the 1980s, much of Egypt's Mediterranean coast and inshore waters were out of bounds for security and military reasons (in Alexandria, for example, Silsila was to become a rocket base, Qait Bey, a military zone). All along the coast, diving was severely restricted, since there was fear of enemy sabotage, particularly after 1967 and during the War of Attrition. If Abul-Saadat had access to some sites, it was only as an individual and due to what his half-brother Ezzat Mohamed Sadeq describes as 'his excellent relations with the Navy which often called upon his help.' Hence the great significance of his observations.

It is to be recalled, too, that if major archaeological operations were to be undertaken in the 1960s, these were the salvage of Pharaonic monuments in Nubia and Upper Egypt, prior to the construction of the High Dam at Aswan. Into this less than nurturing context – enters Abul-Saadat, this amateur with no academic credentials, always going on about columns and sphinxes underwater and constantly sending the antiquities department and the Governor of Alexandria lengthy appeals for the salvage of submerged artefacts. Not surprisingly, he was regarded as something of a pest.

To return to the Isis statue: the survey of the two submerged sites, off Qait Bey Fort and off the Silsila promontory, undertaken by frogmen from the Navy, was a matter of verifying Abul-Saadat's report and photographing the artefacts. The actual raising of the so-called Isis statue, which is 7 m in length and weighs 25 tonnes, was a major operation that was effected over several weeks, between tying up its two segments with metal chords (which snapped while the upper part of the statue was being raised) and hauling them out.[9] Finally, when the barge carrying the statue reached the Navy docks, it was left there during the weekend. Meanwhile, a storm caused the barge to capsize and the statue was to remain under water for six months.[10]

Some time later, Abul-Saadat demanded of the antiquities department an honorarium for having discovered the Isis statue and the headless Roman-male statue and having guided the frogmen to them. This presented a problem:

how to rate the monetary and archaeological value of the two statues. The committee that was formed for the task rated the Isis statue at £E700, 'for overall, its features are not clear, due to its long submersion underwater', as the antiquities authorities' report goes.[11] As to the Roman-male statue, it was estimated at £E50. Given the appraisal, Abul-Saadat's honorarium of £E125 (approximately $35) was a princely sum.

But if Abul-Saadat received little recognition from the antiquities department, he gradually drew a small group of supporters who understood his passion and saw the value of what he was doing. Each helped in a different way. There was Sami Dessouki, then Alexandria correspondent to *Al-Ahram*, who often wrote about Abul-Saadat and his projects, thereby providing the diver with a platform for his campaigning.

---

[9] Report by Sami Dessouki, Al-Ahram, *16 October 1963; reprinted in* Hadarat Ghariqa *(Sunken Civilizations), Selim Morcos. Cairo: Dar El-Maarif, 1965, pp. 138–9.*

[10] Eye-witness account by Mr. Mohamed Abdel-Hadi, overseer of excavations at the SCA. Personal interview. March 1997. When the statue was finally raised, Abdel-Hadi adds, it was left in the sun on the Navy docks for about a year. Meanwhile, when Hamdi Ashour, the Governor of Alexandria in the 1960s, announced his intention to place statues in public squares, the antiquities organization proposed the granite 'Isis', recalls Youssef El-Gheriani. But the suggestion did not meet with municipal approval, since the female figure – whose dress had been all but obliterated by erosion – was deemed too immodest for display in a public square, El-Gheriani adds. Eventually, the decision was made to display it in the grounds of Pompey's Pillar from which it was moved to the lawn of the Maritime Museum a few years ago.

[11] Memo dated 7 March 1978, from the Director of the Graeco-Roman Museum in Alexandria (signature illegible) to the Head of the Egyptian Antiquities Organization. The occasion for the memo, which narrates the entire episode, was a request made by Abul-Saadat in 1977 for a re-assessment of the honorarium. Indeed, from a previous memo from the head of the Graeco-Roman Museum to the Inspector-General, the General Inspectorate of the Legal Department, Egyptian Antiquities Organization (dated 18 August 1977), we learn that Abul-Saadat's honorarium was paid in two installments, the first time he received the sum of £E75, the second £E50. See the SCA's files on Abul-Saadat.

And then there was the informed support Abul-Saadat received from Professor Selim Morcos, at the time teaching oceanography at Alexandria University, and later to become a senior UNESCO staff member in the Division of Marine Sciences. Since 1965, when he published *Hadarat Ghariqa* (Sunken Civilizations), Professor Morcos has written extensively on Alexandria's potential for underwater archaeology and its links with oceanography.

The two men became acquainted when Abul-Saadat, having read *Sunken Civilizations*, took issue with what he saw as a cursory reference to his discoveries. In a letter to Morcos, dated 15 May 1966, Abul-Saadat detailed the work he had done in the Qait Bey, Silsila and Abu Qir sites, ending on a *cri de coeur*: 'As you know, sir, these discoveries, far from being easy, are highly difficult and fraught with danger. I have exerted great effort, for I used to dive in winter – January and February – for more than five hours a day. This is because of the wind which is inopportune except in winter, in terms of underwater visibility in areas that are turbid due to Nile water or sewage which pollutes the sea. Yet, despite these huge exertions, there is, very sadly, neither encouragement nor interest from the antiquities organization or from men of science like yourself ...'

In his reply to Abul-Saadat, Morcos explained the importance of documentation and report publishing. Later, he was to act as a sort of academic mentor, encouraging Abul-Saadat to adopt more professional practices, and record his sightings and sketch objects seen underwater. Morcos also 'provided [the diver] with hydrographic maps and documentation on the Battle of the Nile which later helped Abul-Saadat in identifying [some of] Napoleon's sunken vessels'.[12]

In the sixties, Abul-Saadat produced a series of approximate maps identifying locations of antiquities in the Eastern Harbour and around Silsila. To the east of Silsila, in addition to the headless male statue which was lifted in 1962, Abul-Saadat had found two sarcophagi, and further to the east, at Chatby beach, he had found some limestone pavements (still not excavated).[13] As noted above, access to the Silsila promontory was barred after 1967 when it became a rocket base. Abul-Saadat's

maps were to prove invaluable and the only source of guidelines for a team of underwater archaeologists from the Supreme Council of Antiquities (SCA) who surveyed the site in May 1997. The survey was made in response to the threat posed to the site by the military authorities' decision to dump concrete blocks around the promontory – atop the antiquities. According to SCA archaeologists Ibrahim Darwish and Sameh Ramses, both of whom participated in the survey, the divers saw fragments of granite columns and a number of granite blocks, aligned side by side. Partly hidden by rocks was a big sarcophagus, probably one of those mapped by Abul-Saadat.[14]

In the waters off Silsila, to the west, Abul-Saadat had found what he described as 'a submerged pavement, part of it buried in the sand, which may be part of the Ptolemaic Royal Harbour'.[15] Interestingly, Abul-Saadat's suggestion about this being part of the Ptolemaic Royal Harbour was corroborated by the 1996 findings of the cartographic mission directed by Mr Franck Goddio. Despite the huge gap in the means of mapping – Abul-Saadat using the naked eye, Goddio's mission having the use of a 'differential global positioning system', a technique which holds possibilities of accuracy that would have been mind-boggling for the Alexandrian diver – their findings were similar.[16] Also worth noting about Abul-Saadat's maps of the Eastern Harbour is the fact that large portions of the submerged antiquities he identified have yet to be surveyed.

The friendship between Morcos and Abul-Saadat was to have other ramifications, too. In his capacity as an academic and a 'name' in his field, Morcos, unlike Abul-Saadat, was

[12] Morcos, Selim. Personal interview. April 1997.
[13] See Abul-Saadat's 'Map number 3 of antiquities submerged in the Eastern Harbour, discovered in 1968–69 by Kamel Hussein Abul-Saadat ...' as the legend reads; map in the SCA's files on Abul-Saadat.
[14] See 'Making Waves in Chatby', Home page, Al-Ahram Weekly, 5–11 June 1997, issue no. 328.
[15] See Abul-Saadat's 'Map number 3'.
[16] See my article 'Harbours unparalleled', Front page, Al-Ahram Weekly, 7–13 November 1996, issue no. 298.

also in a position to contact key figures and institutions in an effort to draw attention to Alexandria's submerged antiquities. From 1966 onwards, Morcos pleaded the cause of Alexandria's submerged sites with prominent figures in the field of underwater archaeology, among them Joan du Plat Taylor, George Bass, Peter Throckmorton and Honor Frost.[17] This effort finally bore fruit when Dr Selim Abdul-Hak, head of the Museums and Monuments Division in UNESCO, responded in 1968 by sponsoring, in co-operation with the Egyptian government, a survey mission by pioneer archaeological diver Honor Frost and geologist Vladimir Nesteroff.

Remarkably, this survey took place in 1968, only one year after the June defeat. Among other extraordinary factors concerning the survey was the fact that, before coming to Egypt, Frost had not been informed about the exact nature of the task and so had packed only 'a mask, fins and a wet suit'.[18] Her first two dives, with Nesteroff, were without breathing apparatus as there was no compressor to be found in Alexandria. For the remaining four dives, Frost had to borrow some bottles of compressed air from a group of French divers who were working for an oil company in Mersa Matrouh. Likewise, theodolites had to be borrowed from the Polish mission in Alexandria. Meanwhile, on her second day at the site, Frost 'saw a man with mask and fins sitting on the shore. He told me (in French) that he knew the site well and offered to show me what was there. His name was Kamel Abul-Saadat'.[19]

Once again, Abul-Saadat was there on his own initiative. The man who had 'discovered' the site, who was behind the raising of the statue, who knew the changes in the area over the years, and who was indirectly responsible for Frost's presence, had not been called upon by the antiquities authorities to accompany the UNESCO mission. Therefore, Abul-Saadat had trouble with his employers over taking time off, and the antiquities department did not help.[20] Despite the fact that Kamel 'was neither academic nor highly educated', Frost 'found ... all [his] observations absolutely reliable' – and describes him as 'an amateur of the very best kind'.[21]

In her report published in the *International*

Journal of Nautical Archaeology, Frost marshals the documentary and the archaeological evidence linking the ancient lighthouse of Alexandria with the morphology of the site and submerged elements, and lists some 17 of the more important pieces of statuary and masonry, writing that 'such evidence would be multiplied a hundred-fold after a complete survey'.[22]

But this complete survey was not to take place until 1994 when the French-Egyptian mission, headed by Professor Jean-Yves Empereur, started working on the Pharos site. Frost herself repeatedly tried to get a permit to resume work, but the Egyptian antiquities authorities never answered her letters.[23] Meanwhile, Abul-Saadat roped in his Italian friend, film-maker and journalist Bruno Vailati, to film the site in 1979. Vailati's team also raised from the site one of a number of huge granite blocks (50 to 75 tons in weight) which are now believed to have formed part of the masonry of the lighthouse.[24]

In the interim between Frost's 1968 survey and the current French-Egyptian mission, much had

---

[17] I am grateful to Professor Morcos for providing me with a copy of his 'Memorandum on Submarine Archeology in Alexandria Waters', sent in September 1966 to key figures in underwater archaeology, as well as copies of the answers he received from Joan du Plat-Taylor (dated 7 October 1966), George Bass (dated 8 October 1966), Honor Frost (dated 21 October 1966), Peter Throckmorton (dated 28 December 1966) and Selim Abdul-Hak (dated 29 December 1966).
[18] Frost, Honor. Letter dated 25 March 1997.
[19] As in [18], above.
[20] As in [18], above.
[21] Frost, Honor. Telephone interview, 23 March 1997, and letter dated 25 March 1997.
[22] Frost, Honor (1975). The Pharos site, Alexandria, Egypt. The International Journal of Nautical Archaeology, 4.1:128.
[23] In a letter (25 March 1997), Frost writes that 'I refused to return [to work in Alexandria] without official Government permission (my letters were never answered).'
[24] A report on Vailati's work on the Pharos site was published in the Italian magazine Oggi, No. 6, of 8 February 1980; a photograph printed with the article (page 57) shows the granite block on land. I am also grateful to Ms. Frost for supplying me with a photograph sent to her by Abul-Saadat, taken during the Vailati expedition, showing a floating crane raising the granite block. See also note [4].

changed at the Pharos site. Despite the fact that the authorities knew of the submerged artefacts, it was the antiquities department itself that ordered the dumping of concrete blocks in two different parts of the site, to reinforce the existing jetty and to construct a breakwater to protect Qait Bey Fort. Thus, Frost's map of the site and her list – compiled with Abul-Saadat's help – were to prove of great value for the present mission, helping them to determine the changes in the morphology of the site and to locate missing statuary and masonry. For example, buried under the new reinforcement of the jetty are several elements from Frost's list, including two papyriform columns, a sarcophagus-like box and a block carrying the Roman numeral IV.[25]

Among a number of hypotheses put forward by the French-Egyptian team currently working on the site, one is of relevance here. Initially, the colossal female statue raised in the early 1960s was thought to represent Isis, a hypothesis endorsed by the iconography of the figure and by the fact that Pharos island was also the site of the shrine of Isis Pharia, patroness of mariners. But given that this female statue was found beside one of a male, of the same proportions (which the French-Egyptian team has raised from the site), it is now speculated that the two colossi represent a Ptolemaic royal couple in Pharaonic guise. 'Among other things, we learned from Honor and her map, which incorporated information given by Abul-Saadat, that the two colossal statues, that of Isis, and that of Ptolemy-Pharaoh, were found side by side and the bases of the two statues were found side by side', says Empereur, 'hence the conclusion that these statues stood at the foot of the lighthouse is a sort of royal propaganda on the part of the Ptolemaic kings who wanted to associate their image with the most celebrated monument of the city –the lighthouse.'[26]

In 1973, Frost had arranged for Abul-Saadat to give a talk on his discoveries in London at the congress of the World Underwater Federation (CMAS, Confédération Mondiale des Activités Subaquatiques).[27] To raise money for his ticket, Abul-Saadat sold his diving equipment to a friend, Captain Mohsen El-Gohari.[28] When Abul-Saadat got to the airport, however, he found it closed: it was the Sixth of October War. But by the late '70s, things began to look up for Abul-Saadat. He had gained a measure of recognition, not least thanks to Frost's crediting of him in her 1975 report published in the prestigious *International Journal of Nautical Archaeology*. And there were lesser rewards, such as an honorary membership of the exclusive Alexandria Yacht Club.

More importantly, one side-effect of late president Sadat's Camp David Accords with Israel was a gradual relaxing of the military grip on coastal areas. Thus, in 1979, Abul-Saadat accompanied divers from the California-based Mobius Group during their explorations of the Eastern Harbour. The group's investigations were guided by a comparison between the visions and extra-sensory perceptions of a number of mediums and the findings of the side-scan sonar; the team was accompanied by Professor Harold Edgarton who took readings with the sonar. The Mobius Group's main quest appears to have been Alexander's tomb, a not uncommon obsession in Alexandria.[29]

Although Abul-Saadat could not resist joining the Mobius Group, he did not believe that they could find the Soma, according to his half-brother Ezzat Mohamed Sadeq. In Stephan Schwartz's *Le projet Alexandrie*, the American team enquired of Abul-Saadat about the process and the rate of silting on the sea bed, whereby antiquities once located later become hidden. Abul-Saadat describes it as a game of hide and seek, and gives the example of the wreck of a ship carrying statues he had once seen; after a storm, he never found it again.[30] Schwartz, who led the Group, describes the Alexandrian diver thus: 'Sadaat [sic] looked awesome, with his two-day beard, his silvery sunglasses, his thick arms

[25] *Frost, Honor. Telephone interview, 23 March 1997, and letter dated 25 March 1997.*
[26] *Empereur, Jean-Yves. Personal interview. March 1997.*
[27] *Frost, Honor. Letter dated 25 March 1997.*
[28] *El-Gohari, Mohsen. Personal interview. March 1997.*
[29] *In the 1950s and '60s, an Alexandrian Greek waiter, Stellio, often obstructed the traffic in different parts of the city by his random digs in search of the Soma or Alexander's tomb.*

and huge belly. But he was an amiable man who dived because, he said, it gave him a sense of 'freedom' ... he was the most indefatigable diver I have ever known [...] Sadaat was always the first in the water and the last to come out, and could hold his breath for an incredible length of time'.[31]

No account of Abul-Saadat's contribution would be complete without a mention of the work he did in Abu Qir. Through a painstaking investigation of Abu Qir Bay, and by interviewing local fishermen, Abul-Saadat had, in 1965, managed to identify the location of at least one of Napoleon's vessels, *Le Guerrier*, sunk by Nelson in 1798, together with other structures he thought were wrecks and a number of cannons.[32] More appeals to the authorities were typed up by Abul-Saadat – to no avail.

In a letter dated 11 March 1969, Abul-Saadat told Ms Frost that he had 'found four 'Battle of the Nile' wrecks, including Napoleon's flagship, *L'Orient*, which carried the silver Napoleon had sacked from the Maltese Cathedral,' together with jewelry and coins. Among the coins brought out was one bearing the legend 'Frederick IV D G SICILIA R...INFAN... 1798... HSPANIR'.[33] In 1972, Abul-Saadat had succeeded in obtaining sponsorship from *Al-Ahram* via his friend Sami Dessouki and help from a number of French divers from a company called Co-océan and thus returned to Abu Qir Bay. It is not clear what work was done by this team apart from the fact that they lifted a coin, the details of which are not clear from the extant photo.[34]

For a full survey of Napoleon's sunken vessels, Abul-Saadat was to wait until the early 1980s when the late French lawyer Jacques Dumas, then president of the CMAS, undertook the task. This time, the antiquities department officially called upon Abul-Saadat to offer guidance to the French team, which included Napoleon's great-nephew. Eventually, the team, with Abul-Saadat's help, was to identify not only *L'Orient* and *Le Guerrier* but also L'Artémise. While the fabled Maltese treasure was not found, the team produced a treasure trove of the ephemera of daily life – brandy bottles, coins, cutlery and crockery, and pieces from a lead

type of Arabic and Latin letters, in addition to a number of cannons, among other things. But Abul-Saadat was not to see the work through. He died in Abu Qir Bay on Friday 22 June 1984. At the time, newspapers and magazines such as *Al-Ahram*, *Al-Gomhouriya*, *Akher Sa'a*, *Al-Mussawir* and *Rose El-Youssef* made allegations of foul play about Abul-Saadat's death.[35] True, Abul-Saadat had the unmistakable aura of a tragic hero – noble but flawed (though in his case the flaw lay more in the times he lived in) – and thus unknowingly and ineluctably headed towards his own downfall.

Yet the suspicions were not altogether unfounded. Dumas had claimed that Abul-Saadat had died in the shower of the search ship, *Le Bon Pasteur*. However, the doctor who was to write Abul-Saadat's death certificate had announced to his family that the diver had died of asphyxia, that his body bore the marks of violence and that one of his ankles was dislocated, recommending that an autopsy be undertaken.[36] Meanwhile, Abul-Saadat's half-brother, Ezzat Mohamed Sadeq, disclosed that the diver had spoken of pressures from the French team to keep quiet about some of the gold finds and that Abul-

[30] *Stephan A Schwartz.* Le projet Alexandrie. *(Translated from the English by Laure de Lestrange). Paris: Les Éditions Sand, 1985, pp. 288–9.*

[31] Le projet Alexandrie, *pp. 289: having been unable to obtain a copy of the English original of the book,* The Alexandria Project, *the foregoing is my translation from the French edition.*

[32] *See Abul-Saadat's map of Abu Qir Bay, the legend of which reads: 'A copy of a contour map showing some pieces of the French fleet sunk in Abu Qir Bay, in the aftermath of Napoleon's Egyptian campaign in 1798; discovered by Kamel Hussein Abul-Saadat in 1965'. Map courtesy of Professor Morcos.*

[33] *As quoted in a letter from Ms. Frost dated 25 March 1997.*

[34] *According to the handwritten note accompanying a photo of the coin sent to Professor Morcos.*

[35] *See* Al-Ahram, *29 June 1984,* Al-Gomhouriya, *2 July 1984,* Akher Sa'a, *4 July 1984,* Al-Mussawir, *6 July 1984 and* Rose El-Youssef, *9 July 1984.*

[36] *Sadeq, Ezzat M. Personal interview. March 1997. See also the newspapers and magazines quoted in note [35].*

Saadat had asked him to see to the formalities necessary to end his secondment.[37]

By the first week of July, the omens of a diplomatic crisis loomed on the horizon: foreign correspondents and journalists from international publications had turned up in Alexandria to investigate the circumstances of Abul-Saadat's death; in Cairo, meanwhile, the French ambassador asked the cultural attaché to compile a full report on the matter.[38] Eventually, the autopsy and forensic report concluded that Abul-Saadat had died of a heart attack.[39] Although Abul-Saadat was officially delegated to work with the French team, he had not been insured by the Egyptian antiquities department nor had he even been given a medical check up. A lawsuit launched by Abul-Saadat's family demanding that the Egyptian authorities pay compensation came to nothing.[40]

Today, visitors to the Qait Bey Fort Museum enjoy the display of artefacts brought up from Napoleon's sunken wrecks in Abu Qir Bay. A sign on the wall narrates the story of the excavation, going to great lengths to credit all the authorities involved. One name, however, is missing from the list: Kamel Abul-Saadat. Thirteen years after his death, it is indeed time that Abul-Saadat's singular achievement find its way into the official history of Alexandrian underwater archaeology.

---

[37] Sadeq, Ezzat M. Personal interview. March 1997. See also Al-Ahram, *29 June 1984,* Al-Gomhouriya, *2 July 1984,* Rose El-Youssef, *9 July 1984, among others.*

[38] See Al-Mussawir, *6 July 1984. According to* Al-Sharq Al-Awsat *of 25 July 1984, 'an unofficial statement from the French Embassy has it that all that has been written on the subject in the newspapers lately is devoid of truth. [...] In any case, France did not stand accused. Rather, the accusations targetted Mr Dumas and those with him on the ship. As a lawyer he can, if he so wishes, demand amends for unjust accusations ...'.*

[39] Copy of the second forensic report, by Anhar Al-Sayed Ghoneim, dated 26 June 1984, courtesy of Mr. Ezzat Mohamed Sadeq. See also Akher Sa'a, *11 July 1984. The fact that Egyptian TV had been filming the work on the day of Abul-Saadat's death also helped tip the balance in favour of clearing the French team of the accusation; see* October, *12 August 1984 and* Al-Mussawir, *6 July 1984.*

[40] I am grateful to Mr Ezzat Mohamed Sadeq for allowing me to look at the memoranda of the lawsuit.

Underwater archaeological investigations of the ancient Pharos

JEAN-YVES EMPEREUR
Centre d'Études Alexandrines, Alexandria

During 1994–1998, a Franco-Egyptian team conducted a salvage inspection of the submerged ruins of the famous ancient lighthouse of Alexandria – the Pharos. The need to protect from the northerly storms the fortress constructed at the end of the 15th century AD by the Mameluke Sultan Qait Bey on the Anfouchy peninsula at the eastern tip of the ancient island of Pharos, led to the construction of a submerged concrete wall at a distance of several dozen metres in the sea. It was quickly realized that this wall would cover an ancient archaeological site at a depth of 6–8 m. In the autumn of 1994, the Egyptian Antiquities Service asked the Centre d'Études Alexandrines [Centre for Alexandrian Studies] to undertake an urgent underwater investigation, a near-natural extension of our rescue activities on land in the centre of modern Alexandria.[1] Thanks to the means placed at our disposal by the Director of the Institut Français d'Archéologie Orientale (IFAO) since 1994, then, in 1995, by the ELF Foundation, later joined by the EDF Foundation, we have been able to undertake a major underwater archaeological investigation covering more than twelve months of field work, occupying on average some 30 divers.[2] The objective of the salvage operation was to delimit the archaeological zone and to determine its nature. We therefore plotted a topographic map and developed graphical and photographical documentation for each element. Obviously, even before the first dive, we already had some idea of the site, thanks to the pioneer work of Kamel Abul-Saadat in 1961 and a UNESCO mission in 1968, following which Honor Frost published a preliminary report with some drawings which

revealed the importance of the site.[3] However, in spite of these indications and those of amateur divers[4], the site remained more or less forgotten, owing to the nearly permanent state of war in which Egypt found itself since the beginning of the Second World War. Coastal surveillance led to a general prohibition of diving, with rare exceptions, and if underwater tourism has developed in the Red Sea, the turn of the Mediterranean [coast of Egypt] has not yet come.

It was, therefore, with surprise that we, in turn, discovered the extent of the site: over an area of 2.5 hectares, 2,500 pieces of stonework of archaeological interest were scattered about: columns of all sizes, in their hundreds, column bases and capitals, sphinxes, statues, and some immense blocks of granite which, given where they lie, certainly came from the famous lighthouse. Hundreds of columns, mostly in pink granite from Aswan, but some of marble, range from the small modules of the small columns of Proconnesis up to the huge granite column shafts which reach 2.40 m in diameter; that is, the width of Pompey's Column. This column was erected in honour of Diocletian and is one of the few monuments of [ancient] Alexandria still standing. This monolith is made of pink Aswan granite; it is 29.7 m high with a diameter between 2.7 m at its base and 2.4 m

---

[1] See Leclant, J. and Clerc, G. (1995). Fouilles et travaux en Égypte et au Soudan, 1993–1994. Orientalia, 64:229–233.

[2] See the preliminary report published in BCH, 119:424–457 (1995). Other accounts will appear regularly in forthcoming issues of the BCH and of the BIFAO.

[3] Frost, H. (1975). The Pharos Site, Alexandria, Egypt. International Journal of Nautical Archaeology, 4:126–130.

[4] See Mondo Sommerso (1980) and Schwartz, S.A. (1985). Opération Alexandrie. pp. 237–270.

at its peak. The capitals belonging to these columns are of composite-Alexandria style, with floral volutes, sometimes in white marble or black granite. There were also several large bases of Ionic form in white marble. Alongside these architectural elements of Greek style, there were some pieces from pharaonic monuments, notably six papyriform columns, of which one bears Ramses II's insignia. There were four obelisks; three were consecrated by Sethi I (Fig. 1) and the other is from a much later period, belonging no doubt to one of the Ptolemies. The first three thus date from the XIX dynasty, near the end of the 14th century BC, and the latter, from the early 3rd century BC.

Several sculptures belong to the pharaonic era; there were 28 sphinxes, bearing the insignia of the Pharaohs Sesostris III (XII dynasty), Sethi I, Ramses II (XIX dynasty) and Psammetic II (XXVI dynasty) (Fig. 2). Their dates therefore range from the Middle Kingdom up to the last dynasties, or the mid-19th century BC to the early-6th century BC. The presence of some pharaonic elements cannot fail to surprise us. Fortunately, two egyptologists from IFAO, Jean-Pierre Corteggiani and Georges Soukiassian, were team members; underwater, they deciphered the hieroglyphics that most of the monuments bear. Several facts must be pointed out immediately: each sphinx is different from every other, so we must exclude the possibility that they formed part of an approach to a monument. All the inscriptions describe scenes of offerings to the divinities of Heliopolis, as do the inscriptions on the obelisks found at the underwater site. In the Hellenistic era, the venerable sanctuary of Rê was no more than ruins; Strabo described them as being abandoned. The sanctuary was burned down and thereafter became a veritable quarry. Strabo tells us, 'Among the obelisks, two that

had not been totally destroyed were transported to Rome'.[5] This was about 25 BC, and this exploitation of the Heliopolis site [as a quarry] had begun during the reign of the Ptolemies. Obviously, the transportation posed hardly any problems, crossing the Canopic Branch of the Nile then the canal that arrived at Alexandria between Lake Mariout and the southern part of the city wall. Given the good state of conservation of some of these monuments, we must suppose that they served to decorate the city, as did certain discoveries at the terrestrial archaeological sites.[6] Cleopatra's Needles, the two obelisks that had been placed in front of the Caesarium in 13 BC, also came from Heliopolis.[7] It is not

Figure 1.
An obelisk of Sethi I
at the moment
of its discovery.
Photo: Stéphane
Compoint/Sygma.

[5] Strabo, XVII(27).
[6] For example, a lintel of Ramses II discovered in the emergency excavations to the north of the Radio Cinema, BCH, 119, p. 425 (1995).
[7] Gorringe, H. H. (1909). Egyptian Obelisks. The engraved inscription on a bronze crab which served as a support for one of the two Cleopatra's Needles gives the date of their transportation and erection as 13 BC.

the place, in this paper, to draw up a list of the pharaonic monuments of Alexandria that we know from the ancient authors or archaeological discovery; we need simply note that the excavations at Qait Bey contribute a new group belonging to this ensemble. Some of the monuments had apparently been transported whole from Heliopolis, as one of the obelisks of Sethi I shows (Fig. 1): in one part of the excavation, we found three fragments and two larger parts of the base. It seems unlikely that they would all have arrived at the one place by coincidence.

Other pharaonic pieces have been re-cut; for example, papyriform columns, two sides of which have been cut smooth, and a sphinx well and truly quartered. They have visibly been re-used as building material. The quarry of Heliopolis was responding to other, less glorious, demands.

It may be concluded that the Greek city founded by Alexander the Great must have seemed exotic in the eyes of its citizens and its visitors, with monuments in the Hellenic tradition decorated with pharaonic elements.

Even if these discoveries show us an unexpected aspect – not one we were hitherto unaware of, but on an unexpected scale – the presence of pharaonic monuments older by several centuries, indeed, by one and a half millennia for the sphinx of Sesostris III, does nothing to change the foundation of Alexandria or its history. We are clearly dealing with monuments taken from outside the city, as the inscriptions prove. Nothing has changed the traditional image we have of the Egyptian fishing village, which no new archaeological discovery at the terrestrial excavations can put in doubt.

Fragments of five colossal statues were found. First, there was the body of a Ptolemy represented as a pharaoh, in rose granite from Aswan. In its present state it measures 4.55 m from the base of the neck to the middle of the thigh. The visit of French President Jacques Chirac to the site in April 1996, provided us with the opportunity to bring up a colossal head which proved to fit the body just mentioned. It was a Ptolemy with young features and an almost female form. If one

Figure 2. Site of the Pharos of Alexandria: raising a fragmentary sphinx with no inscriptions. Photo: Stéphane Compoint/Sygma.

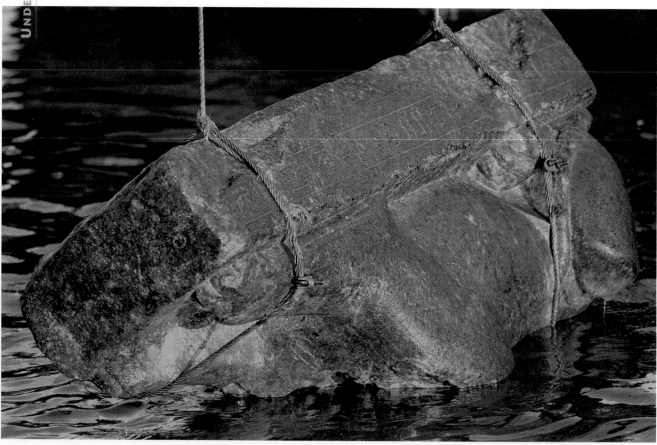

aligns this statue with one of the bases and adds a double crown, the total height of the original would have been close to 13 m. This reminds us that a colossal statue of Isis had been found at the same site by Kamel Abul-Saadat in 1962. We learned from Honor Frost that the Pharaoh Ptolemy had lain parallel to this royal spouse represented in the form of the chief deity of the Ptolemaic world; and their bases (2.2 m high) were found only recently under water, next to each other. They were one of the royal couples whose images stood at the foot of the Pharos. At least three such couples were so represented, judging from the fragments (two other heads wearing a *nemes*, and a female bust) and from the bases of half a dozen colossal statues that were found during the excavations (Fig. 3). These royal colossi stood at the foot of the Pharos and bore witness to the care the Ptolemies took to associate their image with the most celebrated monument of the city. Each traveller entering the port passed in front of the statues. The place was very well chosen for this royal publicity. Was it to the 'Saviour

Gods' that Sostratos of Knidos dedicated the Pharos? That would mean getting involved in a very long-lived debate, which would require much more development. Even so, it is remarkable that, in this Greek city of Alexandria, the Ptolemies chose to represent themselves as pharaohs. Of course, this way of representing royal figures was not unknown, as, for example, the couple representing Cleopatra with her husband, which was found in the last century in the suburb of Hadra.[8] No doubt, the idea was to point out to visitors to the city that they were entering the realm of the Ptolemies, masters of all Egypt, the pharaohs of their country, divinities standing above the ordinary kings of the region. These new discoveries reinforce even more the Egyptian-like decoration of the Greek city. It was a deliberate choice of the Lagide kings, the significance of which would require deeper consideration using the body of knowledge represented by the *Aigyptiaka* now being prepared in Alexandria.

Besides these statues, among the thousands of architectural elements, there is a series of

Figure 3. Crown of Isis of Athyr; the crown was worn by one of the female colossi. Photo: Stéphane Compoint/Sygma.

granite blocks that catch the eye by their extraordinary size: they are often more than 11 m long, weighing 75 tons each. Twenty or so of these blocks are arranged in line starting from the foot of the Mameluke fort (Qait Bey) and running for about 60 m towards the north-west. Some of them have been broken into two or even three pieces, which indicate that they have fallen from a certain height. Being thus of an extraordinary size, arranged in a line, and broken in several fragments after falling, constitutes a strong temptation to attribute them to the famous Lighthouse, when it is known from ancient and Arab authors that these blocks stood precisely at the eastern tip of the Island of Pharos[9] and that tradition – which is not so very old, after all – recounts that the Sultan Qait Bey built this fortress on the ruins of this same tower. True, we have not found the statue of Zeus that stood on top of the tower, nor the dedicatory inscription of Sostratos of Knidos, which would remove all doubt. Yet, to what other extraordinary monument could we attribute these extraordinary blocks? The fact that they were of white stone (but not necessarily of marble, an unfounded deduction transmitted from one interpreter to another)[10], does not appear to be an obstacle to recognizing them as elements of doors – jambs and lintels – or window frames of the Lighthouse, parts that required the use of more solid material for pieces of this size. It is possible to produce larger elements from granite than from marble, and the use of this local material reduced the need to import it, while allowing the traditional techniques of Egyptian builders to be applied.

Obviously, we can never reconstruct the Lighthouse from the objects the archaeologists have found so far, but the desk-top work now underway allows us to hope that soon we shall have a more precise image of this tower, thus refining and correcting the image given to us by Hermann Thiersch at the beginning of this century.[11] The German scientist fixed our vision of the Lighthouse for nearly a century; now we can add new information from documents published since his book came out. They include newly found ancient representations of the Lighthouse (of mosaics, glass, precious stones etc.) and descriptions by writers who visited the monument.[12] These

documents, as well as some information from our own archaeological investigations, show that this building was, far more than expected, a mixture of Greek and traditional pharaonic styles, illustrating well the particularity and originality of the Alexandrian world. The representations of the bas-reliefs of temples and pharaonic tombs describe for us the mastery of transportation and erection of obelisks and monoliths, the biggest of which exceeded 300 tons.[13] Thanks to these decorative scenes, to the perennity of the pharaonic techniques that allowed the erection of the magnificent Ptolemaic temples of Upper Egypt, and doubtless thanks also to the huge effort to translate Egyptian texts into Greek, starting at the time of Ptolemy II or even from the reign of his father[14], the Greek engineers profited from this experience. One therefore saw the multiplication of treatises on applied science, especially mechanics, in Alexandria. The architectural result is this tower, destined to guide travellers arriving at the Egyptian coast; a tour de force that greatly impressed its contemporaries who were soon to consider the Lighthouse one of the Seven Wonders of the World.

The 1998 campaign of underwater investigations on the Lighthouse has lead us

---

[8] The male head decorates the garden of the Graeco-Roman Museum of Alexandria, and the upper part of Cleopatra can be seen at the Mariemont Museum. See also M.-C. Bruwier (1989), Chronique d'Égypte, pp. 224–237 and Musée Royal de Mariemont, Choix d'Œuvres: 1, Égypte, No. 40. (1990).

[9] Strabo, XVII(6).

[10] Ibidem.

[11] Thiersch, H. (1909). Pharos.

[12] A useful review of these new documents is given in Daumas, F. and Mathieu, B. (1987). Le Phare d'Alexandrie et ses dieux: un document inédit. Academiae Analecta, 49:43–55.

[13] The obelisk of Hatshepsut at Karnak weighs 323 tonnes, not to mention the incomplete obelisk still half cut in a quarry at Aswan; its weight is estimated at 1,168 tonnes! See Habachi, L. (1984). The Obelisks of Egypt, pp. 17, 60, 94, 155 etc., for their weights, and pp. 27–37, for their transportation and erection.

[14] See the article by Alain Le Bolluec, Sagesses barbares: Alexandrie IIIᵉ siècle av. J.-C. Autrement, 19:63–77 (1992), evoking Greek translations from Jewish writings since the reign of Ptolemy I (p. 76).

to think, together with geophysicists, about the constitution of this site; apparently, subsidence is particularly strong in this region – from 5 to 7 m since Antiquity. It is therefore quite probable that, in ancient times, a good part of the site east of the Qait Bey Fort was above sea level and that, at the end of the age of antiquity, a dump had been established there, a sort of quarry where all the bits and pieces of dismantled monuments from various parts of the city had been accumulated. Only a few of them had been reassembled at this place and it is very difficult to distinguish these from the rest. The blocks of the Lighthouse were exceptional because of their great size which must have made their transportation difficult. It is notable also that nearly all the blocks at this site are made of Aswan granite, the marble and limestone having disappeared, probably into the lime kilns or to be used in new buildings. They were incorporated into construction work for the Qait Bey fort or even for the city the Ottomans started to build in 1517 on the isthmus that had developed on either side of the Heptastadium. The pieces of granite, a material much harder to work, were left, to become covered by the sea little by little at a time that is difficult to specify.

This subsidence phenomenon is corroborated by a discovery made in the autumn of 1996: about 350 m to the north of the Lighthouse, we found about forty Greek and Roman ship hulls dating from the 4th century BC to the 7th century AD. Their preservation was remarkable and, besides the usual wine amphorae, there were oil lamps, bronze vases and even ship anchors (Fig. 4). These vessels, which came from all over the Mediterranean – Crete, Palestine, Rhodes, Asia Minor, Tripolitania, Italy etc. – provide first-rate information for retracing the commerce of Alexandria. Here, I shall only deal with the conditions under which they were sunk: all sank within about 350 m of the entrance to the port of Alexandria,

at a time when the Pharos was operating. The danger of the Egyptian coast arises from its lack of relief, so that mariners only see it at the last minute – and in that respect the Lighthouse was primordial in averting such danger – but also, as Strabo pointed out[15], from rocks at the sea surface or only slightly below it. We were able to follow this rocky bar parallel to the coast; it is now at a depth of 12 m. Given that the maximum swell is about 5 m, we must suppose a subsidence of 7 m to be able to imagine how, in a heavy storm, the unfortunate ships' captains ran aground on this bar even though they could see the monuments of the capital of the Ptolemies on the horizon.[16]

Figure 4. An area about 300 m north of the Pharos: a lead anchor stock from one of the sunken ships. Photo: Stéphane Compoint/Sygma.

[15] Strabo, XVII (6).
[16] The excavations of the Lighthouse and its surroundings is underway and we have only given the preliminary results. Two new campaigns are foreseen and the field work should be finished by the end of 1999.

Underwater archaeological survey of Alexandria's Eastern Harbour

FRANCK GODDIO
Institut Européen d'Archéologie
Sous-Marine
(IEASM)

Mission objective

Figure 1. The Eastern Harbour of Alexandria showing the submerged lands discovered during the IEASM surveys.

The main objective of the mission was to carry out a detailed and systematic underwater archaeological survey to establish precisely the contours and determine the geographical locations of the submerged land and ruins in Alexandria's Eastern Harbour.

Surveys

On the basis of our 1992 electronic mapping mission, all the work performed during the present mission was achieved by diving. A total of 2,500 dives were made during the June–July and September–October missions of 1996. The teams of divers were sent to pre-selected points and charged with marking bottom contours by fixing buoys on visible targets. Work was greatly facilitated by the unexpected relatively light sedimentation on the sea bottom. In cases of uncertainty, due to the presence of sedimentation, additional soundings were carried out.

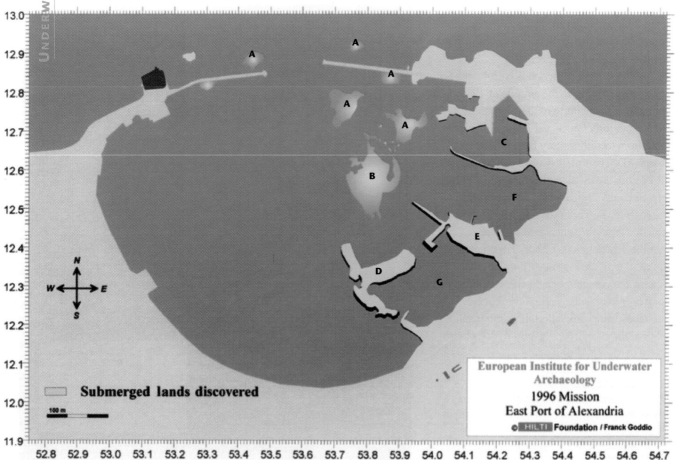

Submerged lands discovered

100 m

European Institute for Underwater Archaeology
1996 Mission
East Port of Alexandria
© HILTI Foundation / Franck Goddio

Any archaeological remains discovered were also identified by means of surface buoys. All buoy positions were rechecked precisely by using:
(a) a differential GPS – a global positioning system allowing 50-cm precision, and
(b) actual underwater on-site measurement.
For the purpose of this mission, we developed and used for the first time ever in underwater archaeology, an underwater differential GPS, which has enabled us to fix the geographical positions of more than a thousand points. Each point was referenced in an orthometric system, as well as by charting geographical latitudes and longitudes. Several maps were drawn; e.g.:
(a) working maps for each site at a scale of 1:500;
(b) a general map summarizing all the data at a scale of 1:2500, with latitudes and longitudes;
(c) several maps at a scale of 1:1250 with the positions of all artefacts discovered during the missions; and

(d) separate maps of two of the main archaeological sites at a scale of 1:100 (including latitudes and longitudes).

Survey results

We were able to achieve complete and exhaustive mapping of all the submerged land in the Eastern part of Alexandria's East Harbour (Fig. 1). For the first time, the complete panorama of the *Magnus Portus* can be precisely described and visualized instead of the so far theoretical interpretation based on known descriptions of Alexandria in antiquity (Fig. 2). This new charting and description is based exclusively on actual findings.
Some areas are covered by modern structures, most probably hiding ancient remains. This primarily concerns the areas covered by the modern piers, and breakwaters, as well as the Cape Silsila structural complex. Still, luckily, these areas represent only a small part of the Magnus Portus.

Figure 2. The Eastern Harbour of Alexandria, as it is today (in grey), showing the contours of submerged lands discovered during the IEASM surveys (in blue). Superimposed (in red), is the outline of the harbour as interpreted from ancient texts.

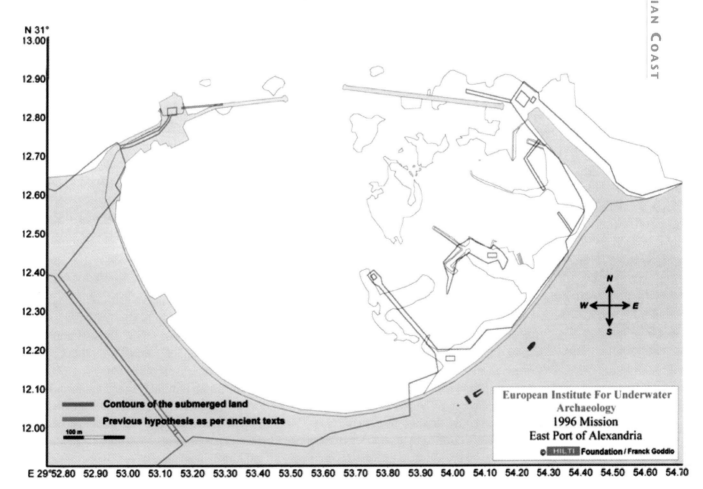

The preliminary maps drawn so far of the two archaeological sites, at a scale of 1:100, can be used for future excavations. The general maps are helpful for the archaeological interpretation of the general topography of the Magnus Portus. On the general map of the discovered submerged land, we have indicated all archaeological artefacts, which will provide a future basis for exhaustive excavations in the area.

Topographic comments on the general map of Magnus Portus

On entering the harbour (as Strabo did, for instance), we perceive, from north to south and east to west (Fig. 1):

Submerged reefs

These are to the west and east of the entrance (A). They are now partially covered by the modern piers. There is no evidence of any construction or presence of artefacts on them.

A low islet

This islet (B) is surrounded by reefs, on which were discovered only a few archaeological vestiges: the foundations of a small wall, coarse with uneven stones and mortar; other foundations of a small wall of the same quality in the south-eastern part; and a small pier which reinforces the eastern part of the islet.

An inner harbour

This harbour (C) is surrounded on its eastern and northern sides by land and closed towards the south by a 240 m-long by 15 m-wide pier protruding from the ancient seashore. This pier is built of limestone and mortar from its western end and is well preserved. The eastern part is built mainly of limestone alone (without mortar). The pier divides the inner harbour into two basins, the eastern basin being partly covered by the modern structures on Cape Silsila. Towards the east, it continues as a natural rock platform, partly paved.

On the northern part of this harbour is located a very well preserved pier, 100 m long and 22 m wide, built of limestone blocks. The upper part of this pier is flat and well paved with limestone.

The bottom of the central part of the harbour is of the natural bedrock, which has probably been artificially levelled to deepen the main basin. The topography of the eastern part of this harbour is difficult to describe, since it has been partially covered by the modern pier of Cape Silsila.

An island 350 m long

This island (D) is situated to the south of the above-mentioned low lying islet, which is paved over almost its entire surface. Its northern part forms a kind of peninsula protected by important blocks of mortared limestone. It has been totally paved to create a pier, probably to protect the island against an easterly swell.

On this island, important archaeological remains were discovered. On its western shore, we found an important quantity of granite column drums of diameters ranging from 90 cm to 120 cm (a map, showing the positions of all visible remains, was drawn at a scale of 1:100).

The site continues into a 350 m-long alignment of archaeological remains, mostly drums of red-granite columns, ending at the tip of the island. Within this alignment, there is an obviously dense concentration of ruins in an area 120 m from the eastern tip of the island. Another map, on a scale of 1:100, was drawn also showing the visible remains.

An important peninsula

This peninsula (E) lies to the east of the island just described, protruding from the ancient seashore; it is about 350 m long and some 100 m wide, pointing north-west. It has several noticeable features:

A very important pier extending towards the low islet. It is 200 m long and 25 m wide, built of limestone blocks, its upper part being flat and paved. At its base, numerous intact and broken amphorae were discovered. There are no remains of construction on this pier.

Another important pier situated at the start of the previously mentioned pier, at the tip of the peninsula, prolonging the peninsula towards the island in a south-westerly direction. This pier, built of limestone blocks, is 100 m long, 35 m wide, and carries a well paved walkway 14 m wide.

A 50 m-wide platform located at the tip of the pier, well paved and covered with scattered ruins, mainly limestone, wall blocks and red-granite column drums of 90 cm diameter.

The main peninsula, paved in several places. Its southern and northern shorelines are built of mortar and limestone blocks, and are well preserved. There are two lesser piers on the northern shore of the peninsula, one built of limestone, and a smaller one built of limestone and mortar, and very well paved with limestone and mortar. There are several dense concentrations of ruins on this peninsula.

An additional inner harbour

This is situated between the northeastern harbour and the peninsula just described, very well protected by a pier protruding, from the peninsula on its northern side. This ancient harbour (F) is about 500 m long and 250 m wide. The bottom is muddy and scattered with amphorae.

A third harbour

This is situated south-west of the peninsula (G) and is closed on its western side by the island; it has its entrance between the eastern tip of the island and the platform projecting out from the peninsula.

A vast area of submerged land

This land lies to the east of the inner harbour. It is partially covered by the complex of modern buildings of Cape Silsila. Some archaeological vestiges have been located in this area.

The ancient seashore

This links the area east of Silsila to the above-mentioned peninsula. The ancient seashore

can also be seen to link the peninsula to a platform just in front of the island. From this paved wharf a pier (also paved) projects towards the island.

Numerous archaeological remnants have been discovered and positioned all along the ancient seashore from Cape Silsila to the above-mentioned paved wharf (in front of Ramley Station). These remains are particularly dense between the peninsula and the wharf facing the island. Between the island and the wharf is a 50 m-wide channel with a muddy bottom scattered with amphorae and antique stone anchors. The wharf is in front of the place where the two obelisks known as 'Cleopatra needles' used to be.

General remarks concerning the zone

All contours and archaeological finds were accurately positioned and their bearings recorded.

Most of the contours of the submerged lands were rather easy to mark, since they consist of wharves or piers built of limestone blocks or blocks of limestone with mortar. In some protected areas (inside the various harbours), the limits of the lands can be distinguished by the presence of pavement made mainly of limestone with borders of limestone blocks. An important part of the submerged land is paved. In some areas, the pavement is made of hard stones (granite, quartzite). The precise bearings of such areas were obtained.

Evidence of an important earthquake (and/or tidal wave) can be found in many places. For example, huge pieces of mortar and limestone (up to 3 m thick), from disintegrated wharves, tilting in the direction of the landslide; accumulation of column drums which had tumbled down the slopes created by the displaced wharves, etc. In many places, the column drums, hard stone blocks, column capitals etc. are lying on the pavement only slightly embedded in the sediment and covered with concretions.

From Byblos to Pharos:
some archaeological considerations

HONOR FROST
Underwater archaeologist

Introduction

A poet put the theme of my paper quite clearly when he wrote:

And the seas go on with sculpturing the capes
When harbours have silted and the fish are
dead. (David Wright)

These lines evoke two archaeological questions: the reasons for, and the origins of, harbours, as well as the variations in sea level and other geological changes that can occur after the building of harbour installations, including lighthouses.

Some ancient harbours, Phalasarna in Crete and Seleucia Piraea in southern Turkey, for instance, are truly bereft of fish, for they have been raised by earth movements so that they can now be visited on dry land, several metres above the present sea level. Elsewhere, as in Alexandria itself, or at the not too distant Caesarea Maritima (which is roughly 600 km to the north), the picture is less simple, for, although in both places some ancient installations are now as much as 6 m below the present sea level, others are not, because different parts of the same harbour can go under at different times and for different reasons. Geological factors are so complex that they make all harbour archaeology both multidisciplinary and long-term. Caesarea well illustrates this point, for after thirty annual seasons of investigation, it was only last year that a very localized geological fault was identified as the cause of one particular jetty being several metres below the surface, while on the nearby shore a rock-cut fish-tank of the same period remains in its original position.[1] Again, it is essential to study geological factors when considering the origins and functions of any ancient harbour installation.

The geological complexities of Alexandria's Eastern Harbour have yet to be worked out in detail. It is, however, already clear from the documentation of one well known landmark, Diamond Rock, that more than one factor affected the relatively small area containing the remains of the Pharos (which was toppled into the sea during the Middle Ages by earthquakes of known date). Diamond Rock, which is at the north-eastern limit of this underwater spread of fallen Pharos masonry, is now a formless shallow covered by some 3 m of water, but when one of Napoleon's topographers recorded it around 1798 for the *Description d'Égypte* (Fig. 1), it was a rock well above the surface, towering above the human figures beneath it. What is particularly significant is that these figures are standing on a flat shelf under the main mass, and this kind of shelf is a common phenomenon, known to geologists as an 'erosion trottoir'. Consequently, whatever the other causes of subsidence, at this particular point in the Eastern Harbour, wave-erosion also made a major contribution to the disappearance of this particular land-mark.

Lighthouses:
functions and origins

The Pharos is known as the Seventh Wonder of the Ancient World, not because it was the first lighthouse, but because it was the biggest in a line of evolution. Why are lighthouses needed? The answer is that any vessel –

[1] Raban, A. (1996). Underwater excavations in Caesarea 1995–1996. C.M.S. News Report, 23:7-13.

ancient or modern – sailing across open water has to have some reliable mark on the coast to tell it where it is situated. I stress this point because of a longstanding archaeological fallacy which still lingers on. Before nautical archaeology became a discipline in its own right, archaeologists, in interpreting texts, used to generalize about ancient craft never losing sight of the coast, never travelling by night and never sailing except in summer weather, whereas every sailor knows that he often has no choice, because he will inevitably meet conditions beyond his control. Winds change, blowing him off course; mists come down so that he cannot see the coast; accidents cause delays which force him to sail by night; and sailing too near an unfamiliar coast is in itself dangerous.

Archaeologically, there is no doubt that vessels were already crossing open water in prehistoric times. One proof is that a volcanic glass called obsidian (used for making Stone Age knives and other tools) has been excavated on certain islands to which it is geologically foreign, so that it must have arrived by boat, and that the boat containing it must have crossed open water. Obsidian from Anatolia has been found in Cyprus. Even more significantly, two distinct types of obsidian, one from the Island of Lipari (Italy) and the other from the Island of Pantelleria, have both been excavated in 6th-millennium contexts on the Island of Gozo (adjoining Malta). It follows that, very early, craft must not only have had to find their way across

open water, but that (whatever the visibility) they had to be able to pinpoint a sheltered anchorage.

Even when sailing within sight of land, adverse conditions often create the need for signals from the shore. Fire signals are the obvious answer, for smoke can be seen by day and light by night, even from so far out to sea that the earth's curvature renders low-lying features invisible. Furthermore, there are many ways of controlling fires so that their light appears intermittently, thus producing different patterns of light, each pattern representing a specific port. Modern lighthouses emit flashes at irregular intervals, thus producing a code that identifies one particular lighthouse. By counting the time between flashes, sailors can know which lighthouse they are seeing (and when in doubt, modern sailors look up the code in a pilot-book).

Nevertheless, even after having identified a port, a foreign sailor may have difficulty getting into its harbour, because, unlike local fishermen, he will not know the rocks, shoals and reefs at its entrance. Such hazards encumber the mouths of most Levantine harbours, and Alexandria is no exception. The solution is for a harbour master either to provide vessels with a local pilot or keep a safe channel marked with beacons and buoys. In the case of Alexandria, the recent discovery of artefacts of all periods spilled over the bottom outside the Eastern Harbour does not suggest that the Pharos had been inefficient,

Figure 1. Diamond Rock as it appeared in 1798 (engraved for the 'Description d'Egypte'). Note the shelf of rock on which the figures are standing. Worn away by wave action, this shelf, or 'trottoir', is a measure of the part played by galloping erosion in the disappearance of this rock which is now some 3 m below the surface of the sea.

but rather that the ancient harbour-masters were occasionally negligent. Let us now examine the evidence for primitive forms of lighthouse at Bronze Age ports.

Early lighthouses

Byblos

Starting with Byblos (in Lebanon), it must be admitted that no visible trace of its ancient harbour survives. However two clues to its existence are worth examining. The first comes in the story of the Egyptian priest Wenamon who, around the 12th to 11th century BC, was sent from Thebes to bring back wood for repairing the temple-boat sacred to Amon. Trees, including cedar, grow on the mountains above Byblos, whence they were brought down to the sea as huge trunks, often some 30 m long. One such trunk can still be seen in the infrastructure of the Step Pyramid of Djser; another now forms the 23 m-long timber placed centrally in the hull of the Cheops ship. It follows that embarkation quays must have been big enough to take such trunks, and this rules out the very small natural basin formed in the rock, currently used by the few 6 m fishing

boats belonging to the village of Gebail, which has taken the place of ancient Byblos. Except for this little basin, Gebail and the excavations of ancient Byblos, which cover a small promontory, are now shelterless, the shallow bays that flank the promontory being open to the prevailing south-west wind. Submerged shallows, which might once have been a reef, now destroyed by either erosion or earthquake may exist, and if this were so, it would have afforded protection to the southern bay, but this question has still not been studied.

The story of Wenamon recounts that, as he was negotiating with the King of Byblos, they saw, out to sea, eleven pirate ships. However, as the harbour itself, the whereabouts of the residential quarter and the King's palace remain unknown, because only the headland has been excavated and it represents only the town's temple area. The bay to the south is the most logical site for the ancient harbour; however, not only has it filled with silt, but earth from 40 years of excavation on the promontory has been dumped into it. A contour map, provided by Maurice Dunand when discussing the possible location of the ancient harbour shows the site as it was before excavation started.

Dunand had also been most generous in helping to retrace the votive stone anchors he had found over the years, inside most of the Bronze Age Byblian temples, and it is this that leads to a re-evaluation of one very curious and architecturally significant 'tower temple' (which, alas, he did not live long enough to publish fully). He dated the building by the Egyptian finds it contained to the 23rd century BC, a dating that is not contested by Dr Muntaha Saghieh in her reassessment of Byblian stratigraphic datings.[2]

This tower temple was on high ground overlooking the sea on the southern side of the promontory. Contrary to the plans of most temples, access to the tower was by a single door up a flight of steps, the first of which was entirely made out of stone anchors (Fig. 2). Unlike the other Byblian temple anchors, the

Figure 2. Anchors forming the first step (those above it having been removed) of a flight leading up to the unique entrance of the 'Tower Temple' at Byblos, Lebanon. Note, firstly, the imprint of the second step which had covered the rope-holes; secondly, the smoothness of the top surfaces of the anchors in contrast with the underside of the one that has been turned upside down and laid across the furthest of the anchors (see also Fig. 3).

[2] Saghieh, M. (1983). Byblos in the Third Millennium BC. Ed. Arris and Phillips, Warminster. pp. 72 and 85.

Figure 3.
The undersides
of all the anchors in
the 'Tower Temple's'
first step were
found to be either
rough-hewn, or
entirely un-cut.

3

SUBMERGED HERITAGE SITES AROUND THE MEDITERRANEAN BASIN

backs of these 6 anchors were unfinished (Fig. 3) and their rope-holes were covered by the second step. Their positioning had therefore been deliberate and not a mere re-use of discarded anchors. This is not surprising, for anchors have symbolic significance; in the Christian religion they are still the emblem of hope. The reasons are obvious, for anchors often stand between a sailor and death, because only their hold can prevent a storm-tossed ship from being wrecked. Consequently, in this particular case, the use of anchors as the first step of a flight, in a tower dominating the sea, reinforces the interpretation of the building as a lighthouse, and strengthens the case for the harbour having been in the bay below the building to the south. Again, a geological survey of the bay is needed to settle the point; meanwhile, corroboration of the use of tower temples as lighthouses also exists at Ugarit in Syria.

Ugarit

While Maurice Dunand was excavating in Lebanon, Claude Schaeffer was excavating the Bronze Age town of Ugarit, north of Tartous in Syria. He started during the 1920s and work still continues, for in 1980 he was succeeded by Professor Marguerite Yon. At Ugarit, the problem of signalling to ships far out to sea was very different from the problem at Byblos, for Ugarit is some 2 km inland, on the slopes of a tell 20 m high, whose summit is crowned by a concentration of temples. On the shore, at Minet el Beida, Ugarit's port town was discovered and partially excavated. As the name implies, there is some shelter, although the whiteness of the rocks is inadequate as a landmark, because they are too low-lying to be seen from far out to sea; similarly the mountains in the hinterland are too far off to guarantee reliable landmarks in indifferent visibility. Consequently, the acropolis on the 20 m-high tell was the best base for any artificial landmark, and indeed two tower temples were found on it. Built on podia, recent research shows them to have been over 20 m high.[3] And excavation indicates that they were dedicated, respectively, to the Earth God, Dagan, and the Weather God, Baal. It was in the Weather God's temple and its precincts that all the votive stone anchors were concentrated. Five of the largest, each weighing about half a ton, still lie beside the entrance to the temple's cella.[4] The cella

[3] Yon, M. (1990). The end of the Ugarit kingdom. In: Acts of the Symposium 'The Crisis Years: 1200 BC'. Brown University, Providence, R.I., May 1990.
[4] Frost, H. (1991). Anchors sacred and profane. Ugarit-Ras Shamra, 1986: the stone anchors revised and compared. Ras Shamra-Ougarit VI, ERC Paris, pp. 355–409.

itself contained the flight of steps leading to the top of the tower. Whether the votive anchors had originally formed the cella's threshold (an equivalent placing to the Byblian tower temple anchors) is uncertain, for they had been moved by the 19th century Ottoman excavators who preceded Professor Schaeffer on the tell.[5] Luckily, the Ugaritic evidence does not stop there.

Byblos and Ugarit both produced written matter: Byblos boasts the first example of an alphabet, while Ugarit produced whole libraries in the form of clay tablets. A recently discovered tablet refers to offerings being burned on the roof of the Temple of Baal.[6] Sacrifices were probably made on a regular basis, and certainly their fire could have been seen by ships at sea. It may well be that, at Late Bronze Age Kition in Cyprus, one of the towers on the sea-wall (which also contained anchors) was used to lead ships into the harbour, but this would now be hard to prove, for the sea has retreated and the land between the excavation and the shore is now overbuilt. Elsewhere, and at later periods, in the northern and central Mediterranean, temples and sanctuaries were often sited on capes and headlands, so that their altars could well have had a secondary use as landmarks for ships approaching the coast.

The height above sea-level of the fires on the roof of the Weather God's temple at Ugarit would have been less than half the height of the reflectors on top of the Pharos (estimated at around 100 m). Symbolically, as anchors hold a vessel away from danger, a light held high leads it towards safety. E. M. Forster's lines about the Pharos eloquently express the spiritual element: "It beaconed to the imagination, not only to ships at sea, and long after its light was extinguished, memories of it glowed on in the minds of men." It is appropriate that a long-term, multidisciplinary programme of investigation, directed by Professor Jean-Yves Empereur, should have started on the most fascinating of all lighthouses: the Pharos of Alexandria.

---

[5] Schaeffer, C. F. A. (1931). Deuxième Campagne. *Syria XII (9). Paris.*
[6] Yon, M. (1984). Sanctuaires d'Ougarit. Temples et Sanctuaires. *Lyon. pp. 44–45.*

The port of Sabratha, Libya

NICOLA BONACASA
Istituto di Archeologia
Università di Palermo

For its maritime trade, the Phoenician *emporium*, which flourished in the 6th–5th century BC, exploited the natural conformation of the shore, after occupying the stretch of coast that later was to become the area of the Forum of Sabratha. The latter, in fact, very probably coincides topographically with the square of the Phoenician market. With regard to the traditional use of the area for trading purposes, it must be remembered that, east of the Justinian Basilica, there is a commercial and residential area with substantial remains of pre-Roman Sabratha,

including a rich-oil factory. It would indeed appear that this quarter – certainly belonging to the Punic tradition of the Hellenistic age – corresponds to the final period of the *emporium* (1st century BC) and coincides with the founding of the Roman city, which eventually spread and incorporated the Punic quarter, extending along the coast, with houses and ancillary buildings, giving rise to rapid urban development that was completed in the second half of the 2nd century AD (Fig. 1).[1, 2]

[1] Matthews, Jr., K. D. (1957). Cities in the Sand: Leptis Magna and Sabratha in Roman Africa. *pp. 17–20, 48–9. Philadelphia.*
[2] Haynes, D. E. L. (1981). The Antiquities of Tripolitania, *pp. 52–3. London, Rome (4th edition).*

Figure 1. Sabratha: Plan of the ancient city. From E. Joly.

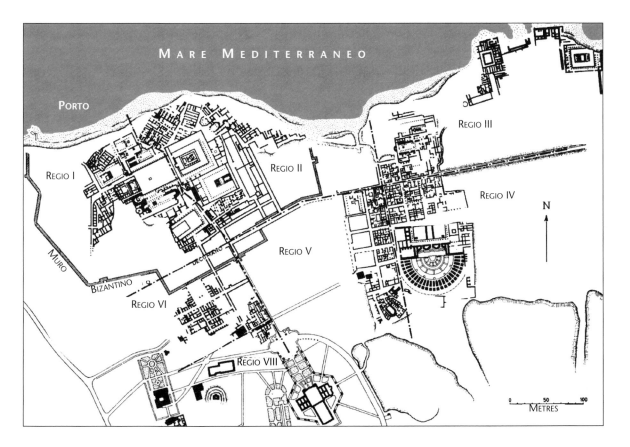

MARE MEDITERRANEO

PORTO

REGIO III

REGIO I

REGIO II

REGIO IV

N

MURO

DECUMANO

REGIO V

BIZANTINO

REGIO VI

REGIO VIII

0   50   100
METRES

The port structure at Sabratha is fairly limited in extent and ranks as one of the minor landing-places in North Africa. With its basin protected by an interrupted series of harbour walls, it is a fairly typical kind of half-natural half-artificial port, used mainly for passenger and goods traffic. It is highly unlikely that the port of Sabratha was ever intended to be used for defensive purposes (Fig. 2).

It thus belongs to the well known category of external ports which present the gradual enclosure of the stretch of water off the coast by artificial infrastructures.[3] These were quite high but not heavy, partly constructed and partly based on natural defences just above or below the sea surface, like the succession of rocks and islets running parallel to and sufficiently far from the shore-line. This system of using coastal islets (*nésoi*) for the construction of ports is common to numerous Mediterranean settlements: Sabratha, Oea, Leptis Magna, Caesarea of Mauretania, Eretria, Mytilene, Halicarnassus, Ephesus and Alexandria (but not Carthage). At Sabratha, we have, broadly speaking, the same situation as at Oea and Leptis Magna, though naturally with different solutions. At

Sabratha, there is a landing area protected by natural prominences and sheltered from the north and north-west winds, which is typical, in the first place, of Phoenician and, here, of Libyo-Phoenician *emporia*, although the technique was also exploited by Roman engineers, who continued to build their ports on the same principle. As is often the case, the quays along the shore must have been lower than the other functional quays, facing out to sea, not only along the south side of the port, inside the basin, but also east and west of the port area, since, to the east, numerous traces of quay structures have been found, as well as ruins of numerous warehouses, at least as far as the 'Seaward Baths', near the Temple of Isis.

Also at Sabratha the use of foundation blocks and concrete made it possible to create an effective series of protective harbour walls defending the port basin from the open sea, with equipment placed on the walls themselves. However, because of the poor

Figure 2. Sabratha: the harbour, showing locations of visible features. From R.A. Yorke.

[3] Lehmann-Hartleben, K. (1923). Die antiken Hafenanlagen des Mittelmeeres. Klio 14, Beiheft, p. 280, No. 245.

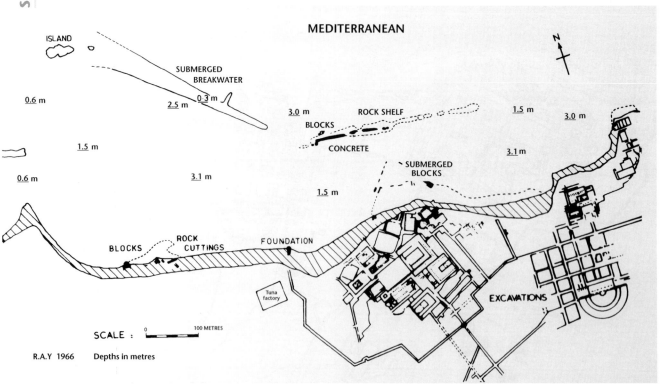

quality of the remains, we are unable to determine whether the harbour walls at Sabratha, which originally, without any doubt, were of the natural rock type with lateral escarpments – as at Leptis Magna in Africa and at Centumcellae in Latium – were all replaced by monolithic concrete walls with ashlar facing, the so-called *opus pilarum* of Suetonius.

Whatever the case, in the ports in Tripolitania and elsewhere, the moles delimiting the *kothon* (the port basin) are consistently more functional and better buttressed to the north and north-west, so as to withstand the north-west/south-east currents and therefore to obviate the constant danger of silting up. With regard to these technical aspects, there is no lack of excellent examples along the North African coast, one of the most prestigious certainly being the one at Leptis Magna.

The only underwater exploration of the port of Sabratha was that carried out by the Cambridge University Underwater Exploration Group in 1966. The results of this initiative were concisely described by Yorke.[4, 5] It is superfluous today to consider other earlier minor initiatives (Fig. 3).

The Cambridge University Group systematically investigated a stretch of water 1 km by 500 m, paying attention first of all to the rocky reef running parallel to the coast.

The original structures seem to have been built right on this natural rock – which is about 180 m long – immediately to the north of what was to become the centre of the Roman city. This is suggested by the cement works and structures which, although in a poor state owing to erosion by the sea, are still recognizable. Later, in the same direction as the 'Seaward Baths', the quays stretched out to sea and towards the north and the centre of the reef, forming in the end a kind of large seawall

of triangular shape, over 70 m long. The port structures extended considerably westwards, with the construction of a breakwater over 230 m long that stretched as far as a natural islet in the north-western part of the bay. This outer sea wall, still recognizable 30 cm below the surface of the water, protected the inner harbour walls and the quays up to 75 m from the western end of the reef. The opening between the natural rock and the eastern end of the breakwater constituted the main entrance to the port basin. Opposite this entrance, it is still possible to discern on the shoreline the foundations of a circular construction which must have been those of the lighthouse located east of the Tonnara (tunny fishery) with, we may suppose, overlying structures and receding floors. The lighthouse must have been similar in type to the one at Alexandria, which set the standard. The lighthouse at Leptis Magna which, together with the city port, has been sufficiently excavated and studied, also has precise points in common with Alexandria.[6]

[4] Yorke, R. A. (1986). pp. 243–5, in: P. M. Kenrick (ed.), Excavations at Sabratha 1948–51. Journal of Roman Studies, *Monograph 2. London*.
[5] Yorke, R. A. (1967). pp. 20–2, in: Archéologia. *Juillet-août 1967*.
[6] Bartoccini, R. (1958). Il porto romano di Leptis Magna. Bollettino Centro Storico. Storia Architettura, *Supplemento 13. Roma*.

Figure 3. Sabratha: the harbour, showing details of submerged remains near the 'Seaward Baths'. From R. A. Yorke.

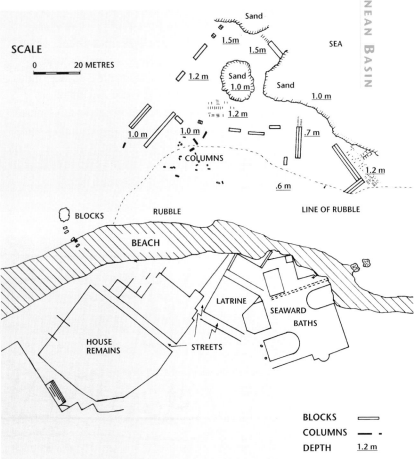

Sabratha possessed a fairly ample port basin, similar in layout to that at Oea, but oriented in exactly the opposite way; also here at Sabratha, the port basin is slightly decentralized towards the west-northwest, away from the city centre, to which it is, however, closely connected. This decentralization must have facilitated the direct links with the caravan routes which stretched south towards Gebel, reaching the mythical Cydamus and the great Sahara Desert territories in the area of Hamada el-Hamra, bordering Fezzan.

It is therefore not unreasonable to affirm that, at Sabratha, there was a long and deep-rooted tradition with a natural progression from Punic-Hellenistic to Imperial-Roman culture, for both of which the port was of indubitable commercial importance. But there is more to the question. In the Imperial age, the links with Rome and Ostia must have become more intense, also as regards passenger traffic. Thus, the port at Sabratha, which originally had purely commercial functions, related to the fertile coastal strip and above all to the desert hinterland, served another function. It conveyed, particularly to Rome, slaves, exotic animals and quality goods such as ivory, timber, textiles and precious stones, which came up from the south along the trans-Saharan route. Indisputable evidence of this is provided by the eloquent symbol of the celebrated *statio Sabratensium*, an elephant, in the Piazzale delle Corporazioni at Ostia. In addition to the well known elephant in the market place at Leptis Magna, it is useful to recall that, here in Sabratha, there is a marble

Figure 4. Sabratha: Church 1, showing marble relief with the Indian Triumph of Dionysus. Drawing by A. Cellura, from N. Bonacasa.

relief with the Indian Triumph of Dionysus, now to be seen on the inner quay against the south wall of Church 1, formerly the Judiciary Basilica, built in the southern part of the Forum (Fig. 4). We believe that it must have been brought here from a building in the square – possibly a great quadrangular base for a celebratory monument – some considerable time after the destruction of the Forum in the late 4th century AD. Thereafter, it was reused here as reinforcement material between the early-5th century and about 450 AD, when it is certain that the old Roman Basilica, which, in its last phase, had two opposing apses, was replaced by Church 1. It is certainly for this reason, and also because of the pagan and symbolic nature of the relief, that all the figures in it were meticulously chiselled and drilled away to a great depth.[7]

With regard to this relief, we are most interested in the first of the three surviving blocks of marble. This presents a particular aspect of the Indian Triumph, with a Bacchic *thiasos* (procession) and exotic wild beasts, an *unicum* of exceptional interest among the sculptures of Sabratha and in the figurative repertoire of the three *emporia* in Tripolitania, for a number of reasons: the absolute originality of the representation, which pertains to symbolic and religious matters; the great importance of its meaning, which

[7] Bonacasa, N. (1996). pp. 49–60, in: Scritti di antichità in memoria di Sandro Stucchi, II. Studi Miscellanei, 29. Rome.

concerns a historical and celebratory theme; the undoubted public destination of the relief; and the propaganda-image nature of the subject. I am sure that the relief is a free and audacious local transposition of the basic compositional patterns of the Indian Triumph of Dionysus. In the first block, the iconographical theme and symbolical atmosphere flow freely from authentic Dionysiac religious iconography to the triumphal interpretation of a real episode. For this reason, the narration has three fundamental characteristics: the presence of *ferae libycae*, small African elephants without any ornamentation or trappings (unlike the Indian elephants on the Roman sarcophagi), and exotic felines, together with Maenads and hunters; the absence of male figures of the Dionysiac *thiasos*, Satyrs and Sileni for, example, at least in the surviving block; the sequence and 'manner' in which the subjects have been elaborated locally and expressed in a realistic and fluent style with a precise and up-to-date evocative objective which did not therefore reflect well known contemporary typologies. And, most importantly, I believe that, in view of the subject and the official nature of its destination, the relief is in fact tangible evidence of the links and the trade between the Mediterranean coast of Proconsular Africa and inner Africa, between Sabratha, in particular, and the vast regions to the south served by the trans-Saharan caravan routes.[8]

A commercial city par excellence, Sabratha was *civitas libera* under Augustus, obtained the concession of *civitas romana*, probably in 110 AD, and finally the title of *colonia* in the time of Antoninus Pius; the creation of the extensive quarters west, north and east of the theatre, along the *decumanus* to Oea, dates from the age of Antoninus and Commodus.[9, 10] It is certain that Severus Alexander solidly fortified Cydamus (Gadames) to protect the caravan route from the Sabrathan coast towards the hinterland, and it is likely that, after the raids of the Austurians (363 AD) and one year before the earthquake in 365 AD, Sabratha was elected to be the seat of the Tripolitan Assembly. The hypothesis is controversial, but the inscription remains a palpitating testimony to city life. It was formerly situated in the Forum at Sabratha and is now located along the south wall of Church 1, once the Judiciary Basilica, in honour of the governor Flavius Vivius Benedictus, the restorer *post ruinam* of the two cities of Sabratha and Leptis Magna, under the emperorships of Valentinian and Valens. For there is no doubt that Benedictus not only renovated the thermae (which certainly correspond to the great 'Seaward Baths') and the aqueduct that supplied them, but also activated the port of Sabratha.

[8] Di Vita, A. (1982). pp. 588–95, in: Aufstieg und Niedergang der Römischen Welt. II, 10, 2. Berlin, New York.
[9] Haynes, D. E. L. (1981). pp. 107, 122–33, in: The Antiquities of Tripolitania. London, Rome (4th edition).
[10] Barton, I. (1995). pp. 7–11, in: North Africa from Antiquity to Islam. Bristol.

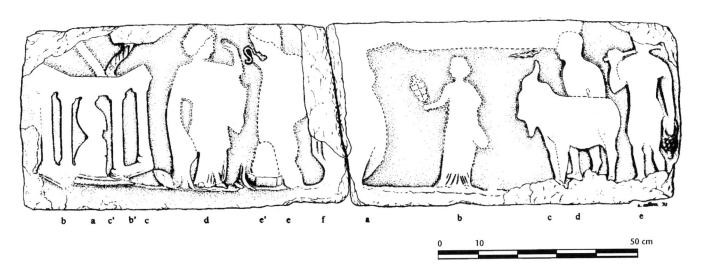

The ancient port of war, Thasos, Greece

ANGELIKI SIMOSSI
Greek Department of Underwater Antiquities

The island of Thasos is in the northern Aegean Sea, near Thrace, from which it is separated by a narrow strait 8 km wide. To the north of the island, Limenas Bay offers sailors today, as yesterday, a refuge against the often redoubtable seasonal winds and even against the north and north-easterly winds.

In about 680 BC, colonizers from Paros, one of the Cyclades [islands], established a colony on Thasos. The Parians occupied the acropolis of Thasos and the whole island all at the same time, thereby dominating the coastal area of the mainland, then setting up trading posts there.

By the end of the archaic period, their city had grown rich enough to allow the construction of a rampart built of gneiss and marble, with city gates decorated with bas-reliefs, enclosing an urban area of more than 4 km in circumference.

The ancient port opened onto the bay to the west, near the middle of the rampart; it was built seawards as an out-jutting fortification. A description of the vestiges of the closed port of Thasos has been facilitated today by the underwater archaeological investigations conducted between 1984 and 1992 by the Greek Department of Underwater Antiquities, under my direction, and by the French School of Athens, under the direction of J.-Y. Empereur.

The military port of Thasos is situated in the middle of the western part of the ancient city. The basin is protected by a fortification projecting seawards and connected to the city wall. Two gateways provide access to the city on the eastern and western sides, but both gateways (the Char gate, to the east, and the Polemarchos gate, to the west) are outside the port proper. Nevertheless, each is very close to a seaward projection of the rampart. The plan of the port is quadrilateral, the south-west side of which separates the port area from the city itself

The northern part of the port wall is separate from the city wall to the west of the Char gate and extends in a SE–NW direction (Fig. 1, line A–B) for a distance of 148.6 m. It turns in slightly less than a right angle southwestwards for about 45 m (Fig. 1, line B–C). This wall, which is quite close to the Char gate and about 3 m wide, is connected to the city wall at right angles and, at its start, its dimension can be compared to that of the city wall.

They are identical, with huge blocks of embossed marble, and are typical of the construction at the beginning of the 5th century BC. The presence of a modern jetty right on top of the ancient walls does not allow a direct view, but the alignment of the ancient wall is beyond doubt.

Along the line B–C, it has proved possible to map a part of the fortification that remains intact beneath the modern jetty. Here it can be seen, at shallow depth in the sea, that the conserved part of the wall, of 3 m width, is made up of two faces of roughly hewn schist plates, with filling between them. Here we are in the foundations; the marble wall elevation has disappeared.

The line H–G (Fig. 1) is straight from the gateway near the Museum (the Polemarchos or 'maritime' gate). It starts at H and is connected to the city wall. The wall's structure along H–G can be seen at H, but even better so to the north-west of the port basin, in front of the modern quay.

The facing towards the middle of the basin is rectilinear and made up of huge embossed marble blocks superposed in regular rows and clearly identical with those of the rampart (between the bastions) at the beginning of the

5th century BC. Behind the facing is a rubble-work of small stones. Certain blocks penetrate more deeply, as foundation stones, at fairly regular intervals of about 2 m. A sample excavation showed that the height of the above-mentioned facing, resting on six marble foundation stones, was 2.13 m.

The section F–G (Fig. 1), which turns back towards the north-east for 31 m is partly covered by the modern jetty. Between D and F (Fig. 1), the fortification there at the beginning of the 5th century has been lost.

The excavations that have been carried out have, in particular, provided us with information on an early Christian city. In the present situation, dating from the mid-19th century (AD), the port entrance, 55 km wide, is situated between the red harbour light (to the left on entering at E) and the green harbour light (to the right on entering at F). Then, between D and E, the modern mole describes a curve (D–E) about 115 m long, then continues in a straight line, after a bend, for 35 m between C and D. This alignment goes back to the early era, as the excavations have shown. The present entrance therefore has every chance of being the same as was used in the early Christian era.

This entrance has been deepened and dredged in modern times, to the extent that the investigation between E and F has revealed nothing new about the ancient city. Between C and D, the present mole has an early Christian foundation, but in this section we are quite sure that no more ancient structure ever existed.

Between D and E, the traces of an ancient city, repeatedly occupied by palaeochristians, have been found only at E. It comprises blocks arranged in alternation either in a diamond-like pattern or crosswise [only one end exposed]. These blocks are joined in an original manner. On the adjoining surfaces, dovetail slots have been cut out and then filled with molten lead. The dating of this construction could not be determined during the investigations, but it is unlikely to be younger than the 4th–3rd centuries BC, and could be even older. In any case, this foundation roughly follows the alignment of the mole D–E of the early Christian then modern eras.

It is probable that the closed port of the 5th century BC was, since the beginning, closed on this side by the extension of the fortification G–F. It is quite likely that the line D–F was closed by a continuous fortification that obstructed the present passage and extended roughly beneath the present mole. The ancient entrance would have been at the northern corner between C and D following a layout the details of which escape us.

If this hypothesis is accepted, the plan of the port, from the very beginning, was that of a closed port, designated precisely by Scylax as 'κλειστος λιμην'. This expression clearly evokes a fortified military port with access reserved to naval vessels that harboured there.

The ship hangars [νεωρια] are to be expected in a naval port. They were, in effect, essential to the ancient naval vessels, from the 6th century BC onwards, up to Roman times. The even foundation defined in the plan is that of a

Figure 1. Arrangement of the ship hangars in the closed port of Thasos, identified by J. Y. Empereur and A. Simossi, and verified by F. Salviat. Drawing by M. Borely based on the designs of Nikos Lianos and T. Koselj.

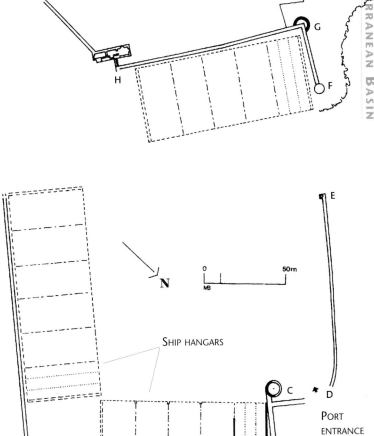

corner of a hangar in service in the mid-5th century BC (Fig. 2).

The north side has a foundation 40 m long and 1.1 m wide. It contains a double wall made of flat schist blocks of regular form. At the end of this wall, no change of angle is evident: it is a wall end. The length of the wall to the east is 20 m and it continues a further 2 m towards the south-east. All this construction is identical. Another wall, also with an identical structure, goes towards the west. Here again, large schist blocks, up to 2 m across, are employed. These blocks are knotched at regular intervals on their loadbearing surfaces to improve their grip.

The undisputable link in this layout defines a plan that suggests a building covering a considerable surface with several juxtaposed cells. Here we have the elements of a rectangular cell 44 m × 20 m, approximately, and part of a neighbouring cell immediately to the south. These cells open onto the port basin. The obvious interpretation is that these are juxtaposed ship hangars. Their length corresponds acceptably to that of a trireme, the hull of which was about 36 m long, and which would have been dragged from the water into the hangar. The width of the cells would have allowed each cell to take three vessels (beam width about 6 m each). Within each cell, it would have been necessary to have rows of supports for the hangar roof, separating the ramps up which the ships were dragged.

At greater depth there is another foundation, made of irregular blocks of schist in a double-walled structure; these vestiges date from the beginning of the 5th century BC.

Historical sources establish the existence of a Thasian fleet at the end of the 6th century BC. The texts show that Thasos had a well equipped navy of considerable size. At the surrender to Cimon's forces in 463 BC, the Thasian navy was able to sustain a loss of 33 triremes in naval combat, yet still be strong enough to sustain a prolonged siege. It is obvious that the loss of 33 vessels did not constitute the whole of Thasos' naval forces; in any case, she kept some reserves in her arsenals. A total of 50 triremes, as a standing navy, kept in the ship hangars of the closed port, seems an acceptable hypothesis.

It seems possible to reconstitute a group of hangars along the wall A–B (Fig. 3). This group could have extended over 100 m for 15 triremes (5 groups of 3). Also, along the wall G–H, over a distance of 100 m, one could reconstitute a similar number of hangars for 15 triremes (also 5 groups of 3); this would amount to 30 triremes. To get to 50, another set of hangars must be imagined; they could have been at the end of the port between H and A. The elevations could be reconstituted, with continuous covers, forming a saw-tooth roof the slope of which, towards the interior of the port, would follow the slopes of the slide ramps on which the vessels were moved. A double-sloped roof for each group of 3 triremes could be imagined (two roof surfaces covering about 20 m wall to wall).

The ramparts of the 6th and 5th centuries BC, with their massive high defensive walls, provided sufficient defence so long as the art of the siege remained little developed. Progress in the design of catapults, ballistas and battering rams led the engineers of the 4th century BC to imagine even more complex protection and to construct counter-batteries in the existing fortifications. With this, the number of towers grew quickly.

The city walls of Thasos therefore underwent improvements in response to new siege

Figure 2. Excavation in the port area: remains of the ship hangars; see A, B and C in Figure 1.
© EFA

strategy. They took the form of the square towers built inland and were erected against the city walls between existing archaic bastions.

It was also natural that the port fortifications should change, by the addition of new structures better adapted to resisting the new forms of attack. The machines that, on land, could smash city walls, were just as effective when mounted on heavy vessels or lashed to two hulls side by side. It was at this time, at the end of the 4th century BC, that the fortifications of the closed port of Thasos, designed in the 5th century BC, were reinforced with round towers.

We know of three of them, at B, C, and G. Only the tower at G was known before we started our archaeological investigations. This tower had on one of the facing stones of its walls an inscription in large letters mentioning the name of the person who had financed the construction: 'Herakleodoros, son of Aristonikos of Olynthe, the city's official host to visitors, has consecrated the tower, the forum and the statue to all the gods, using funds from the deposit he had entrusted to Archedemos, son of Histieos.' The date of the tower is given by the inscription. It is after the taking of Olynthe by the Macedonians in 348 BC. The date of the construction of the tower was probably at the end of the 4th century BC; this is confirmed by the findings from the sample excavations of the foundation. The central part of the tower had a filling of stones and that it was probably full, at least up to the top of the rampart against which it was built. The diameter of the tower at its base was only 8 m, hence it was a less massive construction than the towers at B and C (Fig. 1).

The towers B and C, with an average diameter of 10 m, were only loosely fixed to the ramparts and were certainly hollow, with floors equipped to contain catapults and with a platform for ballistas.

They were adapted for the defence of the port and had the same strength as the square towers (9 m wide) of the city enclosure on the landward side. The existence of the tower at C can only be explained if the entrance to the port was between C and D. The date of the towers at B and C is ascribable to the end of

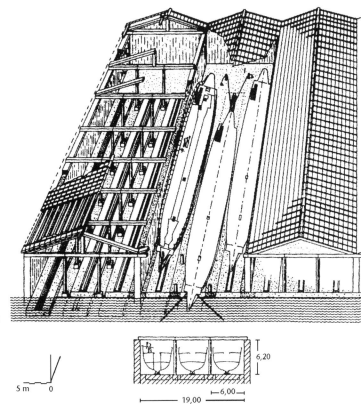

5 m   0

6,20

19,00   6,00

the 4th century BC, by reason of the filling in their foundations.

Outside the closed port, in the vicinity of the angle at G, an external construction pushing the embankment northwards has been observed. It forms a support made of blocks of marble and schist side by side in two rows covering a width of 2 m. The line of this artificial embankment follows a sinuous path from a point near the green harbour light at F to the vicinity of the tower at G; then it becomes more or less straight towards the south-east, parallel to the rampart G–H. There was clearly a land enclosure on the edge of the rampart G–H facing the 'maritime' gate.

There stood the ancient edifice of Soteira who was probably a goddess of protection for the port; and farther to the north, a piece of land recovered from the sea could have borne other constructions. The dedication of Herakleodoros to all the gods, which was mentioned above, and the tower at G, evoke a forum and a statue, which could have had their place on the artificial promontory constructed here.

Figure 3.
Reconstitution of the ship hangars in the ancient closed port of Thasos.
By M. Borely.

Underwater archaeology in Greece

DIMITRIS KAZIANIS
Archaeologist
Former Director of the Department of
Underwater Antiquities, Athens

Introduction

Greece, having 16,575 km of coastline and a history covering many centuries, is the richest country in the world in terms of underwater archaeological sites and shipwrecks. The protection of our cultural heritage, generally speaking, but more specifically of underwater antiquities, is included in the Greek Constitution [article 24], and the Archaeological Law KN 5351/32 includes the basic provisions for the protection of underwater antiquities. This law, in article 1, refers to the ownership of cultural goods. 'All antiquities found in Greece in any state-owned property, including rivers, lakes and the seafloor, either municipal, monastery or private, both movable and non-movable, are property of the state. Accordingly, the right and care for their quest, study, preservation and exhibition in public museums belongs to the state'. As Professor Roukounas clarifies in his study *Cultural Goods on the Bottom of the Sea*, it is understood that the seabed is the one recognized by international law as belonging to the coastal state.

Without a clear and powerful legal system our underwater cultural heritage is in danger from smugglers of antiquities, illegal fishing and illegal harbour construction.

The Department's programme of research and field work

In 1976, a special law (Government Gazette 207/A/10.8.76) established the Department of Underwater Antiquities, based in Athens, as a branch of the Archaeological Service, of the Ministry of Culture, for the protection of underwater antiquities nation-wide.

The Department, within its field of competence and relevance to the archaeological law, and in compliance with the law that was later established, has demonstrated multi-dimensional and interesting research and scientific achievements.

The research programme during the last three years has continued to improve, despite the everyday difficulties, and the inevitable bureaucracy. A brief report of the Department's annual archaeological excavation programme follows.

(a) In 1994, the Department discovered, in the northern Sporades, a 5th-century BC shipwreck, at a depth of 30–35 m with a cargo of amphorae which were being transported from Mendi, an ancient town of Khalkidhiki.

(b) A medieval, post-byzantine shipwreck was discovered at the entrance to the port of Zakinthos (on the Ionian island of the same name); the entire hull is preserved under a thick deposit of mud and sand. The ship's freight consisted of pottery, silver coins, hazelnuts, masses of glass, bullets and cannon balls (made of stone and metal). The shipwreck was found at a depth of 11 m.

(c) Research is taking place on the eastern part of the peninsula of Likithos (in Khalkidhiki) in the ancient port of Toroni. Here, we found remains of podiums, walls and other constructions of different periods. Some of these architectural remains were found in the sea, and others, on the coast.

(d) At Methoni, near Pylos, an extended submerged Middle Helladic prehistoric settlement was discovered. Remains of constructions can be seen under water in various places and the settlement is estimated to cover about 1,000 sq. m. The most important find located so far was a large *pithos* (storage jar) with the funeral remains of a young person inside.

(e) During the third period of excavations (in 1994) at the ancient port of Pythagorion on the island of Samos, we discovered, on the south side of the harbour, part of the ancient wall-breakwater and a part of a sea wall, dating to the Byzantine era. These walls were the continuation of the walls of the city into the sea. They protected the ancient port and reinforced the defences of the city.

(f) In August 1994, during fifteen days, archaeological research was carried out on the western part of the temple of Apollo, near the ancient port of Aigina (near Attica). Ancient harbour constructions were discovered submerged along the coastline. A topographical land and underwater survey was completed.

(g) In November 1994, the Republic of Cyprus's Ministry of Transport and Communications, Department of Antiquities, was interested in finding a shipwreck in the vicinity of Protara-Paralimni. A team of archaeologist-divers of the Greek Department of Underwater Antiquities located the hull of a wrecked ship lying at a depth of about 30 m on the sandy sea floor near Protara. The wreck was covered with *Posidonia* seagrass. Unfortunately, the wreck had been heavily plundered.

(h) A survey of the 17th century warship, *La Thérèse*, is continuing. The ship was participating in a military mission which Louis XIV sent to Handaka to help in the defence of the Venetians (War of Crete, 1645–1669). The warship was sunk after the explosion of its powder magazine during an organized attack from the sea against the Turkish camp. The failure of this attack led to the end of the Cretan War and the total surrender of the island to the Turks. The shipwreck was discovered in the harbour of Heraklion (Gulf of Dermata) in a depth of 17 m, covered by sand. So far, 80 sq. m of the wreck site have been excavated and various parts of the actual ship have been exposed. Also, many personal objects belonging to the crew have been raised to the surface.

(i) An excavation near the Acropolis of the modern fishing port of Avdira (near the modern town of Xanthe, Thrace) is

continuing. Here, an ancient breakwater, 170 m long, remains; it lies in an east-west direction. Two semicircular towers seem to belong to an older period, since one can observe two different construction phases. The eastern and northern sides were built in the Byzantine era. There are important indications that place the first phase in the Archaic Age.

An important scientific activity of the Department of Underwater Antiquities is the study of ancient navigation routes, (ever dependent on progress in ancient ship-building) which facilitated the commercial and cultural exchanges between the islands and the continental regions of the Mediterranean.

Reports of archaeological discoveries – emergency excavations

Besides its systematic research, the Department of Underwater Antiquities undertakes emergency underwater searches as well as preparatory reconnaissance of newly discovered shipwrecks that have been located by recreational and professional divers.

(a) On the indication of a private individual, a shipwreck of the Roman era has been located in the Volimon in the vicinity of Zakinthos at a depth of 30–35 m. A preliminary underwater search took place; photographs of the shipwreck were taken and pottery samples collected.

(b) On the indication of a private individual, a shipwreck of the Roman era has been located at a depth of 40–45 m, in the vicinity of the Parapola islet in the Mirtoon Sea. Its freight consists of amphorae that have retained their caps. Photographs of the shipwreck have been taken and pottery samples collected.

(c) On the indication of a private individual, a shipwreck possibly dating back to 1770 or to at least to the Crimean War (1854–56) has been located on the site of Methones on the island of Limnos. The shipwreck has been photographed and diagrammed.

(d) The shipwreck found near Keratea in Attiki may be mentioned, and the fact that the north Sporades area is gaining particular

interest for underwater archaeological
research, as a result of the indication of other
shipwrecks to the Department.

Preliminary underwater research has been
started at various other sites: (i) Alimnia, in
the island of Rhodes, where dockyards of the
Hellenistic era hewn out of rock have been
located, photographed and measured;
(ii) emergency underwater archaeological
research at Kalo Limani, near Andissa, on the
island of Lesbos, where an arrangement of
rock piles, which have not been dated, has
been located, photographed and measured;
and surveys of the underwater part of a
construction in Dilesi in Beotia and the
ancient arrangements of rocks in Palaiokhora
near Siteia on the island of Crete.

Registration of antiquities with the Department of Underwater Antiquities

A large number of objects, mostly transport
amphorae, found underwater mostly by
fishing trawlers, have been turned over to the
Department. Amongst these was a black-
figure crater (a type of vase) dated to the
Classical period.

The most important object raised to the surface
accidentally by a fishing trawler and turned
over to the Department was the bronze statue
of a young woman, which was found near the
islands of Kalymnos and Pserimos in the
Dodecanese. The statue is of life size [1.90 m]
and resembles the well known marble copies
of the Great Herakliotissa found at the theatre
of Herculaneum. The Young Woman from
Kalymnos is the only bronze statue of its type
and is dated to the Hellenistic era.

The statue, composed of two pieces, the head
and the body, was raised to the surface on
30 December 1994 and was escorted to
Athens by a team of archaeologists from the
Department. In accordance with Greek law, a
large amount of money was granted to the
fisherman who had salvaged this unique
bronze statue. Today, almost two years later,
the statue is undergoing a very slow and
tedious restoration period, but it will soon be
ready to be exhibited, along with the first
scientific presentation.

Modern development and ancient maritime sites along the Tyrrhenian coast

ENRICO FELICI
Associazione Italiana Archeologi Subacquei
Rome

Introduction

Coastal management cannot disregard knowledge of the ancient underwater remains of archaeological interest found there as a result of changes in sea level. These remains were mainly maritime structures destined for residential or practical use: seaside villas, anchorages, quarries, fish tanks and fish-processing equipment, harbours, lighthouses etc. Such monuments are liable to suffer considerable damage from exploitation of the coastal zone in modern times.

The harbours, especially, have suffered heavy destruction; most of the ancient Mediterranean harbours have been lost for human use as anchorages. Moreover, Roman harbours were established in the best nautical locations, and the ruins encouraged their incorporation into the construction of new jetties, to save money in the new construction.

When an ancient harbour is covered by a modern harbour, we lose not only a monument, but also the archaeological remains beneath which are often destroyed by dredging. Above all, any possibility of learning about ancient techniques for building harbours is lost. These techniques are still not very well known; they only recently became better understood as a result of underwater archaeological research and detailed surveys. The concentration of Roman ports on the Italian coast of the Tyrrhenian Sea is understandably great. It comprises small docks for local use and grand commercial and military harbours, such as those at Ostia or Portus Julius.

Roman harbour construction

Firstly, some short accounts of Roman techniques for building harbour moles follow. According to Vitruvius (the Augustan-age author of *De architectura*), one could build maritime structures by casting concrete (*opus caementicium*) in two types of wooden moulds: 'waterproofed' or 'flooded'. In the first, a double-walled mould had to be emptied of water, for use by the 'normal' building method. In the second, a flooded mould was possible, concrete being cast directly in water, but the system needed the addition of volcanic ash, pozzolana (*pulvis puteolanus*), from the Puteoli region, which enables the concrete to harden under water. In both cases, the mould was reinforced by an internal wooden frame of posts (*destinae*, or *stipites*) and horizontal beams (*catenae*).[1]

[1] Dubois, C. (1902). Observations sur un passage de Vitruve. pp. 439–67, in: Mélanges d'Archéologie et d'Histoire. *Rome.*
• *Felici, E. (1993). Osservazioni sul porto neroniano di Anzio e sulla tecnica romana delle costruzioni portuali in calcestruzzo.* Archeologia subacquea, Studi, ricerche e documenti, I:71–104. Istituto Poligrafico dello Stato.
• *Fensterbush, C. (1964).* Vitruv, Zehn Bücher über Architektur. *Darmstadt.*
• *Oleson, J. P. (1985). Herod and Vitruvius: Preliminary Thoughts on Harbour Engineering at Sebastos: the Harbour of Caesarea Maritima. pp. 165–72, in: A. Raban (ed.),* Harbour Archaeology, Proceedings of the First International Workshop on Ancient Mediterranean Harbours (Caesarea Maritima [near Haifa], 1983), *British Archaeological Reports, 257.*
• *Oleson, J. P., Hohlfelder, R. L., Raban, A. and Vann, R. L. (1984). The Caesarea Ancient Harbor Excavation Project (C.A.H.E.P.): Preliminary Report on the 1980–1983 Seasons.* Journal of Field Archaeology, 3:282–305.

(cont'd on next page)

The harbour of Cosa

Recent American surveys interpreted the mole of the Roman harbour of Cosa as being a pier building, dating to the early 2nd century BC (Fig. 1).[2] A later Italian technical survey reconsidered the building system, suggesting that the mole's structure was based on spaced piers as the main loadbearing points, and that the gaps between were filled later. This suggestion is supported by the fact that there are two hollows on the north faces of the piers, one of which was surely due to the insertion of a small amphora in the wet concrete. The hollows served as receptacles for the ends of the horizontal beams of moulds used in the construction of the small pier. This was a cheap way to build an uninterrupted mole (Fig. 2).

Figure 1. Cosa harbour mole, Western side.

Figure 2. Cosa harbour mole, axonometric projection of the building technique.

The interpretation of the mole's structure as a pier building sprang from a gap between piers 2 and 3, but this gap is probably the result of the recent demolition of a part of the mole to facilitate the drainage of a quagmire behind the coastal dune. An indication of this is the modern ferroconcrete mouth of the drain, which partially encased the mole. This is an example of a modern intervention which, by altering an ancient ruin, can induce archaeological misinterpretation.

[1 - cont'd]
• Oleson, J. P. (1988). The Technology of Roman Harbours. International Journal of Nautical Archaeology, 17(2):147–57.
• Oleson, J. P. and Branton, G. (1992). The Harbour of Caesarea Palaestinae: a Case Study of Technology Transfer in the Roman Empire. pp. 389–420, in: Atti del Simposio [Symposium Proceedings], Geschichte der Wasserwirtschaft und des Wasserbaus im Mediterranen Raum (Merida, 1991). Braunschweig.
• Schläger, H. (1971). Die Texte Vitruvs im Lichte der Untersuchungen am Hafen von Side. Bonner Jahrbücher, pp. 150–61.
[2] Gazda, E. K. (1987). The Port and Fishery: Description of the Extant Remains and Sequence of Construction. pp. 74 et seq. in: A. M. McCann et al., The Roman Port and Fishery of Cosa. Princeton University Press.
• Felici, E. and Balderi, G. (1997). Il porto romano di Cosa: note per l'interpretazione di un'opera marittima in cementizio. Archeologia subacquea, Studi, ricerche e documenti, II:11-19. Istituto Poligrafico dello Stato.
[3] Lugli, G. (1939). Saggi di esplorazione archeologica a mezzo della fotografia aerea. Istituto di Studi Romani, pp. 5-6. Rome.
• Lugli, G. (1940). Saggio sulla topografia dell'antica Antium. Rivista dell'Istituto Nazionale di Archeologia e Storia dell'Arte, VII:153 et seq.
• Blackman, D. J. (1992). Ancient harbours in the Mediterranean. In: International Journal of Nautical Archaeology, Part 1, 11(2):79–104; Part 2, 11(3):185–211.
• Gianfrotta, P. A. (1980). Anzio. pp. 9 et seq. in: (cat. mostra) L'aerofotografia da materiale di guerra a bene culturale: le fotografie aeree della R.A.F. Roma.
• Lehmann-Hartleben, K. (1923). Die antiken Hafenanlagen des Mittelmeeres. Klio XIV. Leipzig.
• Schmiedt, G. (1970). Atlante aerofotografico delle sedi umane in Italia. Parte seconda: Le sedi antiche scomparse. Istituto Geografico Militare, Firenze.

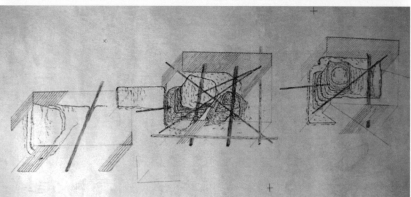

The harbour of Antium

The western dock

This impressive harbour near Rome was, according to Suetonius, built by the emperor Nero. A lot of the main dock was silted up when the adjoining modern harbour was built in the 18th century (by Pope Innocence XII), and later occupied by the modern town. A lot of the eastern mole was encased by the new mole.[3]

Recent surveys have documented the structure of the moles' foundations. The moles appeared to be uninterrupted (Fig. 3), built by flooded moulds reinforced by internal wooden frames made of posts and horizontal beams, and filled with pozzolanic concrete and tuff fragments. The elevations (above the water surface) of the moles were also brick-faced (Fig. 4).

The same technique was used for building the wharf on the western side of the port, on which there are many barrel-vaulted service rooms (Figs. 5 and 6).

The eastern dock

Hitherto, Anzio was known as a one-dock harbour. Plans from the 18th and 19th centuries and photographs from the early 20th century show the *Molo Panfili*, a masonry ruin now encased by a modern tourist wharf. According to the literature, this *pennello* was built in the early 18th century, shortly after the construction of the port ordered by Pope Innocence XII, to limit its siltation. This 18th-century *pennello*, according to some building documents, was built by erecting piles (*passonate*) and filling them with stones (a building technique used by the Papal States); they were abandoned immediately after completion because they were ineffective against siltation.

The photographs otherwise show an obviously Roman construction, made in brick-faced *opus*

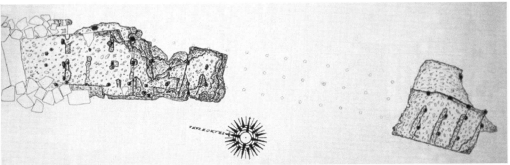
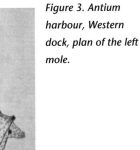

Figure 3. Antium harbour, Western dock, plan of the left mole.

Figure 4. Antium harbour, Western dock, a brick-faced ruin on the seabed.

*Figure 5.
Antium harbour,
axonometric
projection of the
concrete bed's
building technique.*

*Figure 6.
Antium harbour,
barrel-vaulted
service rooms.*

*Figure 7. Antium
harbour, Eastern
dock, the roman
mole in an early
20th century
photograph.*

*Figure 8. Antium
harbour, Eastern
dock, axonometric
projection of the
roman mole's
building technique.*

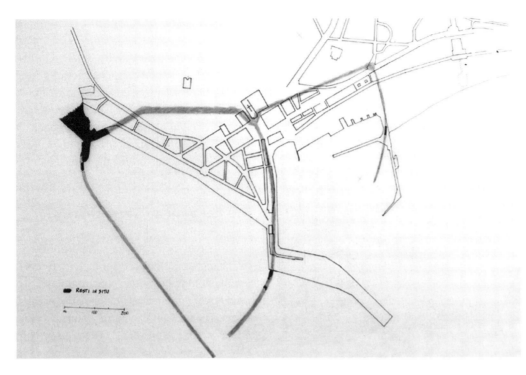

Figure 9. Antium, a new topographical hypothesis on the two harbour docks in a planimetric sketch.

caementicium, most probably built simultaneously with the neighbouring Neronian harbour (Figs. 7, 8). The *Molo Panfili* absorbed these ruins to simplify the construction works, as was often done in Anzio.[4] This method also led to the covering of the lefthand mole of the Neronian port.

Anzio's harbour complex during the Imperial era therefore comprised two docks (Fig. 9), which also explains the discovery, during late 19th-century construction work, of a Roman shipwreck, later sanded in, that had sunk in the eastern dock.

The lost fish tanks at Nettuno

The recent building of tourist wharves destroyed two Roman fish tanks, as shown by an aerial photograph (Fig. 10).[5]

A harbour at Astura

The famous seaside *villa*, complete with a large fish tank and a harbour, owes its preservation to the absence of tourist facilities (it being military property), in spite of some destruction due to wave action. The fish tank and the harbour moles and wharf were built in concrete.[6] The mole's

[4] Felici, E. and Balderi, G. (1997). Nuovi documenti sulla 'topografia portuale' di Antium. pp. 11–20, in: Atti del Convegno *[Conference Proceedings]* Nazionale di Archeologia Subacquea, *(Anzio, 1996). Edipuglia, Bari.*
[5] Gianfrotta, P. A. (1997). Le peschiere scomparse di Nettuno (RM). pp. 21–4, in: Atti del Convegno *[Conference Proceedings]* Nazionale di Archeologia Subacquea-A.I.A. Sub. *(Anzio, 1996) Edipuglia, Bari.*
[6] Castagnoli, F. (1963). Astura. Studi Romani, *XI(6):1–8.*
• *Gianfrotta, P. A. and Pomey, P. (1981).* Archeologia subacquea. *A. Mondatori, Milano.*
• *Piccarreta, F. (1977). Astura,* Forma Italiae. *Regio, XIII. L. Olschki, Rome.*

Figure 10. Nettuno, roman fish tanks in aerial view.

The sea gate of Circeii

This sea gate, perhaps built by Nero, connects the Paola Lake with the sea at Circeii.[8] It has two uninterrupted concrete moles, the righthand one of which has a head that clearly shows the use of moulds in the construction (Fig. 13).[9] The moles were covered by more modern construction during the Papal era.

The harbour of Tarracina

This is one of the important harbours of the Tyrrhenian coast; it is lost for modern re-use. Period photographs show an uninterrupted cement mole provided with pierced mooring stones. The harbour had barrel-vaulted service rooms (storage, workshops, offices etc.).[10]

The Phlegraean Fields

The Phlegraean Fields were an important centre of marine engineering. This region had a strategic position, excellent for navigation on the Mediterranean. Many of the harbour installations discovered were part of a complex system that had complementary functions: military and commercial. Today, most of these ruins are submerged as a result of the geological

Figure 11. Astura's harbour, the left mole, Western side.

Figure 12. Astura's harbour, left mole, axonometric projection of the building technique.

remains (Fig. 11) reveal clearly enough the technique of construction, for which wooden moulds were used (Fig. 12). Some authors have thought the mole was built on piers (*pilae*), but a filling technique applied between the main load-bearing piers was most probably used.[7]

Figure 13. Circeii's gate, right mole' head, axonometric projection of the building technique.

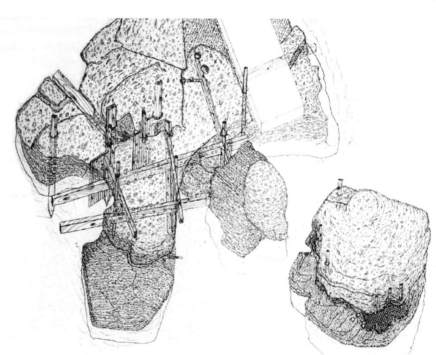

phenomenon (bradyseism) that affects the entire area, and lost for human use.[11]

The mole of Puteoli

An image of the Puteoli mole often appears on souvenir glass flasks such as those made in Prague, Odemira, Populonia etc.[12] It was built as a 372 m-long breakwater (Fig. 14) spanned on arcades supported by piers (*pilae*). It is attested to by many maps drawn in the 17th and 18th centuries. Today, it is completely covered by modern renovation. The same technique (called *opus pilarum*) was also used for the external part of the Portus Julius and more frequently along the Baia coastline. The technique was also used to lengthen the structures built into the sea around the Rione Terra (Pozzuoli, near Naples).

Harbour structures at Nisida Island

Some other similar structures were built on the north-eastern side of the island of Nisida (Fig. 15). Few have survived, but many others, documented by maps of the Bourbon period,

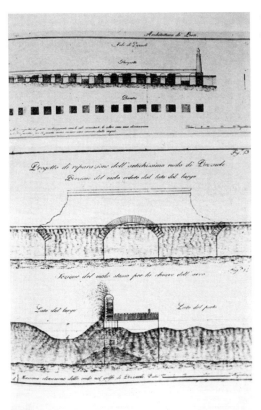

Figure 14. The Puteoli's mole in an 18th century survey.

[7] Felici, E. (1993). op. cit.
[8] Lugli, G. (1928). Circeii, Forma Italiae. Regio, I:2. L. Olschki, Rome.
[9] Felici, E. (1993). op. cit.
[10] Lugli, G. (1926). Anxur-Terracina, Forma Italiae. Regio, I:1. L. Olschki, Rome.
[11] Castagnoli, F. (1977). Topografia dei Campi Flegrei. pp. 41–79, in: I campi Flegrei nell'archeologia e nella storia, Atti dei Convegni [Conference Proceedings] Lincei 33, Roma (1976).
[12] Gianfrotta, P. A. (1996). Harbor Structures of the Augustan Age in Italy. pp. 65–76, in: Atti del Convegno[Conference Proceedings] Caesarea Maritima, a Retrospective after Two Millennia, (Caesarea Maritima, 1995). E. J. Brill, Leiden, New York, Cologne.
• Ostrow, S. E. (1979). The topography of Puteoli and Baia on the eight glass flasks. Puteoli, III:77–137.
• Di Fraia, G., Lombardo, N. and Scognamiglio, E. (1985–1986). Contributi alla topografia di Baia sommersa. Puteoli, IX-X:211–99.
• Di Fraia, G. (1993). Baia sommersa. Nuove evidenze topografiche e monumentali. Archeologia subacquea, Studi, ricerche e documenti, I:21–48. Istituto Poligrafico dello Stato.
• Dubois, C. (1907). Pouzzoles antiques. Bibliothèque des Écoles Françaises de Rome et d'Athènes, 98.

have been covered by modern jetties. Remains of some ancient harbour installations were hitherto unknown, but recent underwater archaeological research has revealed three *pilae* still in place. One of these is perfectly preserved: it is a 'tower' 9.5 m high, the top of which is 180 cm below sea level. It was built in *opus caementicium* with tuff fragments which, on the sides of the *pila*, seem to form a sort of *opus reticulatum*. In some sections, there are holes left by the wooden posts and beams of the double-walled moulds.

Figure 15. Nisida island: a pier jetty in a 19th century plan.

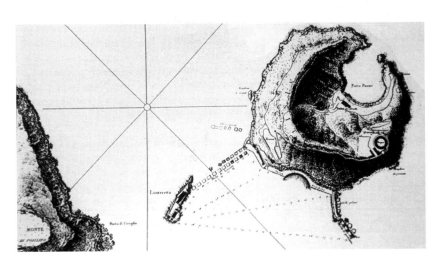

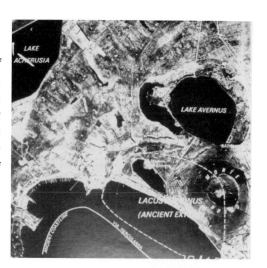

Figure 16. An aerial view of Phlegraean Fields, showing the location of the ancient coastline. Portus Julius occupied the two ancient lakes of Lucrino and Averno.

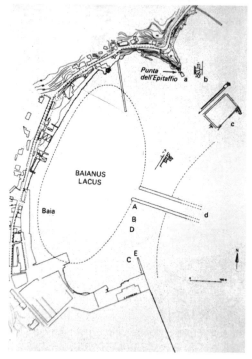

Figure 17. Baia, plan of the submerged evidence and the ancient coastline.

Figure 18. Baia, fragment of an Egyptian 'stele' from the sea.

Harbour structures at Misenum

The same type of construction is found in the breakwaters that protected the two entrances to the harbour of Misenum. On the Punta Terone side, the underwater structures[13] consist of a row of eight *pilae*, most of them still standing. A long breakwater runs alongside them, but today it is hidden by blocks of a modern breakwater. The *pilae* are parallelepipeds; some of them have holes left by the vertical and horizontal beams of the scaffolding. The curvilinear concrete head of the breakwater remains, in which some mooring stones are visible; four can be distinguished, all cut in the middle, with the cut part having been found on the seabed.

The Portus Julius

It was a great military harbour, built in 37 BC by Agrippa in the Lucrino and Averno lakes (Fig. 16).

The submerged town of Baia

This residential settlement is for the most part submerged to depths of 6 to 19 m as a result of bradyseism. In spite of the Archaeology Office's efforts, the ruins have been damaged by the modern activity of vessels loading pozzolana: the keels of loaded ships have, for a long time, abraded the submerged remains. The hulks of some modern ships have been abandoned on top of them. The villas of the Republican and Imperial eras, which have yielded important historical data and sculptures, continue to reveal buildings and objects of archaeological interest (Fig. 17, 18).[14] Among these, also, evidence of the relationship between the Phlegraean coast (particularly the harbour of Puteoli) and Egypt, and perhaps with the harbour of Alexandria, has been found.

[13] Gianfrotta, P. A. (1993). *Puteoli sommersa.* pp. 115–24, in: Puteoli. *Banca Sannitica, Napoli.*
[14] Gianfrotta, P. A. (1983). *L'indagine archeologica e lo scavo.* pp. 25–39, in: AA.VV. *[various authors],* Baia. Il ninfeo imperiale sommerso di Punta Epitaffio. *Napoli.*
• Scognamiglio, E. (1997). *Aggiornamenti per la topografia di Baia sommersa.* Archeologia subacquea, *Studi, ricerche e documenti, II:35–45.*
• Schmiedt, G. (1972). Il livello antico del Mar Tirreno. *Firenze.*

Remote-sensing tools for archaeology

FAROUK EL-BAZ
Center for Remote Sensing
Boston University

Introduction

Much has been learned during the past
three decades about photographing the
Earth from space, through a series of
American, Russian and European space
missions. Starting in 1965, many useful
photographs were acquired by astronauts of
the American Gemini, Apollo, Skylab, the
US/USSR Apollo-Soyuz, and the Russian Mir
missions. In 1972, the Landsat programme
introduced digital imaging from unmanned
spacecraft, from which data were transmitted
to ground receiving stations. The technology
of these systems provides an advanced new
tool for detailed study of the natural and
cultural resources and the changing
environment of the Earth. This is particularly
true in desert regions where the land features
are not masked by vegetation.[1]

Unmanned and manned spacecraft systems
are placed in high, medium or low orbits. The
highest orbits are left to the unmanned
weather satellites, such as Meteosat, which
are propelled to a height of 36,000 km above
the Earth. At this altitude, their motion is
equivalent in speed to the rotation of the
Earth about its axis. These satellites are
termed geostationary and remain above the
same point on the Earth to acquire and
transmit repetitive images as frequently as
every hour. Owing to their high altitude, the
images they collect cover most of one
hemisphere of the Earth at low spatial
resolution, which is ideal for studying global
weather phenomena.

Intermediate orbits are those from 500 to
1,000 km above the Earth, the region where
most unmanned imaging satellites are placed.
For example, the polar-orbiting satellites of
the US National Oceanic and Atmospheric
Administration (NOAA) fly at altitudes of
835 to 870 km; and the near-polar orbits of
the American Landsat and the French
Système Pour l'Observation de la Terre
(SPOT) reach a maximum altitude of 920 km
above the Earth. Images collected from these
altitudes provide greater local detail than is
possible from the high-altitude satellites, but
the area covered by individual images is
reduced.

At the lower end, most manned missions are
placed in orbits below 500 km, to a minimum
of 150 km above the Earth. For example, the
Space Shuttle's operational altitude is about
250 km. From this altitude, images show
greater detail. The Space Shuttle's Large
Format Camera (LFC), for example, provided
images that show features as small as 10 m in
mapping-quality, three-dimensional (stereo)
photographs.[2]

Imaging from space

Landsat: The Earth Resources Technology
Satellite (ERTS-1), the first unmanned digital-
imaging satellite, was launched on 23 July
1972. Four other satellites in the same series,
later named Landsat, were launched at
intervals of a few years. The Landsat

[1] El-Baz, F. (1984). *The desert in the space age.*
pp. 1–29, in: F. El-Baz (ed.), Deserts and Arid
Lands. *Martinus Nijhoff Publishers, The Hague,*
The Netherlands.
[2] El-Baz, F. (1985). *New mapping quality*
photographs of the Earth and their applications to
planetary comparisons. Lunar and Planetary
Science, *XVI(Part 1):207–8. Lunar and Planetary*
Institute, Houston, Texas.

spacecraft carried a Multi-Spectral Scanner (MSS) and, later, a Thematic Mapper (TM) imaging system.[3]

The MSS was carried on Landsat 1, 2 and 3 and produced images representing four different bands of the electromagnetic spectrum (Fig. 1). The four bands were designated band 4 for the green spectral region (0.5 to 0.6 micrometres); band 5 for the red spectral region (0.6 to 0.7 micrometres); band 6 for the near-infrared region (0.7 to 0.8 micrometres); and band 7 for another near-infrared region (0.8 to 1.1 micrometres). Radiation reflectance data from the four scanner channels are converted first into electronic signals, then into digital form for transmission to receiving stations on Earth. The recorded digital data, at 80-m resolution, are reformatted into computer-compatible tapes for processing and analysis. For example, the green band (band 4) most clearly shows underwater features, because of the

Figure 1. The electromagnetic spectrum, showing the range of visible (colour) photographs, infrared and thermal images, and radar (microwave) images.

ability of green radiation to penetrate shallow water, and is useful in coastal studies. The two near-infrared bands, which measure the reflectance of the Sun's rays outside the sensitivity of the human eye (visible range), are useful in the study of vegetation cover.

The TM is a sensor that was carried on Landsat 4 and 5; it covered seven spectral bands in the visible, near-infrared, and thermal-infrared regions of the spectrum. It was designed to satisfy more demanding performance parameters from experience gained in the operation of the MSS with better ground resolution (30 m). At this ground resolution, many small agricultural fields may be accurately characterized.[4] The seven spectral bands (Fig. 2) were selected for their band passes and radiometric resolutions. For example, band 1 coincides with the maximum transmissivity of water. It also has beneficial features for the differentiation of vegetation, along with bands 2, 3 and 4. Vegetation and soil moisture may be estimated from band 5 readings, and plant transpiration rates may be estimated from the thermal mapping in band 6. Band 7 is primarily used for geological applications, including the identification of rock types.[3]

SPOT: This system was designed by the French Centre Nationale d'Études Spatiales (CNES) and built by the French industry in association with partners in Belgium and Sweden. Like the American Landsat, it consists of remote-sensing satellites and ground receiving stations. The imaging is accomplished by two High-Resolution Visible (HRV) instruments that operate in either a panchromatic (black-and-white) mode for observation over a broad spectrum, or a multi-spectral (colour) mode for sensing in narrow spectral bands. The ground resolutions are 10 and 20 m, respectively. For viewing directly beneath the spacecraft, the two instruments can be pointed to cover adjacent areas. By pointing a mirror that directs ground radiation

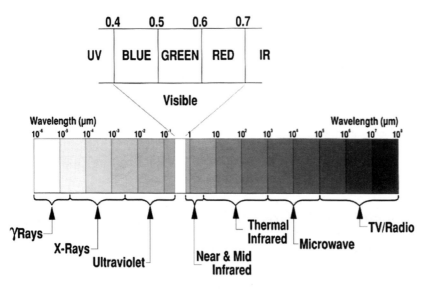

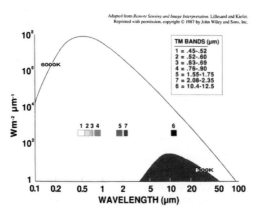

Fig. 2 The wave length range of the seven imaging bands of the LANDSAT Thematic Mapper (TM) sensors. (see also Fig. 1)

[3] Hord, R. M. (1986). Remote Sensing Methods and Applications. *Wiley Series in Remote Sensing, John Wiley & Sons, New York.*
[4] Szekielda, K. H. (1988). Satellite Monitoring of the Earth. *John Wiley & Sons, New York.*

to the sensors, it is possible to observe any region within 450 km from the nadir, thus allowing the acquisition of stereophotographs for three-dimensional viewing.

Shuttle Imaging Radar: Imaging radar instruments transmit waves towards the surface and record the returned echoes. The latter are stronger (bright) from rocky terrain and weaker (dark) from smooth surfaces. On its maiden flight in November 1981[5], the Shuttle Imaging Radar experiment (SIR-A) provided the first indication of the ability of radar to penetrate through sand and reveal buried courses of ancient rivers in the eastern Sahara (Fig. 3). North of this region, in the Western Desert of Egypt, drilled wells in 'East Oweinat' produced water for an experimental, 5,000 acre farm. It is estimated that the ground-water resources in this region are capable of supporting agriculture on nearly 200,000 acres for 200 years.[1] The next flight, three years later (SIR-B), obtained images of the Arabian Peninsula, among other regions. In addition, the renamed Spaceborne Imaging Radar (SIR-C) experiment, returned 25 m-resolution images from flights in April and October 1994. Unlike previous orbital radar systems, SIR-C acquired digital images using a 24 cm [wavelength] L-band and a 6 cm C-band, with each wavelength recording vertically and horizontally polarized waves. Different combinations of wavelength and polarization can be used to produce colour images to emphasize particular features. For example, SIR-C images were used to reveal inconspicuous segments of the Great Wall of China (Fig. 4).

Radarsat: This satellite is a project led by the Canadian Space Agency (CSA) in partnership with NASA and NOAA. It was launched in a polar, Sun-synchronous orbit by a Delta II rocket on 4 November 1995. It features a C-band, horizontally polarized, synthetic-aperture radar (SAR), with flexible beam steering and resolution characteristics.[6] Thus, it is the first SAR to operate in a variety of resolutions (down to 10 m), swath widths and incidence angles. This flexibility is designed to maximize potential applications of the data and the frequency of coverage required for operational use.

Spy satellites: In February 1995, the United States Government announced the declassification of the Corona programme 'spy-satellite' photographs obtained between 1960 and 1972 of various parts of the world.[7] Shortly thereafter, Russia followed suit by declassifying similar products. The DD-5, very-high-resolution, black-and-white images, are among those declassified; the original images, with 0.7 m resolution, are degraded by digitization of photographic prints to a resolution of about 2 m prior to their sale for civilian use outside Russia.

Figure 3. Left, part of the eastern Sahara as depicted in two LANDSAT scenes (width of composite is approximately 185 km). Right, the same area with a strip showing the palaeochannels as revealed by the Shuttle Imaging Radar (SIR-A) mission of the Space Shuttle in November 1981.

[5] Elachi, D. et al. (1982). Shuttle Imaging Radar experiment. Science, 218: 996–1003.

[6] Raney, R. K., Luscombe, A. P., Langham, E. J. and Ahmed, S. (1991). Radarsat. Proceedings of the IEEE, 79(6):839–49.

[7] McDonald, R. A. (1997). Corona between the Sun and the Earth: the First NRO Reconnaissance Eye in Space. American Society of Photogrammetry and Remote Sensing, Bethesda, MD.

Figure 4. Spaceborne Imaging Radar (SIR-C) images of a segment of the Great Wall, about 700 km west of Beijing, China (L and C bands, horizontally, H, and vertically, V, polarized combinations). The bright line from top to bottom in the L-HH image is the younger wall (600 years BP). The discontinuous line in the L-HV image is an older segment (1,500 years BP). Vegetation types can be distinguished in the C-HH and C-HV images.

Future systems: In addition to data already available, four commercial entities are presently planning to launch digital-imaging satellites. These will be the first privately supported ventures, with no government subsidy whatsoever, proving that satellite images are commercially viable products. The new system will be able to reveal small features on the Earth's surface. These digital-imaging systems will be designed to produce multi-spectral data with a resolution of 5 to 15 m, and panchromatic, stereo-images with 1–5 m resolution.[8] These characteristics would allow use of the data in detailed archaeological investigations.

Field instruments

In conjunction with data from the imaging systems, archaeologists are increasingly utilizing geophysical sensors. The latter are similar to those used by geologists to investigate subsurface layering in petroleum and groundwater exploration.[9] Foremost among these are the following:

Electromagnetic conductivity sensor: This instrument measures differences in conductivity between surface and subsurface soils and features. It provides direct readings of terrain conductivity to a depth of about 6 m. Thus, it can be used to map either superposed layers of soil or subsurface cavities, such as tombs.

Ground-penetrating radar (GPR): This is a special type of low-frequency radar that is capable of 'seeing' into the ground. Conventional radars use microwaves, which can penetrate only a few centimeters into rock. A GPR uses much lower frequencies (close to those used by FM radio or television stations), emitting a brief pulse of radio-frequency energy lasting only a few billionths of a second. When the radar pulses travel down into the ground, they pass through various layers of soil, sand, clay, rock, or man-made materials. Each interface between layers produces an echo. These echoes return to the surface, where they are detected by an antenna. The deeper the reflecting layer, the longer its echo will take to return to the surface.

Magnetometers: The magnetic field of the Earth is influenced by subsurface features that have a different magnetization from that of the surrounding soil. Small localized features near the surface are easily detectable and deeper geologic structures are also observable if the survey is extended across large areas. The proton magnetometer, the most widely used in archaeological investigations, can measure very small variations in magnetization; for example, those due to the presence of an ancient hearth.

Resistivity instruments: In the resistivity method of prospecting, an electric current is

[8] *Fritz, L. (1996). The era of commercial earth observation satellites.* Photogrammetric Engineering and Remote Sensing, *January 1996:39–45.*
[9] *El-Baz, F. (1997). Space age archaeology.* Scientific American, *277(2):60–5.*

produced in the ground by two contact electrodes, and the differences in electric potential between them are measured. Electrode arrays may be moved along profiles to determine lateral variations in resistivity, thus, pinpointing the location of buried features.

Seismic instruments: Seismometers used by archaeologists are much like those used to detect, magnify and record vibrations due to earthquakes, but are sensitive to artificially generated elastic waves. The detected motions are recorded in charts, which show the time taken for a wave to travel to a reflection or refraction subsurface layer and back again to the surface. The charts are correlated to show the depth of the interface that causes the reflection. Thus, emerges a 'seismic picture' of the subsurface layers and structures.

Examples in Egyptology

Tomb of Nefertari

The author has applied remote sensing tools to the investigation of a tomb that was jointly studied by the Egyptian Antiquities Organization and the Getty Conservation Institute. The tomb was that of Queen Nefertari, the favorite wife of Pharaoh Ramses the Great, who ruled Egypt for 67 years (1304–1237 BC). When it was unearthed in 1904 by an Italian expedition led by Giovanni Schiaparelli, it had lost much of its magnificent wall paintings because of salt crystallization behind the plaster layer on which the ancient artisans had applied the paint. Fear of further damage resulted in the closing of the tomb to visitors during the past 50 years.[10]

The objective of applying remote sensing was to establish the origin of the water that had caused the mobilization of salt and its recrystallization behind and/or on top of the tomb paintings, so as to recommend a

---

[10] El-Baz, F. (1987). *Geographic and geologic setting. pp. 46–53, in:* Wall Paintings of the Tomb of Nefertari. *The Getty Conservation Institute, Los Angeles, California.*

treatment to conserve the remaining paint. Remote-sensing methods and techniques was applied to: (a) map the region in the immediate vicinity of the tomb for developing a hydrologic model of the area; (b) establish whether the deterioration was a one-time event or a continuous process; and (c) study the state of various segments of the tomb's walls to locate areas needing emergency treatment.

To determine the sequence of the deterioration of the wall paintings, we used software that was designed to aid in the study of Landsat images. Photographs of the same wall taken at different times were digitally compared using powerful computers. This indicated that the recent deterioration was mostly physical rather than chemical – pieces that were already separated from the wall by salt crystallization had fallen down with advanced age. On the basis of this information, it seemed unlikely that the chemical deterioration had continued to affect the paintings into recent times.[10]

The study of the state of various parts of the wall was done with multispectral photography. Cameras were used to obtain photographs in the visible, near-infrared and ultraviolet light (Fig. 5). These images indicated which parts of the wall had

Figure 5. Ultraviolet image of a life-size depiction of Nefertari on the wall of her tomb in the Valley of the Queens, west of Luxor, Egypt. The image indicated that there were two generations of paintings – one to establish the form (red lines) and a later one to fill in the colours.

deteriorated without visible signs. Pockets of air or salt not visible to the human eye were detected and helped in locating areas that required emergency conservation.

Second 'solar boat' of Khufu

The author also conducted a non-destructive investigation of the westernmost of two buried chambers at the base of the Pyramid of Pharaoh Khufu. The chamber in question was located in 1954, aligned with another, 18 m south of the Great Pyramid of Giza. During the same year, the eastern chamber was excavated from under a cap of 41 limestone blocks and found to contain a disassembled boat.[11] Gypsum mortar sealed the crevices between the cap blocks. When the first block was removed, the excavators smelled the scent of cedar, which made them believe that the chamber had been hermetically sealed till then. The 4,600-year-old wood was excavated and the assembled vessel was placed on exhibit at the Boat Museum, which was built on the site of the discovery and opened to visitors in 1982.

By 1986, however, the boat had shrunk about 0.5 m from its original length. It was feared that such deterioration may have been caused by the changing environmental conditions inside the museum. By association, the second (western) chamber was thought also to contain a boat. It was hoped that the investigation of its environmental parameters would lead to a better understanding of how best to preserve the ancient wood of the exhibited boat. This idea was the driving force behind the project.

The author developed a research plan that was jointly sponsored by the Egyptian Antiquities Organization and the National Geographic Society, to undertake the following actions: (a) geophysical surveying of the site to develop a profile of the chamber; (b) drilling a 9 cm hole by means of dry drilling motion through the limestone cap rock; the drilling and other operations were carried out in a specially designed air lock to separate the air inside from that outside; (c) sampling the air in the cavity at different levels; (d) measuring pressure, temperature and relative humidity inside the chamber; (e) photographing the interior with a high-resolution, black-and-white, video camera using a fiber-optic 'cold' light, and a 35 mm still camera with colour film; and (f) sealing the drill hole with material similar to that used by the ancient Egyptian builders, without altering the environment of the chamber in any way.[12]

Photography of the interior revealed a disassembled boat (Fig. 6). Much like the one that was excavated in 1954, the second chamber contained stacks of wood with pieces of the cabin arranged on top. This second boat appeared to be smaller than the first and had four small pointed oars. The pressure of the chamber was identical to that outside, indicating that there was communication between the air inside and outside the chamber. The temperature was 27°C and the relative humidity was 85%.

When the air samples reached NOAA's laboratories, atmospheric scientists and physicists began to monitor the contents of the canisters and analyse their components. Results of freon analyses came first: freon-11, 300 parts per trillion; and freon-12, about 540 parts per trillion. These values were higher than, but close to, those of the air measured near Cairo.

Figure 6. Photograph of the interior of the second (western) chamber near the base of the Great Pyramid, Giza, Egypt. The chamber is approximately 30 m long and encloses a disassembled 'solar boat.' The bright angular shapes are mortar that broke off the chamber's ceiling and fell on top of the wood planks of the boat.

An unusually high value was that of the carbon dioxide concentration: 720 parts per million, double the amount in the surrounding atmosphere. Carbon dioxide might have been produced by degassing from the organic materials inside the pit or even by decay of the limestone walls of the chamber. A test to date the carbon dioxide gave an age of 2,000 years, indicating that it was a mixture of ancient air and a modern counterpart.

Coastal zone of Alexandria

The northern coastline of the Nile Delta has undergone numerous changes throughout recorded history. The subsidence of the coastline, which caused the submergence of many archaeological sites, was due to natural processes. However, other changes occurred, owing to human activities, most notably since the construction of the High Dam at Aswan. The formation of Lake Nasser has inhibited the passage of silts and, therefore, the growth of the northern boundary of the Nile Delta. As the eastward-moving Mediterranean currents began to erode the promontories at the mouths of the two remaining branches of the Nile River, segments of beaches received new deposits from the eroded areas. This indicated that a new balance was being established between the water flow from the Nile and the Mediterranean currents. The resulting changes must be understood and monitored prior to undertaking a programme of underwater archaeological exploration along the Alexandrian coastline.

As stated earlier, satellite images provide an exceptionally useful tool to establish the nature of, and to monitor, such short-term changes. This is done through change-detection techniques where an image is compared with another obtained at a different time to define the changes. Landsat Thematic Mapper (TM) images obtained yearly from 1984 to 1993 were recently utilized to characterize the minor changes along the coastline of Alexandria. Results of their analyses may be of significance in understanding the process of burial of archaeological sites.

When the coastal zone environment is understood and a mechanism for monitoring natural and man-made changes is established, remote-sensing equipment can be employed to help uncover hidden archaeological sites and artefacts. The instruments that have the greatest promise for this particular application and which have not been mentioned above include:

(a) Side-scanning sonar: it emits sound waves by an electro-acoustic transducer that is in direct contact with the water. The transducer converts electric energy into acoustic energy (as a loudspeaker), and converts the returned acoustic energy back to electric energy (as a microphone). Buried objects on the bottom generate specific 'echoes' that help define the ranges, bearings and nature of the targets.

(b) Electromagnetic sounder: this produces magnetism by an electric current. Highly sensitive electromagnetic equipment, which may be adaptable to archaeological investigations off the coast of Alexandria, is presently being tested by the Space Research Institute in Russia.

(c) Sub-bottom profiling: to produce detailed profiles of the Mediterranean Sea floor, which may indicate locations of buried sites.

(d) Video and other imaging: where a submersible craft, manned or unmanned, is utilized to provide high-resolution images of targeted features on the sea bottom.

A combination of the above-mentioned methods (satellite-image interpretation and geophysical surveys) is required to fully understand the nature of the coastal offshore region of Alexandria. Such a combination would also be needed to plan a well thought out exploration programme for archaeological structures that may have been submerged beneath sea water. A multi-disciplinary team of investigators would ensure that such a programme would satisfy the exploration goals without harming the coastal environment. In the meantime, the coastline of Alexandria should be protected from further urban development until the archaeological survey is completed.

[11] Jenkins, N. (1980). The Boat beneath the Pyramid. Thames and Hudson, London.
[12] El-Baz, F. (1988). Finding a pharaoh's funeral bark. National Geographic, 173–4:513-533.

Remote imaging of submerged man-made structures

H. ARNOLD CARR
American Underwater Search & Survey, Ltd.

Introduction

Submerged objects can be located, mapped and identified through a variety of techniques including acoustic imaging, optical remote sensing, manned diving vehicles and robotics. Often, a combination of techniques is the best application if the location of the underwater site is not accurately known and the aim is to locate and acquire some detail of the site. Broad aerial surveys are best accomplished using towed acoustic or optical imaging systems. Diving or robotics can then optically examine specific sites or targets identified in these surveys.

Acoustic imaging is commonly preferred if the survey objective is to cover large areas in search of specific submerged objects. Because of its long range and real-time data display, acoustic imaging using side-scan sonar can provide the archaeologist with very short time to target acquisition. Side-scan sonar is also the most efficient means of obtaining a real-time map of an underwater site that is extensive. Sonar is also preferred when the water allows only poor visibility.

Laser imaging can also provide maps of sites. The laser line scan is towed from a vessel in the same manner as side-scan sonar. The advantage of the laser line scan is the resolution it can produce. The system does require a modest surface support craft that will accommodate a special winch because of the size and weight of the towfish. Reasonably clear underwater visibility is also required, since suspended matter in the water column will quickly attenuate the laser beam.

Imaging

Submerged human habitat provides the surveyor or nautical archaeologist with complex challenges. Direct access to the underwater sites and the difficulty of accurately mapping them are two challenges that are encountered in even the most benign underwater locations. Side-scan sonar can help to surmount these obstacles. Side-scan sonar can produce an image similar to an aerial photograph if a sufficient number of features are not totally buried.[1] Under these conditions, sonar can provide a general view of a site such as a village, and will outline streets, homesites and certain landmarks, which may determine priorities for excavation. Side-scan sonar can also be used as a means of periodically assessing the excavation. As excavation or removal of large objects progresses, side-scan sonar can be used to provide intermediate maps of the site. It can assist in determining whether the excavation is complete or what the impact of excavating a primary site is on adjacent sites. At sites where underwater visibility is severely restricted, sonar may be the only means of surveying the site.

Although current side-scan sonars are available in different frequencies, multi-frequency or dual frequency sonars usually have a range between 100 and 500 kHz. The 100 kHz frequency is capable of ranges up to 600 m on each side. The 500 kHz frequency is normally used for ranges between 25 and 100 m and gives higher resolution than the 100 kHz frequency. Sonar equipment can have both these frequencies to enjoy the advantage of range and of high resolution. Higher frequency side-scan sonars are not commonly

---

[1] See: Fish, J. P. and Carr, A. H. (1990). Sound Underwater Images. AUSS, Cataumet, MA, USA. 188 pp.

used, but they are available. They have very high resolving power, but are limited to about 20 m in range.

Survey methods

The most important parameters controlled by a survey team, once on a survey site, are sonar range, sonar frequency, tow speed, towfish 'altitude' [height above sea floor] and overlap. When surveying to acquire an aerial distribution of a large site, a range overlap of 50% is usually sufficient. This amount of overlap is normally enough to offset vessel tracking errors. Operators will also benefit from this amount of overlap, for they will have a second look at targets that appear at the outer edge of any given lane. Typically, the goal of a target distribution survey is not to look at and identify each individual target, but to achieve a broad overview of the site. This type of survey is commonly considered to be a primary survey based upon which a second more discretely dedicated survey can classify, in greater detail, specific sites that may be of more interest.

If thorough imaging of a large site covering several square kilometres or more is preferred, a scaled, high-resolution mosaic of the submerged area can be generated. The generation of high-quality mosaics has advanced significantly recently. More programmes are available to produce these data as long as the surveyor plans in advance for sonar mosaics and uses the proper medium. Sonar surveys dedicated to classifying and geodetically locating discrete sites or individual targets are more likely to use a minimum of 100% overlap. This means that the lane spacing will be equal to the sonar range on one side. An important benefit of this methodology is that this overlap puts sea-bottom and associated target sites that were at the extremes of any one lane, into the near range of any adjacent lane. Side-scan sonars have the characteristic of beam spreading and attenuation which may cause loss of detail at the outer edges of the sonar record. 100% overlap gives two values to the survey: better detail and a second perspective of the insonified bottom.

What area can be covered in an aerial survey that is undertaken with 50 % overlap? If the side-scan sonar is set for a 100 m range (on each side) and the vessel is surveying at a speed of 3 knots (1.5 m/sec), the survey can insonify a 0.4 km square per hour.

At the speed and range mentioned above, a side-scan sonar may emit pings at a rate of 4.9 pulses per metre of forward motion. The pulse rate is a factor of range: a shorter range will have a higher pulse rate, whereas a longer range will have a lower pulse rate. For example, the side-scan sonar previously mentioned, if functioning at a range of 50 m, will have a pulse rate of 9.8 pulses per metre of forward motion. Sonar range, vessel speed and required detectability are critical components of an efficient, successful survey.

Even if the target or feature is displayed on the sonar record, it may not be recognized unless the target has been adequately insonified and the chart speed is appropriate for the eye and brain of the operator to recognize it. Although recent developments in side-scan sonar have provided for repeated data displays in outgoing pulses and for the displayed data to be immediately enhanced, adequate insonification of the target is the primary step to data acquisition. A conservative plan includes a choice of tow speeds and ranges that will allow for a minimum of 12 insonifications (pings) in a forward travel distance equal to the target's least dimension.

The surveyor should make repeated runs on a site, so as to insonify it from many different angles and perspectives. Each pass will provide more information to aid in classifying and enumerating the site.

In general, most surveys are performed with the towfish altitude at approximately 10–20% of the range-setting of the sonar. The optimum 'altitude' of the towfish above the sea bed is a function of range, because, at the outer edges of the record, the angle of incidence of the outgoing pulse on the seabed is one of the factors that determines the properties of the echoes returning to the towfish. If the fish has a high 'altitude', resultant target shadows will be lessened and target recognition reduced. If the fish 'altitude' is low, the reflectivity of the outer ranges will be diminished thus reducing the effective range. Conditions do exist that require a change from this relationship of sonar range to towfish 'altitude'; one such condition would be in very shallow water. In this situation, the reduced effective range may be accepted and the distance between survey lanes reduced.

Recognition of a seabed feature or target is dependent on the knowledge and experience of the operator. For example, review the images illustrated in this article and attempt to determine which lie naturally and which man has manufactured or influenced. Many will probably remain unclassified. However, an

experienced sonar operator has a greater ability to recognize and classify features and targets. A prudent post-survey technique is to have experienced personnel thoroughly review the records.

Quality assurance

The key to obtaining high-quality sonar data is planning, appropriate equipment, deployment methodologies and post-processing of recorded sonar data.

One essential component of the use of sonar in high-resolution imaging and mapping is the deployment and data-gathering team associated with the programme. The quality of resolution and the spatial accuracy in the imaging relate directly to the experience and ability of the personnel deploying the sonar. Experienced sonar crews are commonly available for routine sonar applications, but the application of sonar to this type of specialized mission requires a combination of professional staff that is more difficult to find and verify before the mission.

This team must work in close communication with the principals undertaking the survey. Close, continued association throughout the survey will conclude with the acquisition, interpretation and presentation of the best possible survey data.

Figure 1.
Residential Area:
(A) steel bridge;
(B) survey vessel
track; (C) riverbed;
(D) foundation;
(E) river bank; (F) rise
in topography.

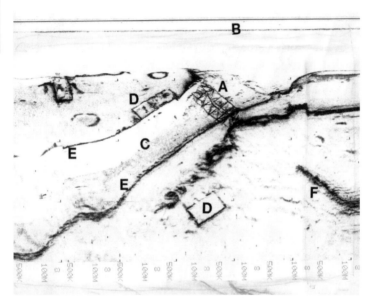

Figure 2.
Steel bridge.
Sonogram features:
(A) horizontal steel
main supports;
(B) shadow from
steel bridge girders;
(C) roadway and
original bridge
footing; and (D) old
riverbed.

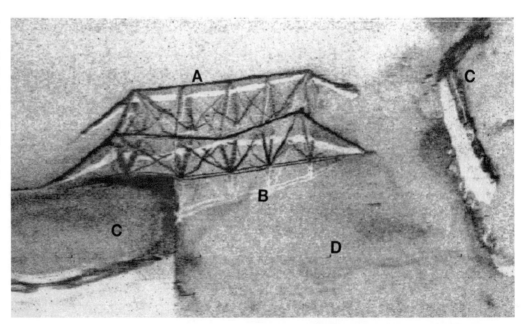

Remote imaging of potential archaeological sites can provide valuable data to authorities. The information obtained can provide the means of establishing plans for sound management and protection.

Sample data

The sonar images shown herein were generated using narrow-beam high-frequency sonar. The system used to map these sites was deployed in a manner specifically designed to image man-made structures. Higher resolution imaging, which would distinguish artefacts smaller than 25 cm, uses a refined application of VHF short-range sonar. This higher-resolution imaging has an application in mapping sites in detail and in better characterizing specific targets.

A once rural residential area that is now part of a flooded river valley is depicted in Figure 1. The site has been submerged for approximately one century. This sonar image was taken at the 100 m range and at a frequency of 500 kHz. The record has little gray scale because the gain is intentionally low. Note the two ovals in the record. These are believed to be cesspools and should be circular. They show that the record is distorted and that the speed of the record was not synchronized with the speed of the survey vessel.

Figure 2, taken at the 50 m range and 500 kHz, gives greater detail of the bridge. The bridge remains remarkably intact except for the bridge roadbed, which is non-existent. During the flooding, the bridge was swept from its footings and now lies with one end canted off the bridge footing, with the other end in the old riverbed.

Two bridge abutments are depicted in Figure 3. Both abutments show an articulated face resulting from the steel cofferdam that houses the reinforced concrete. One abutment has two vertical supports that sit on a footing. The other abutment has one larger vertical support. The sediment around these structures is a combination of fine sand and small cobble. Water flow in the region has caused the scouring evident in the sediment at the base of the structures. This figure is a complete side-scan sonar record which includes the track of the survey vessel and the right and left channels. The two white strips on either side of the vessel track represent the water column where the signal passes from the towfish prior to first contact with the substrate.

Figure 4 shows about 23 granite blocks alongside a road. The dimensions of the blocks are 0.8 m in width and 3–4 m long.

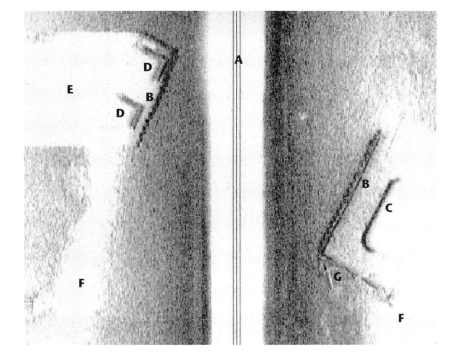

Figure 3. Two bridge abutments.
Sonogram labels include: (A) sonar vessel track; (B) abutment face lined with corrugated steel sheathing; (C) single vertical support sitting on concrete footing; (D) double vertical supports with square configuration; (E) abutment shadow; (F) bottom scouring caused by river current; and (G) construction debris recently lost.

Figure 4.
Granite blocks:
(A) granite blocks;
(B) road;
(C) road intersection.

Figure 5.
Two foundations:
(A) possible old dirt
road; (B) first
contact with bottom;
(C) foundation;
(D) shadow; (E) small
rise in topography;
(F) basement floor.

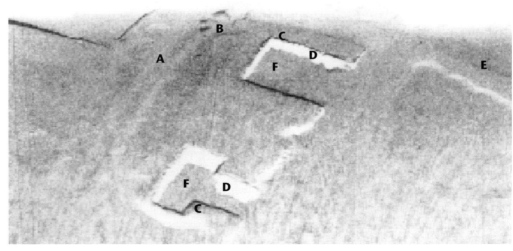

Figure 6.
Large building
complex: (A) factory
foundation; (B)
collapsed chimney;
(C) walkways;
(D) stairs;
(E) subbuilding
foundation; (F) road;
(G) survey vessel
track. This record
was taken at 50 m
range and 500 kHz.

Two foundations are well marked in Figure 5. The white shadow that is prominent in both indicates that the basement floors are significantly depressed relative to the surrounding topography. Geometric calculations shows that the depth of the basement floor within both foundations is 2 m. The lengths of the two foundation shadows differ with respect to their axis perpendicular to the track of the survey vessel because of the distance each is from the vessel track. The record also suggests remnants of an older foundation and road.

Figure 6 is a record of a large building complex. One dimension of this industrial building foundation, as seen in the record,

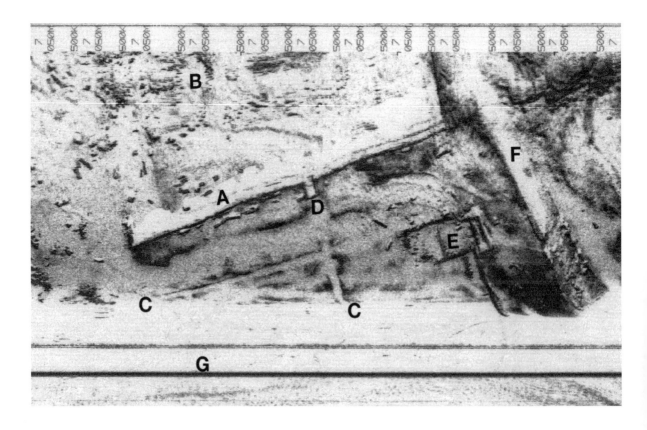

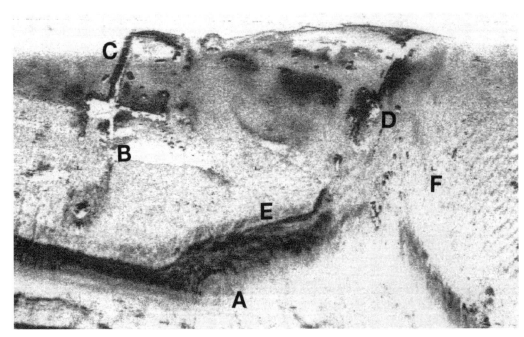

Figure 7. Submerged homesites: (A) an old riverbed; (B) wall remnant and sloping terrain; (C) main foundation; (D) discrete debris field; (E) steep terraced shoreline; and (F) shallow lake bed.

Figure 8. Submerged industrial site: (A) remains of industrial building; (B) banked slope; (C) river bed; (D) hydro power source for factory; (E) water discharge area.

is 44 m long. This foundation wall is not linear because the track of the sonar fish, as towed by the vessel, was not absolutely straight.
Figure 7 shows a residence that is submerged in 40 m of water. This homesite is elevated on land that slopes sharply down to an old riverbed and a nearby ancient lake bed.

A discrete industrial site is shown in Figure 8. The site is next to a river which was the source of power for the factory. The site now remains submerged within a reservoir. Some vertical structure is evident, especially where the building foundations were located.

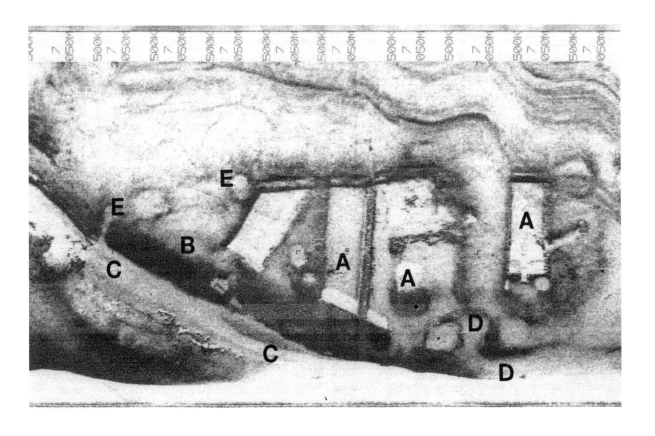

Proposed survey of Alexandria harbours by a sonar sub-bottom profiler

NILS TONGRING AND NEAL W. DRISCOLL
Woods Hole Oceanographic Institution

Introduction

The future of archaeology has been described[1] as involving the increasing application of a number of technological innovations, such as:

• laser ranging (used on land for two decades now, although the blue-green window in water has not been exploited);[2]

• satellite observations and spaceborne radar (the use of satellite images to find prehistoric sites – for example, Acheulean sites in the Sahara[3] is well known; SAT images use three visual windows – blue, green and red – along with three channels in the infra-red; the future Landsat will have 230 channels, with increased resolution);

• expanding non-destructive research methods at sites, like ground-penetrating radar; and

• increased computer use by means of digitizing images.

These technological developments are common to many other disciplines, however. What seems more significant is the still increasing integration of concepts and analysis from other fields.

Interdisciplinary efforts in archaeology are not new. In Egypt, the geologist Elinor Gardner worked with Gertrude Caton-Thompson in the Fayum and in the Kharga oasis[4]; such collaborative work goes back to the 19th century.[5]

Such factors as geological structure and climate change have often been critical in analysing land sites. At the International Workshop on Submarine Archaeology and Coastal Management, Honor Frost (cf. this volume, p. 64) pointed out that geological investigation had discovered a faultline which explained the difference in jetty levels at Caesarea, and that such factors can be the key to interpreting ancient harbour installations. In turn, archaeological data can illuminate problems in geology. For example, Warne and Stanley[6] have used shards from cores to date soil strata, since the deposit and redeposit of organic material by water often leads to overestimation of the age of the sediment layers.

The significance of coastlines, river basins, and deltas in human history has introduced further geological and oceanographic problems into archeology; an important factor in many of these problems has been the effect of sea-level change. The city of Alexandria offers a striking example of this effect on different time scales: the subsidence of the

[1] For example: Smith, B. D. (1996). Remarks on the next 35 years of archeology. The Sciences, New York Academy of Science, Nov.–Dec.

[2] But cf. Medard, J. (1997). Underwater positioning for archaeological and topographic needs. Sea Technology (July), pp. 31–3.

[3] McCauley, J. F. et al. (1986). Paleodrainages of the eastern Sahara – the radar rivers revisited. (SIR-A/B Implications for a Mid-Tertiary Trans-African Drainage System). IEEE Trans. Geosci. Remote Sensing, GE-24:624–48.

[4] Caton-Thompson, G. and Gardner, E. W. (1929). Recent work on the problem of Lake Moeris. Geog. Jour., 73:20–60; The Desert Fayum. London, Royal Anthropological Society. Vol. 2. (1934).

[5] Cf. the discussion in Butzer, K. (1964). Environment and Archeology. Chicago.

[6] Warne, A. G. and Stanley, D. J. (1993). Archeology to refine Holocene subsidence rates along the Nile delta margin, Egypt. Geology, 21:715–18.

Ptolemaic city, first noticed and described by Arab commentators, due to local tectonic changes and the global (eustatic) sea-level rise; the earlier subsidence of the ancient harbours reported by Jondet[7]; and, on a larger time scale, the relative subsidence and landward migration (some 50 km) of the coastline since the last Pleistocene lowstand 18,000 years BP (before the present).[8]

To study in detail aspects of this relative sea-level change, and to supplement the visual archaeological survey being carried out by Goddio, we propose an acoustic imaging of the harbour of Alexandria.

In the last decade, sonar has developed the capacity to penetrate the ocean bottom, and is now able to resolve sediment layers 5 cm thick to a depth of 60 m or more. The application of sonar to archaeology had essentially been limited to the finding of shipwrecks, the 'objects' of marine archaeology. As coastlines are investigated, an obvious application of this technology will be the imaging of structures buried in ocean silt and sand. An example of this kind of sonar, a shallow-water sub-bottom profiler, is being developed at Woods Hole, and our proposal is to use the system to map the Eastern Harbour of Alexandria as part of the general plan to survey the remains of the Ptolemaic city.

If we judge by the silence of the early writers on the subject, the subsidence of Alexandria has taken place in the last 1,000 years. The gradual eustatic sea-level rise for the last 3,000 years is almost linear[9], about 3 m below the present sea level 3,000 years ago and 1 m below, 1,000 years ago. This is too slow to be seen by the contemporary casual observer, but, coupled with tectonic changes, the relative rise was noticed (to find new first-hand accounts from Arab sources would be extremely useful, particularly to improve estimates of the rate of relative subsidence at different historical times). One estimate from archaeological and tide-gauge records is an average rate for subsidence of 1.2 mm/yr over the past 3,000 years.[10] The tectonic factor is difficult to determine, but the levels indicated by submerged Greek and Roman ruins suggest that the total effect has been a submergence of 3–5.5 m in the last 2,500

years. Much of the palace precinct (Cape Lochias) is under the sea; the rest is under great amounts of fill used to compensate for the subsidence when building resumed in the middle of the 19th century.

The late-Quaternary sea-level history is fairly well established. In the recent period, 5,000–1,000 years BP, sea level rose about 5 m.[11]

The first goal then will be to scan the Eastern Harbour, covering with particular care the area surveyed visually by Goddio, from El Manshiya to El Silsila (Cape Lochias) along the corniche, and the area at the base of Qait Bey Fort, the site of the figures recovered by Empereur. The detailed stratigraphy revealed by the sub-bottom sonar can provide the optimal places for taking cores, determining strata, possibly to distinguish the later Roman work from the Ptolemaic, to help in the analysis of the sonar data, and to contribute to determining the rate of relative sea-level rise. Ultimately, the visual and sonar data could be integrated to produce a three-dimensional computer model of the Ptolemaic harbour, a kind of imaging which is already in use; for example, the stored visual images of the Mid-Atlantic Ridge are presently so displayed.

The second goal will be to perform a similar scan of the site of the earlier breakwaters and

[7] Jondet, G. (1916). Les ports submergés de l'ancienne île de Pharos. Institut Égyptien, 9.
[8] That this area was inhabited is likely. Even in the Western Desert of Egypt, human settlement may extend back 500,000 years; cf. Wendorf, F. et al. (1985). Prehistoric settlements in the Nubian Desert. American Scientist, 73:132–41.
[9] Lighty, R. G. et al. (1982). Acropora palmata reef framework: a reliable indicator of sea level in the western Atlantic for the past 10,000 years. Coral Reefs, 1:125–30.
[10] El-Sayed, M. Kh. (1988). Sea level rise in Alexandria during the late Holocene: archeological evidences. Rapports et Procés Verbaux de Réunions, Commission Internationale pour l'Exploration Scientifique de la Mer Méditerranée, 31:108; cf. also El-Gindy, A. A. and Eid, F. M. (1988). Sea level variation in the Mediterranean. ibid, 31:196.
[11] Cf. the discussion in Warne, A. G. and Daniel, J. S. (1993). Late Quaternary evolution of the northwest Nile Delta and adjacent coast in the Alexandria region, Egypt. Journal of Coastal Research, 9:26–64.

dockwork reported by Jondet north and west of Ras El Tin, if possible. Again, study of the sub-bottom may suggest particularly suitable places to extract cores; the structure of the sediment layers and shards may verify and date these early harbours, and yield information on their subsidence. The extensiveness of Jondet's finds and the problem of the lack of any documents or reports referring to the existence of such a harbour, beyond its mention in Book IV of the Odyssey, as Jondet himself points out, must lead to caution in passing judgment on the existence and nature of such structures. The 'karkar' limestone of the type described by Jondet can naturally exhibit channels resembling joints or tiling in the plan view. The mystery of the Homeric Pharos Harbour, first pointed out by Jondet, remains. Finally, the offshore area parallel to the coast could be scanned to complement the land studies[12], and to determine the link between sediment loading and delta migration. Are the limestone ridges fault-controlled as previously proposed?[13] If the ridges continue east, the extent of their bending under the load of the deposits of Nile silt could be determined (with the present scouring and reduced Nile flow, rebounding might be observed).

A description of the system

Originally designed to generate quantitative acoustic data which can be used for classifying sediments and determining their physical properties, the Subscan Sonar being constructed at Woods Hole Oceanographic Institution will permit the collection of high-resolution seismic images in nearshore environments (surf zone to mid-shelf water depths). This system is built on proven and new technology, including advanced signal processing, to make possible the extraction of data under conditions particularly adverse to sonar: shallow water means greater energy trapped in the water column, causing persistence or 'ringing', side echoes and 'ghosts', multiples caused by reflections between the bottom and the sea surface. New beam focussing and CHIRP technology significantly reduce these obstacles to resolving power. CHIRP differs from other sonar systems in that it transmits a linearly swept, frequency-modulated pulse, instead of a constant-frequency pulse. Its frequency therefore changes with time, the resolution possible with CHIRP varies inversely with pulse bandwidth and is not a function of pulse length as in conventional sonar. The CHIRP operating frequency being lower,

Figure 1. Close-up of Subscan Sonar vehicle on sled.

sound absorption is reduced, which, in the sea, is roughly a quadratic function of frequency; in the conventional sonar, reducing the operating frequency would reduce the resolving power of the system. The equipment is deployed on a sled, the total weight being approximately 200 kg, light enough to be handled on a small open boat with an A-frame or davit (Fig. 1). The tow frame is designed to be stable on the bottom while being pulled slowly across the surf zone out to mid-shelf water depths. Outside the surf zone, the vehicle and the towed frame will be 'flown' in a traditional configuration while maintaining a constant depth above the seafloor.

The sonar is wide-band, sweeping from 1 kHz to 7 kHz in 20 ms with extraordinary resolution; matched filtering techniques will allow a resolution as small as 5 cm. With the software developed at Woods Hole for three-dimensional imaging, an unprecedented picture of any structure above and below the bottom to a considerable depth (70 m) will be obtained.

The Subscan Sonar is entirely self-contained with its own power supply, and can fit in a container $10 \times 8 \times 8$ ft (approximately $3.0 \times 2.4 \times 2.4$ m), thus allowing relatively easy transportability.

Supported by the US Navy, the Subscan Sonar will be available for use in a pilot project, and the suitability of the system to the survey of the Eastern Harbour of Alexandria is obvious. The chance for archaeologists to take part in the development and trials of such equipment will improve the potential for its successful application.

[12] Stanley, D. J. and Hamza, F. H. (1992). Terrigeous-carbonate sediment interface (late Quaternary) along the northwestern margin of the Nile Delta, Egypt. Journal of Coastal Research, 8:153–71.

[13] El-Wakeel, S. K. and El-Sayed, M. K. (1978). The texture, mineralogy, and chemistry of bottom sediments and beach sands from the Alexandria region, Egypt. Marine Geology, 27:137–60; cf. Butzer, K. W. (1960). In: The Pleistocene shorelines of Arab's Gulf, Egypt. Journal of Geology, 68:626–37.

Conservation of marine artefacts
Examples from INA-Egypt projects

HOWARD WELLMAN
Director of Conservation
Institute of Nautical Archaeology-Egypt

Introduction

The Institute of Nautical Archaeology is the pre-eminent American organization conducting research into nautical archaeology worldwide, and training nautical archaeologists in the United States. Since the Institute of Nautical Archaeology-Egypt (INA-Egypt) established its permanent base in Alexandria in 1994 to explore Egypt's nautical heritage, it has conducted four major projects focusing on shipwrecks on the Egyptian coast, and intends to continue its work, with an emphasis on research, the training of archaeologists, and long-term care of the artefacts discovered.

Three major components

Long-term research into regional maritime history requires three major elements: survey, excavation and conservation.

Survey
Survey is a necessary part of any long-term research, since the larger picture of where wrecks are located, and the patterns of shipping and trade, figure in the understanding of individual excavations. INA-Egypt has performed two survey projects since 1994: one in the Red Sea, from El Qesir to Ras Mohammed, and one on the Mediterranean coast west of Alexandria, from Sidi Abd Al-Rahman to Ras Hawala. In the Red Sea, over 26 sites were visited

and numerous archaeological sites were identified, including the Sadana Island shipwreck. On the north-west coast, 16 wreck and harbour sites were visited dating from the 4th century BC to the 7th century AD, where amphorae and other evidence of sea-faring, including a stone anchor, and a Byzantine cruciform anchor were found. These objects were measured, documented and raised, and are now in the Alexandria Conservation Laboratory for Submerged Antiquities.

Given INA interest in Mediterranean ships and shipping, future surveys will focus on the north-west coast, looking for information about Egyptian shipping from the Bronze Age into the Medieval period. This is a crucial area, since Egypt was a centre of maritime trade, and we should expect to find ships of all nationalities along its shores.

Excavation
Surveys give us broad pictures of ships and shipping in a region, but to get detailed information about the objects and sites found on surveys, it is necessary to excavate. INA-Egypt does not attempt to excavate every site it finds; it focuses on those shipwrecks that can add significantly to our knowledge of ancient trade and shipbuilding.

For its first excavation, INA-Egypt chose the Sadana Island shipwreck, a 50-m 3-decker ship from the 18th century, carrying a mixed load of Chinese porcelain, Middle Eastern earthenware, copper tools and vessels, including inscribed basins, which allowed us to date more precisely the time of the shipwreck, glass containers including beverage bottles and a perfume vial, and various spices, resins and foodstuffs, which would constitute a low-volume, high-value cargo.

This vessel was chosen for excavation since it was endangered by looting, and it illustrates a poorly documented part of Egypt's place in the modern Red Sea and Arabian Sea trade. In two years of excavation, we have logged 3,000 dives on the site and raised 1,300 artefacts for conservation and study. The ship itself is the largest artefact on the site, and we have uncovered parts of it to reveal that it is of an unknown type of construction. Our third and final season of excavation will focus on understanding the ship's construction and origin.

The surveys and the excavation give INA-Egypt a chance to contribute to the development of professional archaeology in Egypt by training students from various universities, and Inspectors from the Supreme Council of Antiquities (SCA) in the techniques and goals of nautical research.

A critical part of any excavation is the post-excavation treatment of the artefacts. In 1994, INA-Egypt proposed to the SCA the creation of a permanent conservation and research facility based at the National Maritime Museum in Alexandria. Derelict buildings at the National Maritime Museum were the servants' quarters and outbuildings for a royal villa on Stanley Bay. The green house has become the main laboratory, the servants' quarters will become climate-controlled storage, darkrooms, a photostudio and research space. The garage will be used for machine space, the water-purification plant, and treatment of large objects, such as ships' timbers. Other smaller rooms will be used for pumps, compressors, and x-radiography.

Construction of two artefact-storage and desalination tanks was completed in 1995, and the renovation of five buildings was completed in 1996, marking the creation of the Alexandria Conservation Laboratory for Submerged Antiquities (ACL). This work was done with the aid of the Alexandria Businessmens' Association, Bechtel Corporation, and a grant from USAID administered by the Egyptian Antiquities Project and the American Research Centre in Egypt. We shall be able to treat a wide range of materials from submerged sites, as well as conduct high-quality research and documentation.

Conservators from INA-Egypt and the SCA are already working on materials from the surveys and the Sadana excavation. This is an excellent example of how INA-Egypt staff and the SCA can work together and exchange information about modern conservation and research techniques. This laboratory will also be an excellent place to train future conservators from Egyptian universities, and from abroad. We have already been able to show the public what is being done in Egypt to promote the conservation of cultural heritage from underwater sites.

Conservation and research

Conservation is something, however, that cannot be confined to the laboratory. The unique thing about archaeological conservation, and particularly marine site conservation, is the immediacy of treatment – conservation begins before the artefacts are excavated, and never truly ends.

The marine environment can be both harsh and protective. Salt water will corrode metal, etch ceramics and dissolve stone. The sea harbours many organisms that will attack and decay metal and organic materials. But waterlogged sediments will also preserve a wide range of materials, especially rare organic finds. As in any excavation, removing an object from its burial environment means exposing it to changes in moisture and atmosphere that can begin irreversible chemical and biological changes. This is even more extreme on marine sites, where objects can go from anoxic, wet conditions to oxygen-rich, extremely dry conditions in a matter of minutes. At the Sadana Island site, objects were exposed to relative humidities of about 20% and temperatures of about 30°C (a change of 80% in RH and 15°C) within minutes of being raised.

Stabilization

Under these conditions, the most pressing dangers are the formation of salt crystals, the loss of moisture from waterlogged materials, and the physical damage caused by the loss of support and buoyancy. It is the conservator's job on site to foresee these changes and begin immediately to ameliorate the conditions. For preference, stabilization should use passive methods, such as simple wet storage, the creation of physical supports to prevent accidental damage, rather than active intervention. This is so that hasty treatment decisions can be avoided, and allow time to properly investigate before beginning treatment. Immediate stabilization is critical for many objects, since irreversible changes can take place within minutes or hours of excavation.

Simple physical padding and supports can prevent mechanical damage, since the objects are now being handled and have lost the support of the burial sediments. With artefacts from the sea, the most important thing is to keep them wet, since drying out too soon could damage them. Small objects are kept in tanks that were built on site at Sadana, though large objects, such as these storage jars, had to be kept in a sheltered tide pool in the reef.

All objects have absorbed some salt while in the sea, and it is necessary to remove that salt before drying an object. Salt crystals will form on objects that are dried straight from the water, and the crystals forming inside porous materials can exert a pressure of more than 3,500kg/cm2, which will literally explode the object. Salt will also cause rapid corrosion of metals. The objects must therefore be soaked for a period of time in fresh water, until all the salts are removed. There is not enough fresh water on Sadana Island to desalinate there, but the ACL will be fitted with a water-purification plant capable of supplying 5,000 litres of water per day to meet needs. While desalination is taking place, other investigative, cleaning and stabilization treatments can continue.

Cleaning

When most people think of conservation, they think of active treatments, as cleaning and restoration. This process also begins on site, since many of the adherent materials can be damaging to the objects once they are excavated. Heavy concretions can damage the object physically, as well as harbour salts and marine animals. Cleaning and detailed investigation are two things that are closely linked. Many objects from marine sites are obscured by layers of marine concretion laid down by corals, algae and other marine organisms. Metal objects may be covered in layers of corrosion that hide technical details, decoration and inscriptions. Cleaning will reveal these details. To proceed slowly and work carefully to observe small details, mechanical methods of cleaning are preferred to more general chemical treatments. When needed, chemicals can be used to remove tough adherent concretions, or remove stains, but this is usually in the last stage of treatment, and not all objects need this degree of care.

The principle of minimum intervention is applied; it states simply that you do only that which is absolutely necessary to stabilize the object physically and chemically, and that you only clean it enough to reveal the information inherent in it. Archaeology is about revealing information, and careful conservation reveals a lot of information about artefacts. But overzealous cleaning, or the introduction of such foreign materials as acids, adhesives and consolidants, can obscure valuable information, such as inscribed surfaces, organic components of metal tools, carbon-14 and trace elements.

By doing only what is absolutely necessary, we run less risk of changing the artefact. If we change the object to improve the appearance, we shall have lost data. If we lose the data, the artefact has lost its value to the archaeologists. You must also keep in mind that the damage may not be visible for many years. It is often better to do only what is necessary now, and keep a careful watch on the object in years to come. It is always easier to do another treatment later, than it is to try to reverse a previous one that has failed.

Modern treatments prefer to use simple mechanical methods, which are generally easier to control and more localized than chemical methods. The most common tool is a surgical scalpel, used to cut and pick concretions off the surface of the objects.

Pneumatic air-scribes can be used on larger masses of concretion that cement objects together.

As copper corrodes, the original surface is preserved inside the corrosion. With a scalpel you can clean down to that line and stop, but with chemicals it is far too easy to clean past that line to the metal, and then the surface details preserved in the corrosion are lost. We are again invoking the principal of minimum intervention.

Sometimes it is impossible to avoid the use of chemicals, but then they must be used carefully, and the by-products washed away completely. With objects from marine sites, it is best to apply chemical treatments while the objects are still in the desalination tanks, so that the desalination washes away the chemical by-products. Some chemical procedures are better than others, and some have lesser side-effects than others.

Investigation

During all of the above-mentioned treatments, the conservator is constantly observing, investigating, and reporting on the nature of, the artefact. Having a conservator on site means that there is a trained observer looking closely at each artefact, noting materials, technology and fine details of decoration and usage. This constant flow of information going to the archaeologists about the objects can enhance the excavation plan. Similarly, conservators can help excavators with specific advice on how to handle delicate or even dangerous materials.

Careful investigation before and during treatment cannot be overemphasized. Treatment should only be performed after you know what the object is, and what its particular problem is. Even the most obvious problems should be examined, because one small detail may alter everything. This does not need to be complicated; simple microscopy can reveal many details to the trained eye.

Other options include x-radiography, but these are carried out in the laboratory, not on site. Investigation is something that takes place during the entire conservation, as new information is revealed at every stage. X-ray images can show the shape of an iron object obscured in a block of concretion and can be used to guide the careful removal of the concretion from the object.

Other forms of examination could include chemical analysis, or scanning electron microscopy. We are looking for signs of weakness, signs of decay, and clues to the structure and nature of the object.

Packing and storage

Another aspect of on-site conservation, of course, requires getting the objects safely to the laboratory. Simply choosing the correct packing material to protect the objects from physical shock, and to prevent them from drying out, allows us to transport objects from Sadana to Alexandria. Padded well and wrapped in wet foam and plastic, over 1,300 artefacts have been carried across the desert, Cairo and Alexandria to reach the laboratory, with only 5 recorded breakages, and the objects were still dripping water when unpacked.

Drying

In the laboratory, once all the cleaning and investigation is complete, the final stage for marine artefacts is drying. Drying can be very damaging to objects, especially organic materials, since water has replaced organic material, and removing the water causes it to shrink and collapse. Treating waterlogged organic materials can be a long, dirty job, but it is very rewarding, since materials like leather, seeds, wood and other delicate objects are best preserved under water, and are rarely found in bulk in terrestrial excavations. These organic materials need to be stabilized with consolidants before they can be dried out. Waterlogged wood is especially sensitive and must be treated carefully so that the object is not damaged. Plant materials, such as wood and rope, are usually treated by soaking them in a solution of polyethylene glycol, which acts as a filler and lubricant to replace the cellulose dissolved from the wood. The wood or rope can then be carefully dried. These procedures can take several years.

Conservation takes a long time – years to treat a single piece of wood, months to treat a copper basin. For every season of excavation, we commit ourselves to two years of conservation. But after all this, what next? The object goes into the Museum display or onto the store-room shelf. And conservation does not stop: it is based on the knowledge of decay, and on trying to slow it. Objects can deteriorate faster in the Museum or storeroom than they can on site – they are subject to a fluctuating environment, damage by handling, and pollution in the air. This is one reason that INA-Egypt and the SCA wanted a permanent conservation facility at the Museum – to help maintain the collections and to implement the best procedures in the care and supervision of collections.

No conservation job is complete unless the paperwork is done. Conservation is a constant flow of reports and descriptions. All treatments must be recorded so that, in the future, researchers will know precisely what has been done to each artefact and how it has been altered, if at all. We also publish the results of our archaeological and conservation work, in our own publications, as well as in international journals.

Acknowledgements

I should like to acknowledge the help and support of my fellow staff members at INA-Egypt, and the conservators from the SCA. I should also like to thank the many generous private and corporate donors who support the work of INA-Egypt and the ACL, and particularly the Woods Hole Oceanographic Institute which made it possible for me to attend this conference.

Protection of shipwrecks
The experience of the Spanish National Maritime Archaeological Museum

IVÁN NEGUERUELA
Director
National Maritime
Archaeological Museum

Introduction

The call for a Conference, made by the University of Alexandria and the Egyptian Delegation to UNESCO as a result of the discovery of some important archaeological remains of the Ptolemaic city of Alexandria, is a unique occasion for all those of us who work in this field. The great significance of these underwater remains, which were discovered by two French-Egyptian teams of archaeologists, is due to the well known historical implications, size, quality and tourist interest of these remains. When considering the totality of 'what should be done', the biggest problem faced is not a technical one, but an economic one. Although, technically, new solutions must be found that have never previously been used in underwater archaeology, no insuperable difficulty appears to exist in this regard. On the other hand, the economic funding necessary to undertake such an enormous task in a short period of time surpasses by far what any State is able or willing to dedicate to its heritage policies. For this reason, the first consideration must be that the work is likely to take many years. And the question that all archaeologists ask themselves, in a case like this, is: meanwhile, how can we protect the remains? The present paper tries to deal with this aspect of the problem and, more specifically, with the protection of shipwrecks.

We shall set out the main lines along which the system of defence and protection of shipwrecks is being developed by the Museum (which depends directly on the Spanish Ministry of Education and Culture). The brevity required on this occasion only allows me to set out the basic policies we have been following over the last three years. Furthermore, since not all the aspects that this multifaceted system obliges us to monitor have yet been sufficiently developed, this International Workshop in Alexandria will serve to compare and contrast it with the experience of colleagues from other countries, because the complexity of what has been found in this ancient, beautiful and hospitable city is going to force all of us to exchange our respective experiences continually for years to come.

The problem

Firstly, the extreme gravity of the situation of the common archaeological underwater heritage is well-known. We shall not deal with it here, since it has already been the subject of discussion in several international conferences (Athens, UNESCO, European Union, etc.). Out of this grave situation arises the urgency for the administrative authorities of the collective heritage to adopt the necessary measures for its protection. Secondly, the degree of difficulty involved in protecting the shipwrecks lying on our sea beds has also been repeatedly considered. This difficulty arises from the fact that, whereas visual vigilance on land is relatively easy to implement, it is virtually impossible under the sea. Thirdly, the budgetted cost of the protection must be considered, and the difficulty we professionals have in convincing the political authorities to fund projects with a very low profitability.

Fourthly, we are faced with a lack of personnel who are sufficiently specialized in the work to be carried out.

The situation is therefore the following: the successive exploratory campaigns of any marine archaeological research centre gradually detect more shipwrecks over the years, and the action to be taken may be any of three kinds:

(a) The shipwrecks are excavated entirely and extracted: this only happens rarely.

(b) The shipwrecks are documented, completely excavated and left at the bottom of the sea.

(c) The shipwrecks are partially excavated, as in the majority of cases, and not only the ship but also part of its cargo are left on the seabed; however, the ensuing damage caused by natural agents and amateur divers is irreparable.

Our experience

Faced with the set of problems described above, we in Cartagena are trying to impose a corresponding set of solutions. As we shall see below, some are being tested and are proving successful; others are under development, and others have not yet been undertaken, but will be in the immediate future.

We have divided the systems of defence and protection under the following main headings:

Passive protection

By passive protection we mean the procedures that, once implemented, give a reasonable guarantee that the shipwrecks will be preserved in the state they were in at the time

the Museum intervened. Various systems have been studied over the last five years, which can be summarised as follows:

Barrows: These are the most classical solutions and are applied internationally. Basically, they involve covering the shipwrecks with an artificial mound of sand. There are several variations on this theme, the most sophisticated being that used by Stewart *et al.*[1] on the 16th-century Spanish shipwreck of a Basque Country whaler found in Red Bay (Canada).

Some 6–8 years ago, the Museum considered using *Poseidon* seagrass (in co-operation with the corresponding university marine biology departments) and/or metallic shavings. Both options were rejected and it was decided to protect the remains with a classical stratified barrow composed of successive layers of sand, stone and wire netting (Fig. 1). In this regard, it is important that the first layer to be in contact with the wreck be of the same nature as the original bed where it was found, to minimize any changes to the physical/chemical environment of the boat during the centuries it has remained under the sea. The upper layer should be made up of stones mixed with sand.

Among the main advantages of these barrows is the fact that they blend in with the surrounding sea environment very quickly, and, of course, their very low cost. Among the disadvantages is the fact that they can only be used once the excavation of the shipwreck has

[1] Stewart, J. et al. (1994). *Reburial of the Red Bay wreck as a form of preservation and protection of the historic resource.* Materials Issues in Art and Archaeology, *IV, Cancún, Mexico, 16–20 May 1994. We thank Mr. Wellman, of the INA-Egypt, for this reference.*

Figure 1.
A barrow of classical composition.

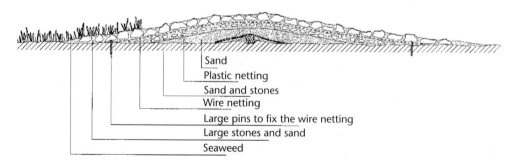

Sand
Plastic netting
Sand and stones
Wire netting
Large pins to fix the wire netting
Large stones and sand
Seaweed

been completed and not during the excavation itself, and their opening or closing for review is very cumbersome. In the case of the Canadian barrow in Red Bay, mentioned previously, a system was thought up to monitor the state of the wood and the medium which surrounded it. However, it must be remembered that, in that case, it was not a shipwreck that was being protected but rather the storage of its dismantled wood: the boat was excavated and then dismantled piece by piece (over 3,000 of them) and fragment by fragment (several thousand) and these were then buried again one by one in a well in which the wood was carefully placed and

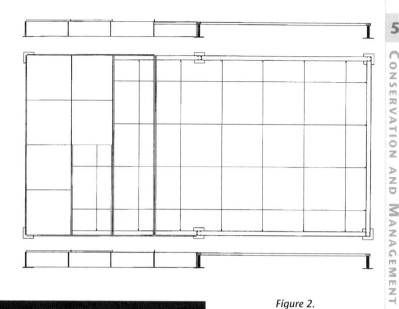

Figure 2.
Strongbox.

Figure 3.
The strongbox can
be closed at day's
end to protect the
excavation site
during the night.

Figure 4.
General aspects of
the strongbox.

stored, without its position in the well bearing any relation to its previous position in the ship. The Museum has not, so far, considered this type of decision (dismantling a ship and then storing its wood at the bottom of the sea).

Strongboxes: Having reflected on the problems presented by the barrows mentioned above, the convenience occurred to us of developing a different system which would provide all the advantages of the barrows while avoiding the disadvantages. The system was originally thought up for shipwrecks that were being excavated, to enable them to be closed at the end of each day and opened again the next. Two basic options were considered for this purpose: a large box-shaped cage installed at the bottom of the sea, or a completely enclosed metallic box (Figs. 2 and 4).

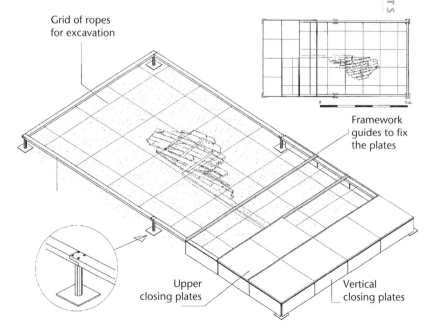

Grid of ropes
for excavation

Framework
guides to fix
the plates

Upper
closing plates

Vertical
closing plates

*Figure 5.
When excavating,
only the necessary
plates are opened,
while the rest of the
box serves as
scaffolding for the
divers.*

We shall set out the option we have developed, after making two important comments: firstly, that this option has now been used by us with satisfactory results in the case of the two 7th-century BC Phoenician vessels discovered at Mazarrón;[2] secondly, that we are continuing to develop a system of shipwreck protection and to perfect the system described here. One of the two vessels is still on the sea bed, whereas the other was transported to the Museum's laboratories on 30 June 1995, where it is undergoing treatment.[3, 4]

As can be seen from Figures 2–6 and Figure 8, a framework to which independent 1 × 1 m plates are fitted, constitutes the large modular metallic 'strongbox'. The framework is positioned on the sea bed first, and later the whole box is closed in, on its four vertical sides and on its upper horizontal side. Once all the plates are in place, they are

*Figure 6.
A strongbox
as used during
excavations.*

secured with long metallic pins and security bolts. The horizontal part of the frame of the box is perforated so that a grid of ropes or elastic cords can be installed there and used to facilitate excavation of the ship and the associated drawing and photography.

The following main advantages are offered by this system:

(a) The box can be opened when the underwater work starts and closed at the end of each day, thus adequately protecting the shipwreck during the evening and night (Fig. 3). This is not possible if a barrow is used.

(b) While the ship is being excavated only the necessary plates are opened up, i.e. the ones situated above the part which is

[2] Negueruela, I. et al. (1995). Seventh century BC. Phoenician vessel discovered at Playa de la Isla, Mazarrón, Spain. International Journal of Nautical Archaeology, 24(3):189–97 (August, 1995).
[3] Gomez-Gil, C. and Sierra, J. L. (1996a). Extracción y tratamientos del barco fenicio (Barco-1) de la Playa de la Isla (Puerto de Mazarrón, Mazarrón). Cuadernos de Arqueología Marítima, 4:217–25.
[4] Gomez-Gil, C. and Sierra, J. L. (1996b). Construcción de un sistema de tratamiento térmico para la conservación de los restos del barco fenicio de Mazarrón. Cuadernos de Arqueología Marítima, 4:245–49.

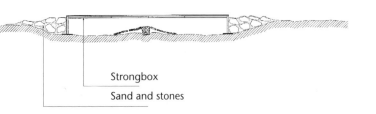

Strongbox

Sand and stones

Figure 7.
The 'windows' of
the strongbox can be
easily opened and
closed as required.

5

CONSERVATION AND MANAGEMENT TECHNIQUES FOR UNDERWATER ARTEFACTS

currently being worked on. Thus, during the excavation made each day, the rest of the box remains closed and the wreck adequately protected (Fig. 5).

(c) When excavation is taking place, the part of the box that is not open serves as scaffolding on which the divers can comfortably move around without altering the ship in any way, and on which all the instruments being used by the archaeologists, restorers, chemists, draughtsmen, etc., can be placed within easy reach (Fig. 5).

(d) Since it is so easy to open and close the 'windows', we can begin by only opening one and, over the course of the day, progressively open and close others (Fig. 7).

(e) The structure itself serves as a frame for installing the grid of ropes used during excavation and documentation (Fig. 4).

(f) Naturally, it protects the remains of the shipwreck against natural agents and unauthorized divers.

Once the study of the shipwreck is complete, either definitively or provisionally, the strongbox remains in place and is in turn covered with a classic barrow, as described previously, whose volume and importance will depend on the time that the shipwreck is expected to remain without further review or study (Fig. 8).

Active protection

In spite of all the foregoing, if 'pirate' excavators locate a barrow and/or strongbox, they have all the time in the world available to them, aided by the opacity of the sea water on the sea bed, to dismantle and violate the passive protection installed by the Museum. A team of well equipped clandestine divers would need several days to force the strongbox, but this could be done if the system is not complemented by other security arrangements.

We therefore recognized the need to co-ordinate this protection with a system of periodic vigilance which we call active protection.

Figure 8.
A strongbox
as used to protect
the wreck for an
extended period.
It combines
the strongbox with
tumulus.

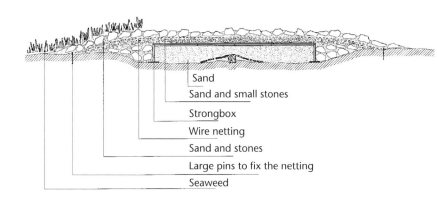

Sand
Sand and small stones
Strongbox
Wire netting
Sand and stones
Large pins to fix the netting
Seaweed

For this aspect of the problem, it was considered essential to involve the police authorities who have jurisdiction over the sea. But the collaboration of diving and amateur submarine archaeology clubs, etc., must be sought too. In our view, the weight of this phase of the project should always basically fall upon the police force, since it has sufficient authority to intervene effectively and expeditiously.

In the case of Spain, this jurisdiction is attributed to the *Guardia Civil* (the Civil Guard, one of the national police forces) which has two related organizations responsible for this task: the *Guardia Civil del Mar* (Marine Civil Guard) and the *Grupos Especiales de Actividades Subacuáticas* (GEAS, or Special Forces for Underwater Activities), the latter being made up of highly skilled, well equipped divers. In the Museum of Cartagena, co-operation with the Civil Guard is being developed with the aim of involving the police in the defence and protection of our heritage.

The Project can be divided into two stages: (a)The development of training courses on underwater archaeological heritage, given by technical staff from the Museum. The first of these courses took place in 1996 with optimum results, both for the Civil Guard and the Museum.[5]

(b)The creation of a small detachment from the GEAS stationed in Cartagena, to work with the Museum. Among its functions is the surveillance of the barrows, general control of the coast, detention of delinquents, etc. All of this is simply an extension of what existed in Spain: the Heritage Civil Guard, which operated on land.

These measures are expected to result in the signing of a series of very ambitious agreements between the Ministries of Defence and Culture, which will enable us in the near future to complete the development of these operations. As soon as the agreements referred to have been signed, we shall set up a network of collaborators among the diving clubs and fishermen's associations; we are already working on the design of the network, which is not yet operational, however.

Conclusion

Combining this double system of passive and active protection, we believe that the protection of shipwrecks defined by ministerial policy can be integrally guaranteed. It is true that the economic cost makes it difficult to protect all the shipwrecks already found, as well as those that have yet to be discovered, but it is also true that a high number of shipwrecks and underwater archaeological zones can be safeguarded for future generations.

The main problem faced in Spain is the enormous length of its coastline. This means it is likely that, in the future, similar models will be created in the main archaeological zones of our country, whether this be the responsibility of the Civil Guard or the corresponding police forces of Spain's autonomous communities.

The funding of the project does not involve inaccessible costs for the institutions, since staff from the Ministries concerned can be used. In fact, the main economic cost turns out to be fuel. As regards the barrows and strongboxes, these can be made with local resources at a relatively affordable cost.

In the case of the shipwrecks that are being discovered near Alexandria, some of the principles set out here could perhaps be applied as a way of protecting them until their study can be undertaken. The decisions to be taken on the enormous concentrations of stone blocks, which we had a chance to see on the occasion of the International Workshop, must obviously be different. But it is also true that, near these blocks, several shipwrecks from the Hellenistic-Roman era have been discovered, and some belonging to the Islamic era are likely to come to light. On the next occasion, after this first and fruitful international contact, we could discuss our ideas on the protection of remains that are not shipwrecks, but related specifically to the architectural monuments found.

[5] Negueruela, I. et al. (1996). I Curso sobre protección del patrimonio arqueológico subacuático. Cuadernos de Arqueología Marítima, 4:239–43.

Data management in underwater archaeology

VINCENZO SOMMELLA
ES s.r.l. - Progetti e Sistemi
Rome

Introduction

In recent years, the techniques of data management have improved significantly. This improvement, in addition to the development of working methods, has brought a change in the way we think about the process that takes place between the archaeological site and the museum.

All the work – surveying, mapping, video-photo documentation, cataloguing, data analysis, book publishing, museum display, and so on, should be considered a unique activity: data management.

Spinoza, in paragraph 31 of his *Treatise on the Emendation of the Intellect* (1661), wrote:

... just as men began by being able to do very easy things using their natural instruments, even if they did them imperfectly and with much effort, and having done these things they went on to do others which are more difficult, and they did them better and more easily, and thus they proceeded by stages, passing first from the simplest works to their necessary instruments, and from these instruments to other works and other instruments, until they came to a point at which they could do a great many very difficult things with great ease – in the same way the intellect proceeds, making for itself intellectual instruments out of its innate strength, through which it then acquires new strengths which enable it to perform new intellectual tasks, and these new tasks lead to the creation of new instruments, and the ability to investigate further; and thus it proceeds by stages, until it reaches the very peak of wisdom ...

In the light of Spinoza's words, I think that the role of data management is to transform information into knowledge or, better, to help archaeologists to do it along the many steps of the same path.

Time destroys, day by day, with a big help from Man, the remains of the past and the memory of things. The only way to preserve our heritage is to record all the data in the best possible way and to make them available to the largest number of people.

This is more urgent for underwater remains which often are in constant danger of being stolen or destroyed. The necessity of collecting data quickly and in the best possible way depends also on the high cost of underwater excavation and, in most cases, on the impossibility of going back and checking the surveying, or the hypothesis, later.

The present workshop is dedicated to underwater archaeology and coastal management; if we want to deal with the two subjects together, we need a common language and a way of sharing data and problems to reach solutions suitable for both fields.

This will be very difficult until we create the three following things:
• a common surveying methodology;
• a common way of describing data, in format and in vocabulary; and
• one or more instruments to manage these data all together and easily.

Obviously several steps have already been taken in this direction and the objective of the present paper is to contribute to the work in progress.

Methods

It is not feasible here to deal with the whole issue of surveying methodology, because that would require a longer paper than the present one; but one aspect of the question may be considered: the importance of planning every survey according to the characteristics of the related data-management programme.

As already stated, we have to consider the data flow, starting from the field survey. A survey is never an objective description of reality; it is a choice of some parts of it or, better, just a choice of some quality of the chosen parts. This establishes a definite responsibility of the surveyors in the final results of the research, because different ways of describing things lead to different ways of studying them.

Every time we look at something that we think we know well, from a different and unusual viewpoint, we discover something new or, at least, new aspects never seen before. This means that we have to plan our system choosing a side of reality and to organize the whole work from the beginning, knowing exactly which kind of data our data-management system requires. We have to know in which formats and with which accuracy and precision our system works; what are the graphic standards and so on.

All this is absolutely necessary to permit the comparison of data and to create a possibility of scientific research.

To take a well known contemporary analogy, we can imagine the kind of approach that we ought to have to projects and to the method of data acquisition, by comparing these processes to the UNI EN ISO 9000 international quality standards. These standards, which now regulate quality control in all manufacturing businesses, whether public or private, require the elimination of any ambiguity from all of the activities of a company. For instance, the precision of the measuring instruments used for quality control must itself be explicitly defined (that is, the minimum unit of measurement that they are able to gauge), their accuracy (that is, their deviation from a perfect measurement in terms of this minimum unit) and their range of tolerance (that is, the variation in dimension that is considered acceptable).

To return to our own field, this analogy suggests that data, if they are to be properly comparable, must either be measured with equivalent precision and accuracy, or at least be translatable into a common standard with the aid of certain reference values. For example, if you measure one distance with a metric ruler made of plastic, and another with a distance-measuring theodolite, the two measurements will not be comparable, unless the accepted level of tolerance is extremely great, or unless there is a coefficient which, when applied, reduces the difference in accuracy of the two instruments to within acceptable limits.

These same ISO 9000 standards require that the operational procedures for every significant activity in a process be defined. Besides ensuring that the correct methods are applied to every stage in the manufacturing process, this requirement guarantees continuity of standards and procedures, even if the personnel applying them change.

In conclusion, we may say that, to obtain reliable data in sufficient quantity and sufficiently quickly to meet our objectives, it is necessary to have a comprehensive vision of the process of study and research as a whole from the very start. Such a vision should include a clear definition of the project's aims, and the instruments to be used in achieving them. It should also be founded on the exact definition of the procedures for collecting and recording data that will be adopted.

The instrument: GIS

GIS is the acronym of Geographic Information System. Beyond its natural field of application – land management – the GIS family is the latest development in data-base software. In fact, a GIS permits contemporary but different types of data to be handled together and has the ability to hold and manipulate large bodies of data of any kind, from vector to raster, from alphanumeric to video, from sound to photo.

The most important innovation is the possibility of linking different types of data and of making queries of graphic and alphanumeric information. This means that we can start by making a query of a map and obtain a list of information, or make a query of an alphanumeric data base to obtain a thematic map as an answer.

To pose such questions as: 'show me all the painted ceramics found on 10 July 1996 in the third stratum' or 'show me all the animal bones of the 2nd stratum that are at less than 2 m from the axe n° 345 and print the list' is a simple way of using a GIS and a great help to the archaeologist in his work.

Moreover, a GIS is able to perform simulations and to produce reasonable hypotheses about any question whose answer could be deduced through algorithms. For example: you have the drawing of an ancient fresco and its damage mapping; it is possible to visualize and calculate the increase in damage during a given time under specified conditions (temperature, humidity, insulation, wall damage, etc.).

Archaeology draws on information from many different governmental and commercial entities, as well as specialist data. It stands to reason, then, that it will be a major benefit if an information system can extract the salient point from these various sources to create maps directly from attribute information from individual or combined data sets. For example, in Alexandria, there is the problem of preserving the Pharos island from sea erosion and, concurrently, of continuing the excavation of the underwater archaeological site and of constructing an underwater museum.

The two or, better, the three problems are dealt with by different specialists with different languages and different points of view. The GIS allows them to find a common ground and an instrument that will merge the languages and the data.

We can introduce into a GIS either data on the archaeological excavation, or those on sea currents, bathymetric contours, the nature of the coast and the rate of erosion. It is possible, however, using appropriate algorithms, to obtain immediate answers to questions about the effects of currents and their ability to change coastal defences, just as it is possible to select and define automatically an underwater path linking

different finds which share certain characteristics, without descending below a given depth.

We have developed a GIS that we called, without much imagination, *Archaeogis*. It was developed to manage the data of La Marmotta site in Lake Bracciano near Rome. This site is one of the most important European Neolithic sites. During the installation of an underwater pipeline in 1989, the neolithic village was found at a depth of about 7.5 m, covered by 2 m of sediment. As soon as we began surveying the excavation area, we understood the necessity of handling many thousands of ceramic fragments, oxydians, stones, wood, bones, vegetables etc., each one with its corresponding card and its picture.

The GIS has a highly innovative characteristic compared with the older data base: it has given to our systems a third dimension, not that of the spatial kind, which is quite common, but the third dimension beyond space and time – the subjects themselves.

The standards

In recent years, we have seen progress in the standardization of archaeological cards and, in consequence, of archaeological data. This progress has lead to a reduction in the numbers of different index cards, from thousands to a regional or national standardization. This standardization does not include, in most cases, either the dimensions and the definitions of data-base fields or the structure and the compatibility of data-base software. This is a problem in Italy and, probably, in the rest of the world, and the situation amongst different countries is much worse.

Here, at an international workshop, the necessity of a common scientific language is very apparent. Everybody agrees that it is useless to own a powerful instrument that is impossible to use because of the lack of compatibility in the data. To make a query we need a vocabulary; to exchange data we need standard cards; hardware is stupid, and if you define a cup as being *biansata* instead of 'con due anse', it could be a big problem, so you can imagine what happens between different languages, different institutions and different software.

The first big problem is the definition of the categories and the sub-categories. This definition is the first step in the data-base structure. This is not a programmer's problem but an archaeologist's. In cartography, for example, there are internationally recognized standard categories, as: buildings, streets, hydrography, orography, etc. Each category has many sub-categories and each sub-category has his own graphic characteristics and its own card. There is, in the most used

system, about 30 categories and 500 sub-categories.

Today in Italy, there is a card-cataloguing system for archaeology which has been established by an agency that is part of the Ministry for Cultural Heritage, the ICCD. This system is specifically designed for cards that are used for archaeological 'objects'. For those who are not familiar with such systems, let me give an example of how ours works: all significant finds are catalogued in the system with a card that is marked RA ('reperto archeologico'). The nature of the find (ceramics, wood, stone, metal, etc.) is described on the card. This description is a free description, since the nature of such finds can be highly diverse. There is no scale of priorities which would define a hierarchical structure for the data. The same is true of the US ('unità stratigrafica') cards, which are used for every independently identifiable element of the site, from a ditch to a wall, from an arch to a mosaic. This lack of a descriptive hierarchy greatly simplifies the work of classification, even if it is at the cost of a certain inaccuracy, so as to cover the widest possible range of cases.

The first problem we encounter if we want to create a GIS for archaeology is the following: in a GIS, every category must have certain graphic characteristics which are fixed; for example, the category 'pavements' would have to be a closed area, and the category 'contour lines' would have to be an open polylinear form. If objects are placed in the category 'US cards' which cannot be described in these ways, then the original categories will have to be sub-divided into sub-categories.

This subdivision – which should also be a priority for other, unconnected reasons – has never been formally defined. As a result, each person chooses only those categories which seem to him or her most significant, and defines them according to those parameters that are most important in his or her work. As a result, we could have one GIS that begins by identifying finds according to their date, another that identifies them according to their material, and yet another, according to the terms in which they are described.

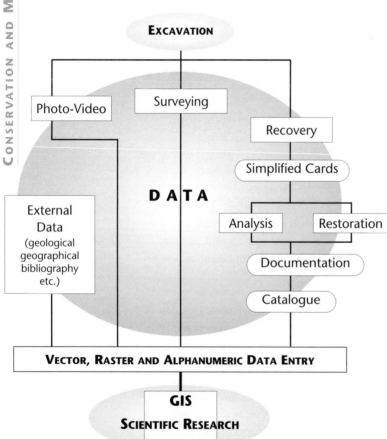

INPUT

EXCAVATION

Photo-Video   Surveying

Recovery

Simplified Cards

DATA

External Data
(geological geographical bibliography etc.)

Analysis   Restoration

Documentation

Catalogue

VECTOR, RASTER AND ALPHANUMERIC DATA ENTRY

GIS
SCIENTIFIC RESEARCH

In addition, the graphic categories used to describe objects have not been formalized either, as a result of which we may have several 'objects' which belong to the same category, but which are defined in such different ways that the various sets of data cannot be used in conjunction with one another.

Finally – though this is not the last of our problems – the question of devising an unambiguous code to replace the traditional inventory numbers has not yet been addressed, nor has the problem of the 'skeleton' which structures the mass of data that has been assembled yet been resolved. In France, the method that is increasingly favoured is that of the 'intelligent' code, from which one can immediately read off the fundamental information associated with the object.

REINS Project

We are currently working on a project that follows the themes described above. The name of the project is REINS (Rete Europea per lo studio degli Insediamenti Neolitici Sommersi); it is co-financed by the European Commission under the Raphael Programme for European Cultural Heritage Safeguard.

The project's partners are: ES Progetti e Sistemi Company, Naples-Rome (Italy), co-ordinator; Museo Nazionale Luigi Pigorini, Rome (Italy); Museu Arqueològic Comarçal de Banyoles (Spain); Archaeologische Denkmalpflege Landesdenkmalamt, Baden Wurttemberg (Germany).

The REINS project includes the development of a Europe-oriented GIS, *Archaeogis rel. Euro*. To develop this software we are comparing the index cards from Italy, Germany and Spain, to create a common standard. This is a vast project. One needs only to think of the difficulty of defining an unambiguous relationship between definitions in three different languages. At the same time, we are trying to define at least some of the procedures for acquiring and presenting the data mentioned above.

In accordance with the concept of data management, this project is conceived around a flow of the data that originates in archaeological excavation, is then rendered in digital form, collected and managed within a GIS, studied using that GIS, is then distributed and compared with other data over the Internet, and is finally used to put together exhibitions, publications (on paper, and electronically, as CD-ROMs), lectures and so on – all of this at only minimal cost at each stage and, above all, with all the data continuously available to provide new answers to new questions.

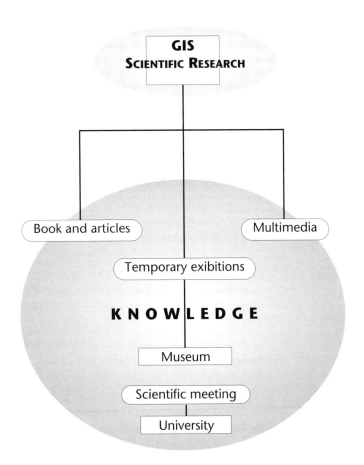

Conventions and laws related to submarine archaeological sites in the Mediterranean

VINCENT NÉGRI
Affiliated researcher
Institut de Droit de l'Environnement
Université de Lyon 3

The Mediterranean is a geographical link that binds together different continents. As a 'complex of seas', it defines a unity that is not only physical, but human, and thus historical, too[1]. It embodies a common heritage which is the source of the high culture generally associated with Western civilisation[2]. Indeed, few people today are not indebted to the culture of the Mediterranean. Where once men and women fought over their inheritance, there is now, for the most part, peace. Yet even this relative calm is not entirely devoid of tension.

On land, the frontiers have been fixed. Where conflict does re-emerge, it remains localized. Instead, those who are ambitious to extend their dominion have turned their attention to the sea. From the time the law of the sea was first formulated in 1930, up until the Law of the Sea Convention of 1982 and beyond, the interests at stake have been growing ever more numerous and more complex. Today, the demand for economic development occupies centre stage. Rather than new territories, debate focuses on the question of rights to the apparently inexhaustible natural resources of the sea. At the same time, the cultural dimension of development policy has come to the fore, and the protection of the environment has emerged as a major issue. The protection of cultural goods has thus come to be seen as integral both to the values of development and to environmental concerns. It was in this context that the law of

the sea sought to address the question of protecting those cultural goods that were to be found underwater. But simply granting the prerogative to the various States concerned as to how the management of these goods should be regulated was not enough to ensure that they would be protected against every possible threat. It thus fell to the Convention for the Protection of the Mediterranean Sea Against Pollution, adopted in Barcelona on 16 February 1976, and its additional protocols, to begin the process of formulating principles by which underwater cultural goods can be brought within the scope of an international environmental instrument. The convention of the Council of Europe of 8 March 1993 on civil liability for damage resulting from activities dangerous to the environment confirmed the extension of the idea of reparation for environmental damage to the cultural heritage. Thus reparation for damage occasioned to wrecks of archaeological interest due to marine pollution, and especially the oil spills, was brought under a clearly-defined legal scheme. Finally, to resume where the law of the sea left off, the Mediterranean States have adopted national laws, some of which deal exclusively with underwater cultural goods, and through which those States seek to achieve a certain degree of control over this part of their heritage.

The law of the sea and the notion of cultural heritage

Partly through the efforts of the Mediterranean States, the law of the sea has gradually come to incorporate certain specific provisions relating to the underwater cultural heritage. In this context, the Mediterranean has often come to serve as the laboratory in which these new concepts were first promulgated and applied.

First steps towards legislation for underwater archaeological sites

The States which border the Mediterranean first raised the question of how to protect archaeological objects found under the sea during the third Conference on the Law of the Sea which began in 1970. Greece, Italy, Malta, Portugal, Tunisia and former Yugoslavia together put forward a proposition, which was also supported by Cape Verde, according to which sovereign rights would be granted to each coastal State over all archaeological and historical objects that were located on its continental shelf. Each coastal State would thus have enjoyed exclusive prerogatives to investigate, salvage, protect and exploit those objects, along with preferential rights should the objects be sold and exported from the country of origin. These preferential rights would have belonged either to the State of cultural origin, or to the State of historical or archaeological origin. The spirit of this proposal, which would effectively have created a series of archaeological zones covering the continental shelves of the various States concerned, was supported by other Mediterranean States, in particular France, Egypt and Cyprus. But it was also strongly opposed by certain States, including the United States, who worked to have the archaeological zone reduced to the contiguous zone. During the negotiation and final drafting of the Law of the Sea Convention of 10 December 1982, this counter-proposal finally won the day. Leaving aside the economic interests of the parties concerned, these debates show how the original idea of an archaeological zone, irrespective of the size of the zone proposed, first emerged in the Mediterranean context, with the support of the coastal States[3]. The Convention contains two articles which make specific reference to the underwater heritage. Articles 148 and 303 deal respectively with archaeological and historical objects found in the zone, and the rights of the coastal State. However, these articles are far from being an adequate mechanism for protecting underwater cultural goods. This inadequacy can be clearly seen in the case of article 303, which can be interpreted as protecting the right to the commercial exploitation of wrecks of historical significance – and thus, in effect, the right to destroy archaeological resources before they can be investigated by scientists[4].

The Mediterranean as laboratory: exploring concepts of heritage

The Mediterranean sea is tightly girded round by land[5], and as such has often served as a model for other enclosed or semi-enclosed seas. Thus the term 'Mediterraneans' has sometimes been used to refer to such types of maritime space[6]. One example of this is the declaration adopted at Santo Domingo on 9 June 1972 by the 15 States which border the Caribbean Sea, in which the Caribbean is referred to as the American Mediterranean. The idea of the Mediterranean thus came to play a crucial role in defining the concept of a patrimonial sea. This concept was intended to solve the problem of reconciling the divergent interests of these States, which could not claim, whether by convention or by unilateral declaration, 'national sovereignty'[7] and

[1] Braudel, F. (1990). La Méditerranée. Volume 1, p. 21. Armand Colin, Paris.
[2] Duby, G. (1986). 'L'héritage', p. 193, in: F. Braudel (ed.), La Méditerranée, les hommes et l'héritage. Champs/Flammarion, Paris.
[3] Leanza, U. (1992). Le régime juridique international de la Méditerranée, p. 253, in: Recueil des Cours de l'Académie de droit international, V, volume 236. The Hague.
[4] UNESCO (1995). Étude de faisabilité sur la rédaction d'un nouvel instrument pour la préservation du patrimoine culturel subaquatique. Document 146 EX/27 (23 March 1995). UNESCO, Paris.
[5] Braudel, F. op. cit., p. 22.
[6] Lucchini, L. (1984). La troisième conférence des Nations-Unies sur le droit de la mer face au phénomène des 'Méditerranées' ou le triomphe de l'État océanique. p. 289, in: Études offertes à C.-A. Colliard. Pédone, Paris.
[7] The interpretation of the nature of the rights to which a nation lays claim will differ from one nation to another. The interpretation that is adopted will not necessarily suppose the application of full sovereign rights. [cf. Castaneda, J. (1972). Les positions des États latino-américains. p. 158, in: Actualités du droit de la mer, Société française pour le droit international. Pédone, Paris].

exclusive jurisdiction over an area of up to 200 nautical miles without thereby each trespassing on the waters of their neighbours[8]. Subsequently, the regime governing matrimonial seas significantly refined this patrimonial concept, by prescribing a sort of commonality of all biological resources which lie beyond the 12-mile limit of national sovereignty. Once again, we must recognise that it was the Mediterranean States who first developed this concept. During the third conference on the law of the sea, the case was plainly stated by the Libyan representatives: 'the wealth of these (semi-enclosed) seas constitute the heritage of the coastal States'[9]. The law of the sea which emerged from the Convention of 1982, and which is dominated by the idea of appropriating maritime areas[10], also satisfied the demand made by one Mediterranean state – Malta – that the juridical notion of a common heritage of mankind be recognized. This notion, as applied to maritime areas, was originally conceived as being advantageous to the developing countries, in that it was thought it would help them to obtain additional

resources for their development[11]. This concept may have had its origin in the most generous feelings. But unfortunately, in the norms governing development, law principles largely predominate over the rules they were meant to inspire. Although these principles are juridical principles – that is, able to dictate juridical rules – their moral or ideological content is very pronounced. Clearly, it is easier to formulate a general principle – and to ensure its universal acceptance – than a rule which dictates a precise form of behaviour[12]. The formulation of article 149, which deals with archaeological and historical objects found within the zone, is thus intended to reserve room for the rights of States relative to the concept of a common heritage, which is nevertheless grandly presented as if it were a monument to the interests of humanity as a whole.

Adapting international environmental norms to protect cultural heritage

The United Nations' declaration on the environment at Stockholm in 1972, proclaimed that 'both aspects of man's environment, the natural and the man-made, are essential to his well-being and to the enjoyment of basic human rights – even the right to life itself.'[13]. Natural resources and cultural productions were thus united without distinction in a single concept: the environment. It is this sense of the term 'environment' that is gradually taken into account in the formulation of environmental norms. The evolution of international law in this area is thus characterised by a series of subtle steps through which heritage considerations have gradually been integrated into texts whose explicit aims are environmental.

First steps towards taking heritage considerations into account
In the preamble to the Convention for the protection of the Mediterranean sea against pollution adopted at Barcelona in 16 February 1976, the contracting Parties declare that they

[8] The maritime zone defined in this way, as the patrimonial sea, is a zone over which the coastal state is competent to exercise jurisdiction and supervisory powers to a specific end, but over which it does not claim sovereignty. Thus the declaration stipulates that 'the coastal State has sovereign rights over the renewable and non-renewable natural resources, which are found in the waters, in the sea-bed and in the subsoil of an area adjacent to the territorial sea called the patrimonial sea'. The patrimonial sea should thus be considered a zone over which the State has economic jurisdiction. The prerogatives that are thus granted are accompanied by both a duty and a right to regulate scientific research conducted in these areas, particularly so as to protect natural resources.
[9] Document Officiel, vol. 1, p. 150. Cited by L. Lucchini, op. cit., p. 302.
[10] Tavernier, P. (1984). Droit de la mer et droit international du développement. p. 230, in: La formation des normes en droit international du développement. Éditions du CNRS, Paris.
[11] Ibid.
[12] Villary, M. (1984). Droit, politique et développement. p. 57, in: La formation des normes en droit international du développement. Éditions du CNRS, Paris.
[13] United Nations (1972). Doc. A/Conf.48/14/Rev.1. UN, New York.

recognize the economic, social and cultural values of the marine environment of the Mediterranean area. Yet the text of the Convention itself reduces the cultural dimension of this programme to a simple matter of the enjoyment of the pleasures which cultural goods can procure for the individual. Article 2 of the Convention thus mentions the degradation of amenities as among the elements which define the notion of pollution.

The Protocol which was joined to the Convention concerning co-operation in combating pollution of the Mediterranean sea by oil and other harmful substances in cases of emergency, adopted on the same day as the Convention itself, extends this approach by including threats to historical and touristic attractions among those related interests which the States must seek to preserve from such damage[14]. These partial, even reductive, approaches to the heritage question, limited by the requirement that the sites in question be deemed aesthetically attractive, were to be considerably extended in the drafting of the additional Protocol of 3 April 1982.

The concept of a protected area applied to archaeological sites

The Protocol of 3 April 1982 concerning specially protected Mediterranean areas places natural resources and sites on a par with the cultural heritage when it comes to defining such areas.

According to the terms of the first article of the Protocol, the contracting Parties 'shall take all appropriate measures with a view to protecting those marine areas which are important for the safeguard of the natural resources and natural sites of the Mediterranean Sea Area, as well as for the safeguard of their cultural heritage in the region'.

Continuing in the same dual perspective, which associates natural sites and resources on the one hand with cultural heritage on the other, article 3 declares that the States will create protected areas in order to preserve from harm both the various elements that constitute natural and ecological resources, and 'sites of particular importance because of their scientific, aesthetic, historical, archaeological, cultural or educational interest'.

To ensure this aim is achieved, the States

must, as specified in article 7, gradually enact the necessary measures, in accordance with international law. As far as cultural heritage is concerned, there is a reference in article 7, paragraph i) to 'the regulation of any archaeological activity and of the removal of any object which may be considered as an archaeological object'.

Concerns regarding the scientific management and development of these areas are specifically mentioned in article 10 of the Protocol: 'The Parties shall encourage and develop scientific and technical research on their protected areas and on the ecosystems and archaeological heritage of those areas'.

As a corollary, this action should be accompanied by mechanisms to ensure public participation and the dissemination of knowledge. Thus article 11 declares that the States will endeavour to inform the public as widely as possible of the significance and interest of the protected areas and of the scientific knowledge which may be gained from them in relation to both nature conservation and archaeology. Such information should have an appropriate place in education programmes concerning the

---

[14] These ideas are to be found in most conventions on regional seas and their protocols concerning co-operation in combating pollution in cases of emergency: Convention of 23 March 1981 for co-operation in the protection and development of the marine and coastal environment of the West and Central African region and its Protocol adopted the same day; the Convention of 20 November 1981 for the protection of the marine environment and coastal areas of the South-East Pacific, and its Protocol; the regional Convention of 14 February 1982 for the conservation of the Red Sea and the Gulf of Aden environment, and its Protocol; the Protocol of 24 March 1983 concerning co-operation in combatting oil spills in the wider Caribbean Region; the Convention of 21 June 1985 for the protection, management and development of the marine and coastal environment of the Eastern African region, and its Protocol. As for the Convention of 25 November 1986 for the protection of the natural resources and environment of the South Pacific region, its supplementary Protocol concerning co-operation in combatting pollution emergencies gives a somewhat different formulation of the relevant cultural interests. Here, the reference is to the cultural value of the region and to the exercise of traditional customary rights within this zone.

environment and history. The Parties should also endeavour to promote the participation of their public and their nature conservation organizations in appropriate measures which are necessary for the protection of the areas concerned.

Co-operation and assistance programmes, especially in the areas of training of scientific and technical staff and of scientific research, should also be established, so as to allow those developing countries that wish to do so to define, establish and manage their own protected areas.

The application of the concept of protected areas to the underwater cultural heritage, as it was defined in the Protocol of 3 April 1982, allows for the creation of archaeological zones according to original criteria. In this sense, this new approach to protecting the space occupied by the underwater heritage corresponds to the concept of a marine reserve or park. Though this concept may be very attractive, it also suffers from two notable limitations, as a result of the fact that its application is limited to territorial waters.

On a practical level, the underwater cultural heritage can only be protected through the creation of protected areas around known or generally recognised sites on a case-by-case basis. This approach supposes that the sites to be protected have already been identified and listed. Although the Protocol says nothing on this subject, these are the classic mechanisms used by international instruments which aim to define protected areas[15]. In the absence of any other specific dispositions, this identification process would inevitably be the responsibility of the coastal States, within the limits of their territorial waters. This last point is implicitly confirmed by the wording of article 2 of the Protocol, which restricts the area of the Mediterranean concerned 'to the territorial waters of the Parties and may include waters on the landward side of the baseline from which the breadth of the territorial sea is measured and extends, in the case of watercourses, up to the freshwater limit'. This text also states that the area thus defined may 'include wetlands or coastal areas designated by each of the Parties'.

There is no ambiguity about the words used here: protected areas cannot be created in international waters, nor in lakes, streams or rivers[16]. By thus limiting the area concerned in accordance with the notion of national sovereignty, the text is deprived of much of its potential force, and the mechanisms for protecting the underwater heritage that it establishes are rendered powerless outside each State's territorial waters.

The regime governing responsibility for damage to cultural goods caused by pollution or by dangerous activities

Wrecks involving several oil-carrying tankers have alerted public opinion to the damage such accidents can do to the environment. But the responsibilities of the authors of what has come to be known as 'ecological damage' could not be fully addressed by mere juridical means. In order to create an adequate mechanism for obtaining reparation, therefore, the Council of Europe introduced a Convention on 8 March 1993 on civil liability for damage resulting from activities dangerous to the environment.

The Convention defines the environment in the same terms as the Stockholm declaration of 1972. Under article 2.10, it states that the environment includes:
• natural resources both abiotic and biotic, such as air, water, soil, fauna and flora and the interaction between the same factors;
• property which forms part of the cultural heritage; and
• the characteristic aspects of the landscape.

These last two points are of particular interest for those whose concern is with the protection of the Mediterranean coastline and environment. They are particularly important because this convention explicitly emphasises the question of reparation for damages sustained by the environment. Article 2.7 in particular distinguishes between damage to persons and to personal property, and damage

---

[15] For example, the UNESCO convention of 16 November 1972 for the protection of the world cultural and natural heritage includes certain dispositions which suppose the creation of such a mechanism.
[16] Strati, A. (1995). The protection of the underwater cultural heritage: an emerging objective of the contemporary law of the sea. p. 86. Martinus Nijhoff Publishers, The Hague.

or loss resulting from some change inflicted on the environment. The conjunction of this distinction and the definition of the environment adopted by the Convention makes this an especially valuable instrument through which to address the protection of the cultural heritage against pollution of all kinds. As for the strict liability of the authors, whether public or private, of damage resulting from dangerous activities undertaken for professional reasons, the Convention established as a criterion that the environmental prejudice suffered should be assessed on the basis of restoration to the prior state and the cost of this work – including appropriate protective measures – or, as a subsidiary provision, the costs incurred to obtain compensation in kind[17]. Under the heading of damage caused by pollution to 'property which forms part of the cultural heritage' and negative effects of dangerous activities, are included any changes suffered by underwater archaeological sites. These sites are particularly vulnerable to such impacts, especially those caused by oil spills. The strong point of these articles is therefore that they establish terms of objective responsibility for such damage. Their weak point lies in the definitions they give of appropriate reinstatement work and preventive measures.

Reinstatement measures are defined in the Convention under article 2.8 as any reasonable measures aiming to reinstate or restore damaged or destroyed components of the environment, or to introduce, where reasonable, the equivalent of these components into the environment. National law may indicate who will be entitled to take such measures. Preventive measures are here defined as any reasonable measures taken by any person, after an incident has occurred to prevent or minimize loss or damage as defined in the Convention[18]. However, the repeated use of the adjective 'reasonable' in these definitions, which seems designed to echo the Anglo-Saxon usage, 'rule of reason'[19], leaves the door open to attempts to attenuate the enforcement of the mechanisms for establishing responsibility created by the Convention.

Nevertheless, these remarks should not be allowed to detract from the importance of this norm, which marked a decisive step forward in ascribing civil responsibility for environmental harm, and which recognized the specific nature of damage to the environment, where environment is broadly interpreted to include among other things the cultural heritage.

While the Convention primarily concerns the European States of the Mediterranean basin, its benefits can also be extended to other States which are not members of the Council of Europe, at the invitation of the Committee of Ministers or at the proposal of the permanent Committee following a decision of the member States taken by qualified majority voting.

Despite its defects, then, this norm does address a number of important questions concerning reparation and compensation for damage to elements belonging to the cultural heritage, including underwater archaeological sites, caused by the dumping of polluting substances.

National legislation

Many of the States which border the Mediterranean Sea have adopted laws which specifically deal with the protection of their underwater cultural heritage. Certain States, such as France and Tunisia, have limited the scope of such laws to supervising archaeological activities and protecting cultural goods to be found within the contiguous zone.

Thus the first article of French law number 89-874 of 1 December 1989, concerning maritime cultural goods, states that maritime cultural

[17] Martin, G. J. (1994). *La convention du Conseil d'Europe du 8 mars 1983 dite convention Lugano. p. 99.* Les petites affiches, *no. 50 (27 April 1994), Paris.*
[18] *Article 2.7 of the Convention in particular defines damage as meaning, among other things, any loss or damage sustained due to an alteration in the environment, where this latter term includes both natural resources and those goods that make up the cultural heritage and the characteristic aspects of a landscape.*
[19] *Martin, G. J. op. cit.*

goods are those sites, wrecks, remains or in general any element which, being of prehistoric, archaeological or historical interest, is to be found in the public maritime domain or on the sea-bed of the contiguous zone.

The second article of Tunisian law number 86-35 of 9 May 1986, concerning the protection of archaeological goods, historic monuments and natural sites in urban areas, envisages that explorations may particularly target underwater remains in any area of water, including inland waters, territorial waters and the contiguous zone which extends to 24 nautical miles from the base lines used to define the extent of the territorial waters. More recently, Tunisian law number 94-35 of 24 February 1994 concerning the code that governs the archaeological, historical and traditional craft heritage, gives to the State the property of all archaeological goods, movable or immovable, that are discovered in both inland and territorial waters.

This regulation then goes on to stipulate that any exploration of underwater cultural sites requires prior authorization, and that in certain cases the State's property in archaeological objects retrieved from the sea bed is accompanied by a pre-emptive right over those objects. In a chapter devoted specifically to discoveries made at sea, the Tunisian archaeological, historical and traditional crafts heritage code of 1994 forbids any form of investigation whose aim is to search for archaeological and historical goods at sea, without authorization from the minister responsible for national heritage. Most States likewise stipulate that underwater archaeological goods are to be subject to the same juridical regime of authorization and supervision as that which applies to archaeological investigations on land.

Other Mediterranean States have extended their control over underwater cultural goods beyond the limits of the contiguous zone.

According to the terms of article 46 of law number 22-80 concerning the preservation of historic monuments and sites, inscriptions, art objects and antiquities, promulgated by the *dahir* number 1-80-341 on 17 Safar 1401 (25 December 1980), Morocco has defined the maritime zone within which it claims jurisdiction over archaeological goods as

identical to its exclusive fishery zone.

More generally, State practice has tended to extend control over underwater cultural goods to cover all or part of the continental shelf. Thus Spanish law applies to movable and immovable goods to be found either in territorial waters or on the continental shelf[20].

In those cases where national law has sought to extend the area of its application, it has done so simply by reference to the continental shelf. Yet such extensions might well have adopted the exclusive economic zone as an alternative criterion. The decision to extend juridical control to the continental shelf alone can be found in the legislations of Greece, Israel, Libya and Turkey[21]. Among those States which initiated the demand for sovereign rights over archaeological and historical objects to be found on their continental shelves at the third Conference on the Law of the Sea, it should be noted that Cape Verde has also manifested this ambition in its law number 102/III/90 of 29 December 1990, which deals with the defence of Cape Verde's cultural heritage.

Yet this kind of legislation contravenes the main thrust of the Law of the Sea Convention, which was to limit the archaeological zone to 24 nautical miles, that is, to the contiguous zone, and which in no case foresaw that a coastal State might exercise any form of sovereign right over underwater cultural goods to be found on its continental shelf.

Nevertheless, the Council of Europe's recommendation number 848 of 4 October 1978 concerning the underwater cultural heritage, which seeks to define the principles which should guide the development of a European Convention on underwater cultural heritage, proposed the declaration of national zones of cultural protection which might extend up to a limit of 200 miles, where geographical conditions made such a distance appropriate. In its annex on minimal legal norms, the recommendation envisaged that national jurisdiction could run up to the limit of 200 miles, with an international agreement

---

[20] Art. 40 of law number 1 6/1985 of 25 June on the Spanish cultural heritage.
[21] According to the indications provided in U. Leanza, op. cit., p. 254.

to determine, on condition of reciprocity, how cultural goods discovered by one country yet belonging to the cultural zone of another country should be dealt with.

The recommendation preferred the 200-mile zone as a norm for the Mediterranean instead of the continental shelf, both because the definition of the continental shelf is imprecise and subject to variation, and because by doing so, the recommendation was able to align itself with the idea of an exclusive economic zone which was just then emerging from the negotiations on the Law of the Sea Convention. It was also then possible to remodel the definition of cultural zones according to the same principles.

Despite this advance, the European Convention for the protection of the archaeological heritage (revised version), signed in Malta on 16 January 1992, returns to the traditional terminology, without taking a position as to the extent of a nation's territorial waters. After having stated in article 1, paragraph 2(iii) that the cultural goods dealt with by the Convention are those which are located in any area within the jurisdiction of the States, the third paragraph of the first article sets out to define the archaeological heritage. This is taken to include structures, constructions, groups of buildings, developed sites, moveable objects, monuments of other kinds as well as their context, whether situated on land or under water. This final precision, added for the sake of completeness to a text which deals primarily with the protection of the archaeological heritage on land, leaves the States concerned a more or less free hand to define the extent of the zone over which they claim rights as regards the underwater archaeology to be found within it. Different national laws may thus define this zone as comprising the territorial waters, the contiguous zone, the continental shelf, the economic zone or even a zone of cultural protection, as they so choose. As a result, an original conception of the State's specific jurisdiction – national zones of cultural protection up to a limit of 200 miles – which could have been defined in the terms laid down by the Council of Europe's recommendation number 848 of 4 October 1978, was effectively sabotaged by the definition of the territoriality of heritage given under article 1, paragraph 2(iii), which simply accepts the practice of dealing with the underwater cultural heritage through the legal dispositions which already apply to the archaeological heritage that is to be found on land. Far from daring to define the territorial terms of cultural sovereignty, the European Convention for the protection of the archaeological heritage (revised version) simply accepts a traditional conception of the zone that is controlled by the State, and thus excludes from the outset any possibility of rethinking the idea of archaeological heritage in the light of new approaches to the definition of national territory. It is therefore to be feared that a similarly traditional approach may yet manage to undermine the conceptual innovations of the European draft Convention on underwater cultural heritage which is to be drawn up according to the recommendation of 4 October 1978.

Conclusion

The Mediterranean Sea constitutes a unique legal context in which issues concerning the environment, both natural and man-made, have had to be dealt with through a series of innovative and original measures. Because the protection of the underwater cultural heritage in several international instruments has been associated with the protection of the environment, it has come to be approached through a normative language in which the key terms are protection, prevention and reparation of damage. In this sense, the precepts that have developed in the region differ markedly from those which typically underpin laws dealing with cultural heritage elsewhere. There may therefore be lessons to be drawn from them which could help in the establishing of new international instruments to extend and complete the provisions already included in the Law of the Sea Convention. Ultimately, it is to be hoped that all these different approaches can be brought together to work for the protection of our cultural heritage and of the underwater archaeological heritage, in the interests of humanity as a whole.

Legal principles for protecting underwater cultural heritage

LYNDEL V. PROTT
Chief, International Standards Section
Division of Cultural Heritage
UNESCO

Introduction

UNESCO has been interested in the protection of underwater cultural heritage for a long time. Its first Recommendation in 1956 was expressly extended to cover it; since then, UNESCO has published two books on the subject: one in 1972, *Underwater Archaeology: A Nascent Discipline* and one in 1981, *Protection of the Underwater Heritage.* Its journal *Museum International* has published three issues of relevance: one on port museums, in 1990, and two on maritime museums, in 1996. The February 1997 issue of *UNESCO Sources* is devoted to the underwater cultural heritage, with a striking picture of one of the finds off Qait Bey on the front cover. Because most of the underwater cultural heritage was not accessible and therefore not threatened until the discovery of the self-contained underwater breathing apparatus (SCUBA), legal principles related to it have only been developed since the 1940s. However, they have not yet been incorporated into the relevant international and national law.

International law

Looking first at the international system, there are several UNESCO recommendations for the protection of cultural heritage, developed by experts from the relevant disciplines and provide guidance for national legislation. The very first of these Recommendations to be developed was the Recommendation on International Principles Applicable to Archaeological Excavations 1956. It sets out basic provisions such as the requirement for excavation permits, conservation, publication and placement of finds primarily in the museums of the host country. It is notable that Principle 1 defines excavation as:

Any research aimed at the discovery of objects of archaeological character, whether such research involves digging of the ground or systematic exploration of its surface or is carried out on the bed or in the sub-soil of inland or territorial waters of a Member State.

Another UNESCO recommendation of importance for regulating the situation confronting the preservation of Alexandria's underwater cultural heritage is that on the Preservation of Cultural Property Endangered by Public or Private Works 1968, Principle 20 provides:

(a) There should be a co-ordinating or consultative body, composed of representatives of the authorities responsible for the safeguarding of cultural property, for public and private works, for town planning, and of research and educational institutions, which should be competent to advise on the preservation of cultural property endangered by public or private works and, in particular, on conflicts of interest between requirements for public or private works and the preservation or salvage of cultural property.

(b) Provincial, municipal or other forms of local government should also have services responsible for the preservation or salvage of cultural property endangered by public or private works. These services should be able to call upon the assistance of national services or other appropriate bodies in accordance with their capabilities and requirements.

...

(d) Administrative measures should be taken to co-ordinate the work of the different services responsible for the safeguarding of cultural property with any other department or service whose responsibilities touch upon the problem of the preservation or salvage of cultural property endangered by public or private works. Yet another UNESCO Recommendation is relevant: that pertaining to the Means of Prohibiting and Preventing the Illicit Export, Import and Transfer of Ownership of Cultural Property 1964. This is relevant because removal of individual elements of the important finds being made under water can distort the archaeological record, so control of access to prevent unauthorized activities is therefore essential.

These principles seem particularly relevant to the protection of the important archaeological sites of Alexandria. The obligation of Member States of UNESCO is to study standard-setting Recommendations adopted by the General Conference, to transmit them to their local authorities and to report on their implementation, or on the reasons why they have not been implemented. In many cases, such recommendations have provided a useful guide for national governments in resolving dilemmas over the protection of particular sites, since they represent the best professional expertise at the time they were drawn up.

There are, of course, also the UNESCO Conventions to look at. Two of those concerned with the protection of the cultural heritage are particularly relevant here. The first is the UNESCO Convention on the Means of Prohibiting and Preventing the Illicit Import, Export and Transfer of Ownership of Cultural Property 1970, which provides international mechanisms for the control of international trade in illegally removed cultural property. Mention has also been made of the UNESCO Convention concerning the Protection of the World Cultural and Natural Heritage 1972. I will address its possible relevance further on.

National jurisdiction to protect underwater cultural heritage

Some States rely on their general legislation for protection of cultural heritage. Newer legislation tends to make express provision for underwater cultural heritage to be included in its ambit (for example, Spain's 1985 legislation), but quite a lot of national

legislation is applied simply by way of interpreting general terms on excavation, protection of archaeological sites etc. without further reference. The Egyptian Antiquities Act would thus appear to apply in this fashion. Other States have quite specific legislation directed expressly to the underwater cultural heritage alone – Australia, France, the United Kingdom and the United States are all in this situation. Often, a State decides to create some kind of special status for an underwater site. The Australian legislation is quite interesting in this regard since it provides for sites which are underwater or partly on land and in the sea. Other solutions have been to use National Parks legislation, or to create marine reserves. On one occasion in the United States, powers were used in respect of a restricted site supervised by the defence forces as part of coastal security. Because of powers under such legislation, the defence forces can be very useful colleagues in the protection of the cultural heritage. To do so, of course, they have to be properly briefed in the importance of the heritage and what kind of activity they have to watch for.

Sites with a special status

It would seem that Egypt has legislation in force that can be used to protect the Alexandrian sites. The Antiquities Act No. 117 of 1983 (and its 1992 amendments) has already been mentioned; the Law on the Environment No. 4 is also relevant; and the Law on Natural Protectorates would appear to give the possibility of creating a special status for the sites by declaring them natural protectorates. Mention has been made of the possible nomination of the Qait Bey/Pharos site for the World Heritage List according to the Convention on the Protection of the World Cultural and Natural Heritage 1972. However, this has to be treated cautiously. The World Heritage Committee has never, so far, accepted an underwater site for inscription. This seems to be due to a variety of deterrents: the practical difficulties of delimitation; the provision of a buffer zone; monitoring; and devising an adequate management plan. None of these requirements is easy to meet, even for land sites, and is much more difficult for underwater sites. The ICOMOS Sub-Committee on the Underwater Cultural Heritage is in favour of their inclusion in the World Heritage List, but the World Heritage Committee will have to be convinced that it is appropriate and that proper management of such sites is possible. Inscription on the List inevitably brings greatly increased tourism and it can be a threat to the survival of the site. This is why the Committee has developed a procedure of close scrutiny of at least 18 months before a site is judged appropriate for listing, even if it is not eliminated at an earlier stage. If the Committee is not satisfied that all the requisite safeguards are in place, it may be delayed until they are.

Law in the making

The international community is taking an increasing interest in the underwater cultural heritage, and in 1994 UNESCO received the Buenos Aires draft convention on the protection of the underwater heritage prepared by the International Law Association (ILA). This text has been studied by a group of experts called together by UNESCO and commented on by States. Following the reports of the meeting and of States' comments, the UNESCO General Conference decided, in November 1997, that UNESCO should draft an international convention on the subject, and a further meeting of governmental experts will be held during 1998. However, the discussions have so far focussed on protection in the area beyond the territorial jurisdiction of the coastal State and this is not an issue in the case of the sites off Alexandria, so I will not go into further detail on its provisions. According to the United Nations Convention on the Law of the Sea 1982, a State has jurisdiction over its territorial sea (not to exceed 12 nautical miles) and can take control of underwater heritage out to 24 nautical miles. There is not yet general agreement on jurisdiction over underwater cultural heritage in the area beyond that, although some States have asserted it (e.g., Australia over the continental shelf and Morocco, in a Dahir of 1981, over the Exclusive Economic Zone – out to 200 nautical miles). However, in connection with the ILA's Buenos Aires draft, the Sub-

Committee on the Underwater Cultural Heritage of the ICOMOS International Committee on Archaeological Sites drafted a Charter on the Protection and Management of the Underwater Cultural Heritage which was adopted at the Plenary Conference of ICOMOS held in Sofia in 1996. These are principles devised by the experts in the subject to set international standards of best practice. The considerations included are important and the text is annexed to this document.

Setting priorities

However, no law can be efficient without two factors: a proper national policy that establishes the priorities; and adequate enforcement. As the 1968 Recommendation discussed above makes clear, co-ordination of policy is essential on important sites, since it is evident that there are often many national and local authorities involved in one way or another with a site. France regulates its programme of underwater archaeology at 4-year intervals, enabling changes to be made in the light of new discoveries, completion of earlier projects, particularly threatened sites etc. In establishing such a programme, it is necessary to have adequate information – first an inventory of known sites and potentially archaeologically rich areas, then an assessment of their relative historical/archaeological importance and, of course, an evaluation of their significance for the cultural dimension of development.

Imaginative protective solutions

If it is decided that these sites have a great potential for development in the cultural dimension, then imaginative protective solutions can be found. There are several possibilities. One that has been mentioned is an underwater museum. There are certain areas where tourists go as divers for leisure, and some of these sites are mixed sites where, for example, coral has grown over an old shipwreck. Some of them are administered as underwater parks. The existing ones are mostly concerned with shipwrecks and natural areas and the Lighthouse site is different: it is an outstanding monumental site. But an underwater museum is more than this and would need very careful planning and development. Another possibility is a mixed land-sea site; this could provide a very interesting tourist experience. Maritime museums are well developed in many areas of the world where it has been decided to raise the underwater finds, but this would not be desirable where the remains are immovable, such as the old port installations in the Eastern Harbour of Alexandria.

Management as a continuing process

The management of a complex site such as the Qait Bey/Pharos site needs to be seen as a continuing process, and legal regulation must allow for this. At this one site, it is evident that coastal management will be a continuing issue and the collection of data to allow informed decisions on future conservation will need to be pursued. Archaeologists still have survey work to do, and the questions of conservation, interpretation and long-term management will need their input.

These issues will also need to be discussed with other governmental agencies likely to have some responsibility for the sites.

Conclusion

The legal issues relating to the protection of the Alexandrian underwater sites do not seem difficult to resolve. Egypt is fortunate in having good legislation in existence which either applies already to the sites or can easily be adapted to give them a special status.

On the other hand, the potential for recognition of the sites as having 'outstanding universal value' (the terminology of the World Heritage Convention) cannot be allowed to obscure the complex management decisions that will have to be made to ensure their continuation in that condition. This is a precondition for the development of a cultural tourism that will not damage the site and for any argument that could be made for the extension of the World Heritage listing to underwater sites.

Annex

THE ICOMOS INTERNATIONAL CHARTER ON THE PROTECTION AND MANAGEMENT OF UNDERWATER CULTURAL HERITAGE

(ratified by the 11th ICOMOS General Assembly, held in Sofia, Bulgaria, from 5–9 October 1996)

Introduction

This Charter is intended to encourage the protection and management of underwater cultural heritage in inland and inshore waters, in shallow seas and in the deep oceans. It focuses on the specific attributes and circumstances of cultural heritage under water and should be understood as a supplement to the ICOMOS Charter for the Protection and Management of Archaeological Heritage, 1990. The 1990 Charter defines the 'archaeological heritage' as that part of the material heritage in respect of which archaeological methods provide primary information, comprising all vestiges of human existence and consisting of places relating to all manifestations of human activity, abandoned structures, and remains of all kinds, together with all the portable cultural material associated with them. For the purposes of this Charter, underwater cultural heritage is understood to mean the archaeological heritage which is in, or has been removed from, an underwater environment. It includes submerged sites and structures, wreck-sites and wreckage and their archaeological and natural context.

By its very character the underwater cultural heritage is an international resource. A large part of the underwater cultural heritage is located in an international setting and derives from international trade and communication in which ships and their contents are lost at a distance from their origin or destination.

Archaeology is concerned with environmental

conservation; in the language of resource management, underwater cultural heritage is both finite and non-renewable. If underwater cultural heritage is to contribute to our appreciation of the environment in the future, then we have to take individual and collective responsibility in the present for ensuring its continued survival.

Archaeology is a public activity; everybody is entitled to draw upon the past in informing their own lives, and every effort to curtail knowledge of the past is an infringement of personal autonomy. Underwater cultural heritage contributes to the formation of identity and can be important to people's sense of community. If managed sensitively, underwater cultural heritage can play a positive role in the promotion of recreation and tourism.

Archaeology is driven by research, it adds to knowledge of the diversity of human culture through the ages and it provides new and challenging ideas about life in the past. Such knowledge and ideas contribute to understanding life today and, thereby, to anticipating future challenges.

Many marine activities, which are themselves beneficial and desirable, can have unfortunate consequences for underwater cultural heritage if their effects are not foreseen.

Underwater cultural heritage may be threatened by construction work that alters the shore and seabed or alters the flow of current, sediment and pollutants. Underwater cultural heritage may also be threatened by insensitive exploitation of living and non-living resources. Furthermore, inappropriate forms of access and the incremental impact of removing 'souvenirs' can have a deleterious effect.

Many of these threats can be removed or substantially reduced by early consultation with archaeologists and by implementing mitigatory projects. This Charter is intended to assist in bringing a high standard of archaeological expertise to bear on such threats to underwater cultural heritage in a prompt and efficient manner.

Underwater cultural heritage is also threatened by activities that are wholly undesirable because they are intended to profit few at the expense of many. Commercial exploitation of underwater cultural heritage for trade or speculation is fundamentally incompatible with the protection and management of the heritage. This Charter is intended to ensure that all investigations are explicit in their aims, methodology and anticipated results so that the intention of each project is transparent to all.

Article 1 - Fundamental principles

The preservation of underwater cultural heritage *in situ* should be considered as a first option.

Public access should be encouraged.

Non-destructive techniques, non-intrusive survey and sampling should be encouraged in preference to excavation.

Investigation must not adversely impact the underwater cultural heritage more than is necessary for the mitigatory or research objectives of the project.

Investigation must avoid unnecessary disturbance of human remains or venerated sites.

Investigation must be accompanied by adequate documentation.

Article 2 - Project design

Prior to investigation a project must be prepared, taking into account :
• the mitigatory or research objectives of the project;
• the methodology to be used and the techniques to be employed;
• anticipated funding;
• the time-table for completing the project;
• the composition, qualifications, responsibility and experience of the investigating team;
• material conservation;
• site management and maintenance;
• arrangements for collaboration with museums and other institutions;
• documentation;
• health and safety;
• report preparation;
• deposition of archives, including underwater cultural heritage removed during investigation;
• dissemination, including public participation.

The project design should be revised and amended as necessary.

Investigation must be carried out in accordance with the project design. The project design should be made available to the archaeological community.

Article 3 - Funding

Adequate funds must be assured in advance of investigation to complete all stages of the project design including conservation, report preparation and dissemination. The project design should include contingency plans that will ensure conservation of underwater cultural heritage and supporting documentation in the event of any interruption in anticipated funding.

Project funding must not require the sale of underwater cultural heritage or the use of any strategy that will cause underwater cultural heritage and supporting documentation to be irretrievably dispersed.

Article 4 - Time-table

Adequate time must be assured in advance of investigation to complete all stages of the project design including conservation, report preparation and dissemination. The project design should include contingency plans that will ensure conservation of underwater cultural heritage and supporting documentation in the event of any interruption in anticipated timings.

Article 5 - Research objectives, methodology and techniques

Research objectives and the details of the methodology and techniques to be employed must be set down in the project design. The methodology should accord with the research objectives of the investigation and the techniques employed must be as unintrusive as possible.

Post-fieldwork analysis of artefacts and documentation is integral to all investigation; adequate provision for this analysis must be made in the project design.

Article 6 - Qualifications, responsibility and experience

All persons on the investigating team must be suitably qualified and experienced for their project roles. They must be fully briefed and understand the work required.

All intrusive investigations of underwater cultural heritage will only be undertaken under the direction and control of a named underwater archaeologist with recognised qualifications and experience appropriate to the investigation.

Article 7 - Preliminary investigation

All intrusive investigations of underwater cultural heritage must be preceded and informed by a site assessment that evaluates the vulnerability, significance and potential of the site.

The site assessment must encompass background studies of available historical and archaeological evidence, the archaeological and environmental characteristics of the site and the consequences of the intrusion for the long term stability of the area affected by investigations.

Article 8 - Documentation

All investigation must be thoroughly documented in accordance with current professional standards of archaeological documentation.

Documentation must provide a comprehensive record of the site, which includes the provenance of underwater cultural heritage moved or removed in the course of investigation, field notes, plans and drawings, photographs and records in other media.

Article 9 - Material conservation

The material conservation programme must provide for treatment of archaeological remains during investigation, in transit and in the long term.

Material conservation must be carried out in accordance with current professional standards.

Article 10 - Site management and maintenance

A programme of site management must be prepared, detailing measures for protecting and managing *in situ* underwater cultural heritage in the course of and upon termination of fieldwork. The programme should include public information, reasonable provision for site stabilization, monitoring and protection against interference. Public access to in situ underwater cultural heritage should be promoted, except where access is incompatible with protection and management.

Article 11 - Health and safety

The health and safety of the investigating team and third parties is paramount. All persons on the investigating team must work according to a safety policy that satisfies relevant statutory and professional requirements and is set out in the project design.

Article 12 - Reporting

Interim reports should be made available according to a time-table set out in the project design, and deposited in relevant public records.

Reports should include :
• an account of the objectives;
• an account of the methodology and techniques employed;
• an account of the results achieved;
• recommendations concerning future research, site management and curation of underwater cultural heritage removed during the investigation.

Article 13 - Curation

The project archive, which includes underwater cultural heritage removed during investigation and a copy of all supporting documentation, must be deposited in an institution that can provide for public access and permanent curation of the archive. Arrangements for deposition of the archive should be agreed before investigation commences, and should be set out in the project design. The archive should be prepared in accordance with current professional standards.

The scientific integrity of the project archive must be assured; deposition in a number of institutions must not preclude reassembly to allow further research. Underwater cultural heritage is not to be traded as items of commercial value.

Article 14 - Dissemination

Public awareness of the results of investigations and the significance of underwater cultural heritage should be promoted through popular presentation in a range of media. Access to such presentations by a wide audience should not be prejudiced by high charges.

Co-operation with local communities and groups is to be encouraged, as is co-operation with communities and groups that are particularly associated with the underwater cultural heritage concerned. It is desirable that investigations proceed with the consent and endorsement of such communities and groups.

The investigation team will seek to involve communities and interest groups in investigations to the extent that such involvement is compatible with protection and management. Where practical, the investigation team should provide opportunities for the public to develop archaeological skills through training and education.

Collaboration with museums and other institutions is to be encouraged. Provision for visits, research and reports by collaborating institutions should be made in advance of investigation.

A final synthesis of the investigation must be made available as soon as possible, having regard to the complexity of the research, and deposited in relevant public records.

Article 15 - International co-operation

International co-operation is essential for protection and management of underwater cultural heritage and should be promoted in the interests of high standards of investigation and research. International co-operation should be encouraged in order to make effective use of archaeologists and other professionals who are specialized in investigations of underwater cultural heritage. Programmes for exchange of professionals should be considered as a means of disseminating best practice.

Human impacts on Alexandria's marine environment

YOUSSEF HALIM
Department of Oceanography
University of Alexandria, and
FATMA ABOU SHOUK
Alexandria Governorate

Introduction

The environmental problems of Alexandria have grown rapidly in recent decades, in proportion to the growth in population and population density, as well as to the urban and industrial development. The rate of development has accelerated considerably since the turn of the century. In 1905, Alexandria's 370 thousand inhabitants lived in an area of about 4 km² between the two harbours. Since then, the city has expanded rapidly eastwards and westwards, beyond its medieval walls, occupying at present an area of about 300 km² with a population ten times larger, 4 million, and a density exceeding 1,200 per km² (Figs. 1 and 2). Modern Alexandria stretches over a narrow and irregular strip of land between the Mediterranean Sea to the north, Lake Mariout (a major coastal lagoon) to the south and Abu Qir Bay to the east. Topographically, the city appears to be encircled by a belt of aquatic environments subject to multiple human impacts.

Environmental issues

In Alexandria, the interface between marine and territorial environments extends along some 100 km of coastline. The city interacts with its aquatic environment in two ways: by discarding all its liquid wastes, domestic and industrial, into the sea, either directly or via Lake Mariout; and by physically altering its coastline, by coastal engineering works.

The total cumulative volume of waste water disposed of into the sea from all point sources along this stretch of coast is about equal to the Nile outflow from the Rosetta outlet: roughly 9 million m³/day; that is, 3.33 km³/yr. But this is not river water.

Figure 1.
The expansion of the city of Alexandria since 1805.

Figure 2. Population growth since 1840.

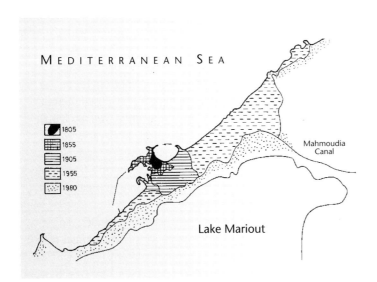

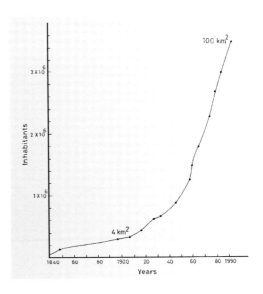

A daily volume of more than one million cubic metres of mixed sewage water is drained from the city. About one third of this is disposed of without any treatment, into the Eastern and Western Harbours and their surroundings. The Qait Bey outfall (Fig. 3), located a few hundred metres from the recently surveyed Pharos site, releases 200,000 m³ of waste water per day. The Eastern Harbour is the recipient of 7 outfalls. This semi-closed harbour remains permanently turbid, and water visibility is drastically reduced.

Two thirds of the city waste water is released into Lake Mariout and subsequently pumped into Mex Bay, west of the city, together with agricultural runoff drained from the north-west part of the delta. Only half this volume of waste water undergoes primary treatment before being dumped into the Lake. On the eastern side of Alexandria, about 2 million m³ of industrial waste water per day are pumped into Abu Qir Bay (see figure on inside front cover).

All of these outfalls add their load of suspended matter and a variety of contaminants to the inshore environment and to the Lake. Such materials, on sinking to the bottom, contribute to blanketing whatever artefacts are lying on the sea bed. They also cause hypoxic or even anoxic conditions at the bottom in some places, enhancing the processes associated with the absence of oxygen, including anaerobic bacterial processes, which end up releasing hydrogen sulphide, and chemical processes, which might accelerate corrosion, thus damaging some of the artefacts.

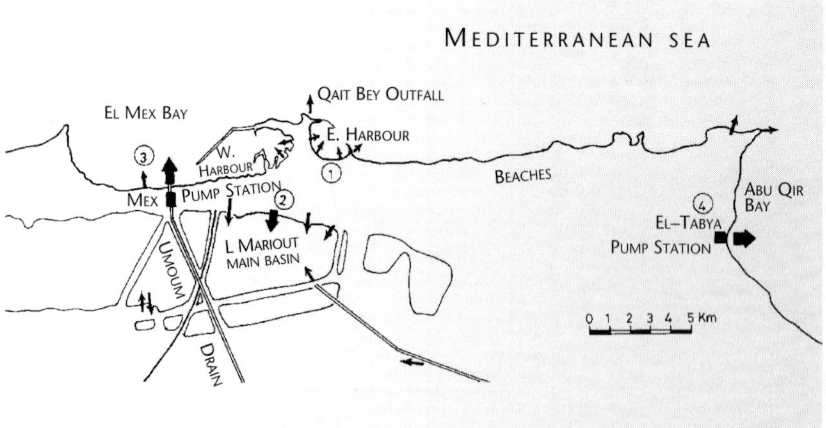

There is, however, an encouraging fact in that remedial action is being taken by the Alexandria Governorate. Work is underway to close the Eastern Harbour and Qait Bey outfalls and divert their share of waste water to the Lake after primary treatment.

Of even greater concern, however, are the far-reaching consequences of ill-conceived and misinformed engineering works which modify the coastline, in response to the pressure for economic development.

There are several issues at stake. We know that the foundations of the 15th century Qait Bey fortress appear to be dangerously eroded, particularly on the eastern side. To protect the fortress, the authorities have dumped more than a hundred concrete blocks weighing 7 to 20 tons each, precisely over parts of the submerged archaeological site recently surveyed. There can be no doubt about the urgent need to protect the fortress from the action of the sea, but other options, based on a still needed hydrodynamic survey of the area, have to be considered to protect the fortress and the adjacent archaeological site. Again, on the eastern side of the harbour, a hundred other blocks are aligned on the Silsila promontory, Cape Lochias, the site of the royal quarter in antiquity and currently a military base. The concrete blocks wait to be dumped to protect this small peninsula from wave action.

New harbours were created east and west of Alexandria, in Abu Qir and Mex Bays, to release the pressure on the main commercial harbour. Breakwaters were built in the vicinity of large effluents, thus preventing the free exchange of inshore waters with the open sea. This led to the accumulation of suspended materials and contaminants inshore. Dredged material from the navigation channels was disposed of at the nearest convenient location. In Abu Qir Bay, infilling with this material covers about 40,000 m² which are now dry land. No one knows what submerged remains have been obliterated by the building of breakwaters and by infilling.

The bathing beaches of Alexandria, an important resource for such a summer resort, are subject to continuous erosion. Each year, large amounts of desert sand are spread over

Figure 3. Main outfalls: 1. Qait Bey and Eastern Harbour outfalls: about 200 x 10³.m³.d-1 untreated waste water. 2. Lake Mariout main basin outfalls: about 500 x 10³.m³.d-1 primary treated + 300 x 10³ m³.d-1 untreated municipal waste water. 3. Mex Pump Station on Umoum drain: about 7,000 x 10³.m³.d-1 agricultural drainage water mixed with the overflow from L. Mariout main basin. 4. El Tabya Pump Station to Abu Qir Bay: about 2,000 x 10³.m³.d-1 industrial waste water. (See Fig. on inside front cover)

MEDITERRANEAN SEA

EL MEX BAY
QAIT BEY OUTFALL
E. HARBOUR
W. HARBOUR
MEX PUMP STATION
L MARIOUT MAIN BASIN
UMOUM
DRAIN
BEACHES
ABU QIR BAY
EL-TABYA PUMP STATION

0 1 2 3 4 5 Km

the beaches to compensate for the lost material, but the added sand will gradually be removed by the unending wave action and by winter storm surges, ultimately to blanket the nearshore bottom.

A project has recently been submitted to the Governorate for the building of a marina in the inner Eastern Harbour precisely on the site of the recently discovered Ptolemaic harbours. It is a relief to know that the project has been temporarily shelved, albeit only on grounds of feasibility.

The foregoing examples and many others point to an unmistakable trend. Cultural and natural environmental resources are often irreversibly damaged by decisions taken and implemented without prior assessment of the consequences. This is a universal problem. Economic development often outweighs the concern for conservation and management of the natural and cultural ressources.

Management issues

The integrated management of the coastal zone can only be achieved through the adoption of a sound policy supported by adequate institutional arrangements. The policy will aim at ensuring that the protection of the coastal zone resources remains an integral part of the development priorities of the country. It will also aim at the co-ordination of the sometimes conflicting interests and uses of the coastal zone.

Institutional arrangements
Several institutions are involved with the coastal zone: the Organization for Coastal Protection (Ministry of Public Works); the Egyptian Environmental Affairs Agency, responsible for the implementation of the National Coastal Zone Management Plan; the Supreme Council for Antiquities; the Governorate of Alexandria; and the Egyptian Navy. There are therefore several decision-making circles, with little communication, very little co-ordination and sometimes diverging views. A functional mechanism for co-operation and mutual understanding between decision-makers in these institutions, on the one hand, and scientists and archaeologists, on the other, has to be established. A standing intersectorial commission or a board with a clearly defined mandate can achieve this link. Among other things, the board will be mandated to carry out an Environmental Impact Assessment (including an archaeological assessment) prior to the authorization for any governmental or private coastal development project.

Monitoring programme
The land-sea interactions and the coastal zone environment must be continuously monitored in relation to land-based activities. The monitoring programme will have to be carried out by an interdisciplinary team of engineers, marine scientists and archaeologists. The programme will focus on the morphodynamic, hydrodynamic and meteorological processes, the relative sea-level fluctuations, the water quality, the rate of erosion, sediment transport and deposition.

International obligations
The submerged archaeological sites of Alexandria being part of humanity's cultural heritage, it is not inopportune to recall some of the relevant principles stated in the UN Convention of the Law of the Sea and in Agenda 21 adopted by the Rio Earth Summit in 1992.

All States are called upon:
(a) to prepare and implement integrated coastal zone management and sustainable development plans,
(b) to prepare coastal profiles identifying critical areas,
(c) to carry out environmental impact assessment prior to any major project and to follow up the impacts and
(d) to improve human settlements, especially the treatment and disposal of sewage and industrial effluents.

While all States have the sovereign right to exploit their natural resources, the enjoyment of such rights shall be in accordance with their duty to protect the environment.

The Egyptian Government, having ratified the UN Convention on the Law of the Sea and being a party to the Agenda 21, is committed to meeting the obligations thereof.

Environmental concerns in Alexandrian underwater archaeology

OSSAMA M.T. ABOUL DAHAB
Department of Oceanography
University of Alexandria

Background and causes for concern

Archaeological discoveries are the principal source of knowledge of ancient cultures. Classical archaeologists are particularly interested in the early cultures of the Mediterranean and the Near East, especially Greece, Rome, Iran, Egypt and Iraq, and in the civilizations of ancient China, Pakistan and of south-east Asia. The majority of archaeological work involves:
(a) surveying, locating, recording and studying the nature of the area; and
(b) excavating or actual digging at the site. The first step in excavation is to make a record of the site before digging begins or before it is changed in any way, to determine the time period and the civilization from which the artefact came (dating may be relative or absolute) and to synthesize data (preparation of historical reports).[1] Recent underwater archaeological searches have been aided by technological improvements, such as satellite photography, radiocarbon dating and the use of computers and metal detectors to locate sites and to record data. One of the most pressing challenges for modern archaeology is to prevent the loss of data, and therefore of knowledge, that results from the destruction of archaeological sites.[2] Artefacts immersed in sea water for long periods may undergo chemical, physical and biological alteration. These alterations depend on the

nature of the artefact, the length of time the object has been in the water and the prevailing environmental conditions, notably pollution and sediment type.

Known archaeological sites

The most known archaeological sites on the Alexandrian coast are the Western Harbour and its surroundings (Mex Bay), Qait Bey, Eastern Harbour, El-Silsila and Abu Qir Bay (the Graeco-Roman site of Nelson Island). These sites are of invaluable importance to human knowledge of ancient history.

State of the environment

The coast of Alexandria is adjacent to two of the most populous, most industrialized and most commercialized coastal metropolitan areas in Egypt: the Abu Qir area, to the east, and El-Mex area, to the west. The city's inhabitants put the coast to a wide variety of recreational, commercial and industrial uses. There are four important harbours in Alexandria, particularly after the market-oriented liberalization of the economy in Egypt.
The coast of Alexandria is continuously subject to degradation and destruction by human pressure, accelerated urbanization

[1] Oxman, B. H. (1988). Marine Archaeology and the International Law of the Sea. Columbia - VLA Journal of Law & the Arts (USA), 12:353.
[2] Strati, A. (1991). Deep seabed cultural property and the common heritage of mankind. International and Comparative Law Quarterly (UK), 40:859.

and land-based pollution. The Alexandrian coast also suffers from several other problems, such as erosion (natural and man-made) and beach degradation, decline of coastal habitats, accelerated loss of coastal biodiversity, destruction and exhaustion of resources, intrusion of sea water into the freshwater aquifers, and the impact of sea-level rise.

Alexandria's coastal environment receives a huge amount of waste water containing mixed agricultural and industrial wastes, and domestic sewage. The sources are sewage outfalls, agricultural drains and industrial outfalls. Several industries also dispose of their waste water directly into the sea at Mex Bay (chemical factories, cement and iron and steel plants, tanneries of various sizes and an oil refinery) and at Abu Qir Bay (food-processing plants and canneries, chemical and fertilizer plants, paper mills, an oil refinery and an electricity-generating station). The Alexandrian coast also receives agricultural drainage water through the Umoum outfall in Mex Bay, the Noubaria Canal into the Western Harbour, the Tabia pumping station and the Lake Edku outlet in Abu Qir Bay.

The disposal of untreated or inadequately treated waste water from land-based sources into Alexandrian coastal waters causes severe pollution problems. The Umoum outfall in Mex Bay is the main land-based source of suspended solids, chlorides, nutrients, pesticides, trace metals and phenols to Alexandria's marine environment. Mex Bay is also subjected to pollution from a chlor-alkali plant (suspended solids, free chlorine, ammonia and mercury), tanneries (chromium and hydrogen sulphide) and from the Noubaria Canal. The sea bottom in the Western Harbour is anoxic in most places and heavily polluted with different types of organic and inorganic pollutants. The direct disposal of untreated sewage at Qait Bey and El-Silsila produced severe pollution problems on the eastern coast. The bottom areas surrounding the end of the sewage outfalls are anoxic and completely devoid of benthic life. The sea bottom in these areas appears to be covered with beds of sewage residues. Abu Qir Bay to the east suffers

unacceptable environmental conditions which do not allow marine life in the Bay. The Tabia pumping station and the Lake Edku outlet provide the Bay with excessive loads of suspended solids, sulphides, ammonia, trace metals and phenols and are responsible for the deteriorated environment in the Bay.[3]

Environmental issues associated with searching, locating, excavating and dating artefacts

These environmental issues can be summarized as follows:

(a) Environmental issues are of prime importance to Alexandrian archaeologists, primarily owing to the co-occurrence of the heavily polluted areas and the archaeological sites.

(b) There is a possibility of interference with surveying techniques by sea-surface slicks, metallic wastes, recently sunken vessels.

(c) There is also a possibility of loss of traces (of archaeological remains) because of pollution and sedimentation.

(d) Alexandria's coastal environment is not safe for divers and archaeologists, because of the severe pollution in most places, and the lack of short-term forecasts of sea state.

(e) There is a possibility of degradation of artefacts. This may be due to chemical or mechanical factors. The chemical factors result from the continuous discharge of untreated wastes into the Alexandrian coastal sea and the mechanical factors result from the dumping of concrete blocks at certain places, the dragging of anchors, unplanned engineering works, as well as erosion and sedimentation.

(f) Excavation wastes may affect some ecologically sensitive habitats.

(g) Chemical pollutants in Alexandria's coastal waters may interfere with dating techniques.

[3] Aboul Dahab, O. (1996). Pollution loads from land-based sources to Alexandria marine environment. p. 160, in: Proceedings of Asia-Pacific Conference on Science and Management of Coastal Environment, Hong Kong, 25–28 June 1996.

(h) There is a possibility of destruction of some archaeological sites along the Alexandria coast by pollution and unplanned engineering work.

Problems that may hamper protection and preservation of Alexandria's underwater archaeological sites and artefacts

These problems can be summarized as follows:

(a) Lack of an operative coastal zone management plan for Alexandria.

(b) Lack of input data required to operate computer models for predicting the most probable movements of water and suspended sediment under various meteorological conditions.

(c) Lack of maps showing the areas of archaeological, ecological, recreational or economical importance.

(d) Lack of information on geographical, nautical and meteorological circumstances which may influence underwater archaeological work.

(e) Lack of modern receiving and treatment facilities for artefacts, as well as lack of trained personnel at the national level.

(f) Lack of rehabilitation programmes for impacted areas.

(g) Difficulty of funding underwater archaeological work.

Alexandria's historical underwater treasures: the development of an ICZM plan for Egypt

Coastal zone management can be defined as a dynamic process in which a co-ordinated strategy is developed and implemented for the allocation of environmental, social, cultural and institutional resources to achieve the conservation and sustainable multiple use of the coastal zone. The Earth Summit (UN Conference on Environment and Development, Rio de Janeiro, 1992) recommended, in section 17.6 of Agenda 21,

that coastal states should establish, or where necessary strengthen, suitable co-ordination mechanisms for integrated co-ordination and sustainable development of coastal and marine zones and their resources, at local and national level.

Integrated coastal zone management (ICZM) involves comprehensive assessment, setting of objectives, planning and management of coastal systems and resources, taking into account traditional, cultural and historical perspectives and conflicting interests and uses; it is a continuous and evolutionary process for achieving sustainable development. The successful management of the coastal zone requires reliable and accurate information which must be available in a 'user-friendly' format. The most effective instruments for providing such information are resource maps and atlases. The resource map needs a comprehensive database which gives a holistic view of the resources, the demands and the various direct and indirect inter-relationships.

Unfortunately, nothing is mentioned about the underwater archaeological resources in the national framework programme for the development of an ICZM plan for Egypt.

The resources, demands, conflicts and issues that can be featured in a map of the Alexandrian coastal area are:

(a) maritime shipping operations and navigation lanes,

(b) ecologically sensitive areas,

(c) tourism and recreational facilities and uses,

(d) administrative boundaries and zones,

(e) coastal erosion, storm and other hazards,

(f) harbour facilities,

(g) discharge points for liquid wastes,

(h) fishery production and methods,

(i) oil and gas exploration and extraction,

(j) conservation of heritage and historical resources,

(k) socio-economic factors in coastal zone management,

(l) power generation facilities,

(m) industrial development and infrastructure,

(n) oil-spill contingency planning,

(o) demographic data for coastal zone use,

(p) seawater uses,

(q) landscape and aesthetic values of the coastal zone and
(i) artificial breakwaters and other constructions.

Recommendations

The following recommendations are made:
(a) Representatives from the Supreme Council of Antiquities and the Ministry of Education should participate in the national committee for ICZM.
(b) Preservation of Alexandria's underwater artefacts and sites should be incorporated into the national ICZM plan as a separate issue aiming at the development of a national underwater cultural heritage preservation plan.
(c) Alexandria's underwater archaeological sites should be mapped and taken into account in the national marine oil pollution contingency plan.
(d) A data base on environmental conditions affecting Alexandria's underwater archaeological sites should be established.
(e) The idea of constructing an underwater archaeological museum should be encouraged and its implementation should consider primarily the prevailing environmental conditions to prevent any possible pollution or damage due to erosion or sedimentation.
(f) Research studies and programmes in support of underwater archaeology should be formulated and implemented.
(g) There should be a contingency fund to enable immediate efforts to preserve the archaeological sites of Alexandria to begin with.
(h) The development of national legislation to protect underwater archaeological sites is urgent.[4]
(i) Environmental monitoring and research programmes on Alexandria's coastal zone should be encouraged.
(j) Intensive training programmes, covering the various aspects of underwater archaeological work, are urgently needed.
(k) It is important to ensure the safety of divers and archaeologists during their field work.
(l) International co-operation and support in the field of underwater archaeology should be encouraged.

_____

[4] O'Keefe, P. J. and Nafziger, J. A. R. (1994). _The Draft Convention on the Protection of the Underwater Cultural Heritage._ Ocean Development and International Law _(USA),_ _25:391–418._

Currents and their variability
in Eastern Harbour and Qait Bey areas

POLLUTION AND EROSION IMPACTS ON COASTAL HERITAGE

7

Ahmed Abdel Hamid El-Gindy
Professor of Physical Oceanography
University of Alexandria

Introduction

The Eastern Harbour of Alexandria lies between 29° 52' 52" and 29° 54' 20" E and 31° 12' 00" and 31° 12' 53" N. This Harbour was once a bay east of the old Pharos island. Qait Bey Fort was built about 500 years ago on the foundation of the famous Alexandria lighthouse site on Pharos island and now forms the end of the western breakwater. The middle breakwater was constructed around 1929, dividing the bay into two outlets. The western entrance has a width of about 300 m with a water depth of 9.5–11 m. The eastern entrance has a width of about 140 m and water depth of 3.5 m. The eastern breakwater and the Harbour itself are strongly exposed to north-westerly waves during winter, which affects the fishing boats, the sea road and the underwater artefacts. The average depth of the Eastern Harbour is about 8 m.

The area outside the Eastern Harbour, off Qait Bey Fort, is a part of the continental shelf where the depth gradually increases to about 50 m at about 8 km from the shore. It is affected by natural forces, mainly currents and waves, and by the sewage discharge which changes the water quality and current intensity and direction.

The wind system in the area is related to the atmospheric pressure distribution over the Eastern Mediterranean and over the North African Sahara, with a prevailing N–NW wind, except that, in winter, the wind direction is more variable and storms persisting for one to several days occasionally invade the region between December and May.

For the protection of the Eastern Harbour and the artefacts on the sea floor, it is necessary to study the current circulation by indirect methods, such as the distribution of hydrographic parameters, and by direct current measurements. This paper deals with previous studies on this aspect and comments on future requirements to fill the present gaps in our knowledge of the circulation.

Discussion

The circulation in the study area was reviewed by El-Gindy[1], including the main results of investigations by Gerges[2], Abdallah[3], Eid[4] and Sabra[5].

[1] El-Gindy, A. A. H. (1988). *The circulation pattern of Alexandria coastal waters in relation to pollution transport: a review*. pp. 286–99, in: Symposium on Environmental Science *(UNARC), Alexandria, 1988*.
[2] Gerges, M. (1978). *Trajectories and speeds of surface currents near the Egyptian Mediterranean coast as deduced from the movement of surface drifters*. pp. 573–87, in: IVème Journée d'Études sur la Pollution, *Antalya, 1978. CIESM, UNEP*.
[3] Abdallah, A. M. (1979). *Study of the currents and the hydrographic structure of the water masses in front of Alexandria coast. M.Sc. thesis, Faculty of Science, Alexandria University. (An internal report of the Institute of Coastal Research of which an abstract was published by IAPSO, Mexico 1988)*.
[4] Eid, F. M. (1979). *Current and water masses in the coastal area from Abu-Kir to Agamy. M.Sc. thesis submitted to Faculty of Science, Alexandria University*.
[5] Sabra, A. (1979). *Wind current and sea-level variations over the continental shelf of Alexandria coast. M.Sc. thesis, Faculty of Science, Alexandria University*.

Gerges, who used surface drifters, found that currents in the nearshore area were in the inshore direction, while, offshore, the current direction was variable.

Abdallah measured the currents at the outlets of the Eastern Harbour using an Ekman current meter. These measurements indicated that, in January and August, water was flowing into the Harbour through the western outlet and out of the Harbour through the eastern outlet. Opposite directions were found in October and May, when a one layer current was present.

Continuous current-meter measurements carried out from July 1977 to July 1978, using an Endeco type instrument, at 30-minute intervals, off the Qait Bey Fort, at distances of 1 and 10 km from the shore, at the surface and at 2/3 of the total depth, were analysed and reported by Anon.[6], Eid[4] and Sabra[5]. The NW current (i.e., inshore flow) was dominant, but in September, February and April, the SW current was also important. At the offshore station, the dominant current directions in August and September, 1977, and in January and March, 1978, were to the NE and SW. In May and June, the NE current was persistent. Current speeds were generally higher at the upper current meter. The nearshore current was slower than the current offshore. The surface salinity distribution along the Alexandrian coast, including the study area,[3, 4] indicated a tongue of low-salinity water extending parallel to the shore to the NE, except in spring when the current was SW. The plume direction was not related to wind or current direction.

Current velocity and hydrographic measurements were carried out at 110 stations inside and outside the Eastern Harbour, using a portable direct-reading current meter, at the sea surface, at mid-depth and above the bottom, by the Institute of Coastal Protection, with the contribution of the author in the data analysis and interpretation, in the periods from 30 May 1984 to 26 June 1984, from 8 May 1985 to 9 June 1985 and from 4 March 1986 to 5 April 1986.[7] Examples of these results are shown in Figures 1 and 2. During the survey (May–June 1984), the surface circulation inside the Harbour (Fig. 1a) was characterized by three eddies, two of which were cyclonic and the third anticyclonic. The current was flowing out to sea through the eastern outlet, whereas at the western outlet the current had two opposite directions. Outside the Harbour, the current was predominantly inshore with indications of eddy motion; the current speed was between 3 and 60 cm/sec, with the strongest current near the Qait Bey sewage outfall. The salinity (Fig. 2a) showed a tongue of low salinity outside the Harbour, going towards the breakwater in the western part of the area, where the strongest current existed. Near the bottom, the current pattern (Fig. 1b) was generally similar to that at the surface, except near the Qait Bey sewage outfall, where there was a cyclonic eddy. The range of current speed was 3–25 cm/sec. The salinity distribution (Fig. 2b) showed a range of 38.75–38.9, outside the Harbour, and of 37.4–38.5, inside the Harbour. The current inflow to the Harbour through the western outlet could be followed by a tongue of high salinity, making a cyclonic eddy inside the Harbour.

Conclusions

The results of the above-mentioned survey, as well as other surveys, carried out in 1985 and 1986, indicated that:

(a) At the western outlet of the Harbour, near Qait Bey Fort, the current enters the Harbour at the surface and at the bottom.

(b) At the eastern outlet, the current is mainly out of the Harbour.

(c) Eddy motion is an important characteristic of the current pattern inside the Harbour at the surface and at the bottom. This evidence is confirmed by the salinity distribution.

The sewage discharge system was changed after 1986, so that the current pattern, which depends on wind stress, tidal force and water-density distribution, is expected to be different from that found in 1986. Since then,

[6] Anon. (1978). The Ministry of Housing and Reconstruction, Arab Republic of Egypt, Alexandria Waste Water Master Plan Study. Vol. 1, Marine Studies. Camp Dresser and McKee, Inc.
[7] Anon. (1987). Data collected in the Eastern Harbour area, Alexandria. Final Report. Ministry of Irrigation, Water Research Centre, Coastal Research Institute, Alexandria, April 1987.

all of the sewage water is discharged through the Qait Bey outfall, hence greater amounts are discharged outside the breakwaters of the Eastern Harbour. Consequently, density currents, which could be relevant in this area, should change drastically. It is therefore necessary to make new current

measurements to determine the present current pattern rather than utilize the previous information. Modelling is also recommended to determine circulation in the area under wind stress from different directions and at variable rates of sewage discharge.

Figure 1. The current pattern in the Eastern Harbour: a) at the surface; b) near the bottom, from 30/5 to 26/6/1984 (Anonymous, 1987).

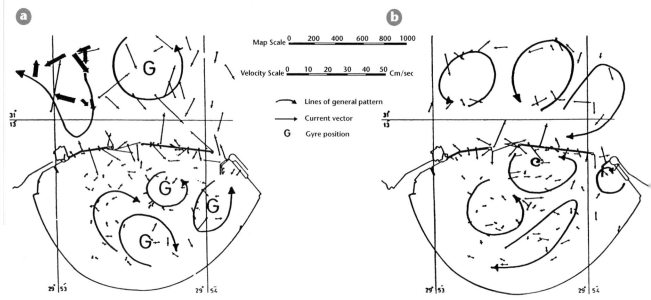

Figure 2. The salinity distribution in the Eastern Harbour: a) at the surface; b) near the bottom, from 30/5 to 26/6/1984 (Anonymous, 1987).

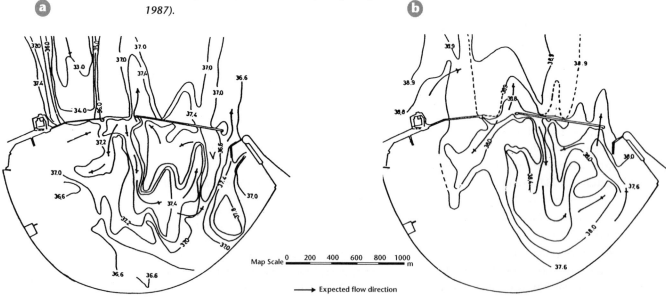

Wave propagation and sedimentation at the Pharos site

DENIS AELBRECHT
J.-M. MENON and
ERIC PELTIER
Laboratoire National d'Hydraulique
Électricité de France

Introduction

The present study lies within the scope of the corporate patronage of Électricité de France (EDF). Dr. Jean-Yves Empereur, the French archaelogist in charge of the Pharos submarine excavations in Alexandria (Egypt), asked the EDF Foundation for a technical assessment of the coastal engineering problems linked to the displacement of a submerged wall. This submerged concrete wall corresponds to the first phase of an uncompleted project on the construction of a large breakwater, and was built in 1994 to protect the Mamelouk fortress at Qait Bey, itself established on the old Pharos foundations. The wall partly covers the submarine excavation site, consequently inhibiting completion of the archaeological work. The archaeologists would like to displace this wall, keeping in mind that the displaced structure would have to meet the following requirements:
(a) protection of the Qait Bey fortress against prevailing waves,
(b) enabling the continuation of the Pharos excavations and
(c) protection of the archaeological site from wave agitation and sedimentation, with a view to creating a 'submarine museum' which could be visited by divers or by observers in glass-bottomed boats.
These constraints, which apply to archaeological preservation and coastal management preoccupations, may not be fully compatible. The objective of the present study is to provide some preliminary results, particularly regarding wave agitation and possible sedimentation, useful for the global understanding of the local hydrodynamic system. Impacts in terms of wave agitation have been studied with the help of numerical modelling using the ARTEMIS software developed at EDF-LNH; sedimentological aspects have been investigated during a short mission to Alexandria, although with only a limited field-data set, and a comparison was made with similar situations already studied. The first part of this report is an overview of the present situation. It is followed by the results on wave agitation from four different schematic configurations describing present or possible future maritime works. The limited sediment data set available just allows a few conclusions on the sedimentological impact to be expected from the installation of new marine structures.

Present context

Alexandria is on the Mediterranean coast of Egypt, and stretches more than 50 km along the shore from Abu Qir Bay to Sidi Krir. The Alexandrian coast is oriented along a SW–NE axis and is characterized by the presence of the Pharos peninsula which separates the Western and Eastern Harbours. A Mamelouk fortress is located at Qait Bey, on the north-eastern part of the Pharos peninsula, and stands on the foundations of the famous old Pharos whose remains have been found near the fortress, 6–8m under water (Fig. 1). In 1994, the first concrete blocks of a breakwater were laid on the site of the archaeological remains and compromised their preservation. An emergency programme was then decided, to undertake systematic archaeological investigations. Since this date,

Figure 1.
Map showing
the site of the
archaeological
remains of Fort
Qait Bey and the
modern submerged
wall intended
to protect
the foundation
of the fort.

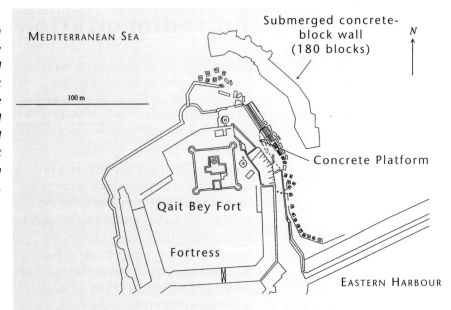

Dr. J-Y. Empereur, Director of the Centre d'Études Alexandrines, has been in charge of this task. More than 2,000 archaeological remains have been located, and it is assumed that the present submerged concrete wall may cover some other remains.

Wave-propagation modelling

The objective of this section is to describe a model of the propagation of waves in a localized area around the Pharos excavations. The method is based upon the following steps:
(a) definition of the wave conditions offshore in deep water
(b) estimation or computation of the wave deformation when approaching the shore line (wave refraction controlled by the bathymetry)
(c) specification of the wave conditions at the boundaries of the local computational domain
(d) digitizing of the bathymetric and shore contours
(e) numerical computations in the local domain using the ARTEMIS software.

[1] Teisson, C. and Bouchard, J-P. (1987). Étude de faisabilité pour la centrale thermique de Sidi Krir (Égypte). Phase I. EDF-LNH Reports, HE-42/87.10 and HE-43/87.21.

Offshore wave conditions

The objective here is to define boundary conditions to be imposed on the local computational domain around the Pharos excavations. Offshore wave climate and the effect of bottom refraction have then to be considered. No criteria have been specified regarding, for instance, the maximum allowable significant wave height in the area of interest. We then focussed our study on wave agitation for annual conditions; i.e., for which a statistical probability of occurrence is about once a year.

The wave climate in the deep water off Alexandria is relatively well known and has been determined in a previous LNH study of the Sidi-Krir Power Plant project.[1] Hindcasting of the wind-induced wave regime and statistical analysis of swell observations by ships provide the following results:
(a) 75% of the waves reaching the coast come from the WNW–NNW sector;
(b) statistically significant wave heights (Hs_0) for statistical return periods of 1 year and 100 years are about 4.0 m and 8.0 m, respectively;
(c) 60% of the time, wave periods are in the range 6–9 seconds for NW waves and 5–8 seconds for NE waves.

Refraction by the near-shore sea floor (depths < 100 m) modifies the wave propagation. We have assessed its effect analytically and finally chose the following 'annual' conditions:

(a) NW waves: $Hs_0 = 4.0$ m; $Tp = 8.0$ s
(b) WNW waves: $Hs_0 = 4.0$ m; $Tp = 8.0$ s
(c) NE waves: $Hs_0 = 3.0$ m; $Tp = 7.0$ s

where Hs_0 = significant wave height; Tp = peak period of the wave-energy spectrum.

The ARTEMIS numerical model

ARTEMIS is a piece of scientific software developed by LNH and commercialized within the TELEMAC system.[2] ARTEMIS deals with wave propagation towards the coast and into harbours. It is based on the Berkhoff, or Mild-Slope, equation (refraction-diffraction equation,[3]), including dissipation through depth-induced wave breaking and bottom friction in shallow and very shallow water.[4] ARTEMIS uses a finite-element formulation and then enables accurate and reliable results in coastal areas of complex geometry to be obtained. ARTEMIS computes wave parameters such as significant wave height, wave incidence, breaking rate, etc.

In this study, bottom-friction dissipation has been neglected, given the short distance covered by the computational domain, whereas wave breaking is taken into account. We used ARTEMIS in random mode to represent the frequency distribution of the wave energy, defined through a typical Joint North Sea Wave Project (JONSWAP) spectrum by the parameters Hs and Tp defined above.[5]

Configuration of the marine structures

The local computational mesh comprises 2233 nodes defining 4236 triangular elements. It covers an area of about 400 m × 500 m around the excavations (Fig. 2). Direction Y is parallel to the North direction. Borders B1, B2, B3 and B5 are liquid limits across which, waves can enter or leave the domain. Border B4 corresponds to a solid boundary made of

concrete blocks. A reflexion coefficient R = 0.3 is assigned to this limit.

With the help of the Centre d'Études Alexandrines, we set up a bathymetric map of the site and assumed it to be constant in time for the numerical simulations. There are no significant sea-level or tidal variations: a free surface at rest is fixed at the elevation 0m, referred to as the Chart Datum. Four topographic/structural configurations have been studied:

C1: The present situation, including the submerged concrete wall next to the fortress (Fig. 3). The wall is represented as a bathymetric artefact, roughly adding the height of two concrete-block layers (+ 4.0 m) to the estimated natural bottom level, and

[2] Hervouet, J-M. (1996). Introduction to the TELEMAC System. EDF-LNH Report, HE-43/96/073/A.

[3] Berkhoff, J. C. W. (1976). Mathematical models for simple harmonic linear water waves – wave diffraction and refraction. Delft Hydraulics Laboratory Publication, 163 (April).

[4] Aelbrecht, D. (1997). Logiciel ARTEMIS – version 3.0. Notice théorique. EDF-LNH Report, HE-42/97/002.

[5] Hasselmann, K. et al. (1973). Measurements of wind-wave growth and swell decay during the Joint North Sea Wave Project (JONSWAP). Deutschen Hydrographischen Zeitschrift, Reihe A (8°), no. 12.

Figure 2. ARTEMIS: computational mesh for wave simulations, comprising 2,233 nodes and 4,236 elements.

COMPUTATIONAL MESH FOR WAVE SIMULATIONS

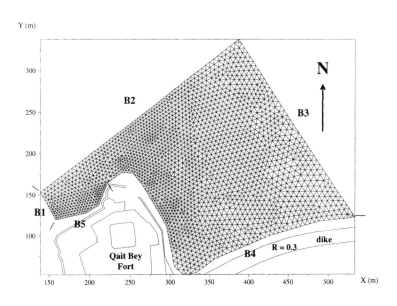

CONFIGURATION C1: PRESENT SITUATION

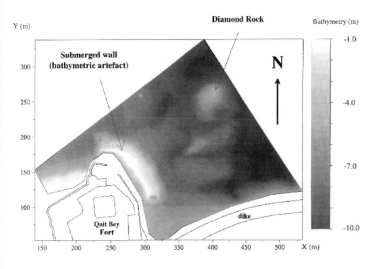

*Figure 3.
Bathymetry
of configuration C1.*

clipping the maximum water depth above the top of the wall at 1.25 m.

C2: The 'natural' topography assuming that the concrete wall is removed. Notice the presence of Diamond Rock in the north-eastern part of the domain (Fig. 4).

C3: The installation of an emerged breakwater, located along the north-western limit of the computational domain (see Fig. 5; the mesh presented in Fig. 2 was designed for this purpose). One length only has been considered: 100 m.

C4: The installation of a submerged breakwater, located along the north-western limit of the computational domain (Fig. 6). Three different lengths have been considered: 100, 125 and 150 m. It is assumed that the

CONFIGURATION C2: SUBMERGED WALL REMOVED

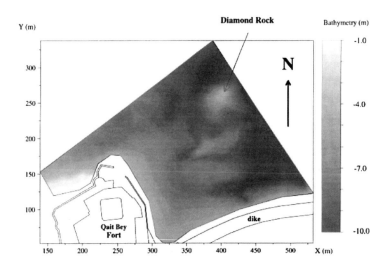

*Figure 4.
Bathymetry
of configuration C2.*

*Figure 5.
Bathymetry
of configuration C3.*

CONFIGURATION C3: EMERGED DISPLACED BREAKWATER

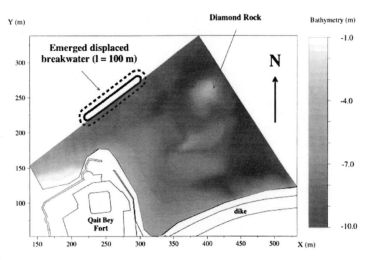

water depth over the top of this structure is 3.0 m, on average, considering that the submerged breakwater corresponds to the displacement of the two-layer block structure in configuration C1.

For configurations C1 and C4, submerged breakwaters have been integrated into the bathymetry. However, Booij[6] has shown that Berkhoff's equation, used by ARTEMIS, can integrate the bottom slope up to 1/3. It is

[6] Booij, N. (1981). Gravity Waves on Water with Non-uniform Depth and Current. (PhD thesis) Technical University of Delft, The Netherlands.

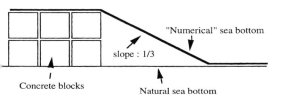

Concrete blocks — slope : 1/3 — "Numerical" sea bottom — Natural sea bottom

not therefore possible to represent the vertical slope of the concrete blocks directly, so we connect the water depths above the natural sea floor and above the top of the submerged wall with a 'numerical' bottom slope of 1/3.

Wave-simulation results

Refraction-diffraction patterns

Figures 7a to 7d show the wave phase field computed for each topographic configuration and each set of wave conditions. This depicts the refraction-diffraction patterns of the wave propagation and shows how the wave length and wave direction are modified in the various configurations and offshore wave conditions used: diffraction behind detached breakwater for NW waves, behind Diamond Rock for NE waves, etc.

Significant-wave-height field

Hs values have been computed for the four configurations and the various wave conditions. For example, Figures 8 to 11 show the results for configurations C1–C4, respectively, for NW wave conditions. Hs profiles along P1 and P2 are also given on the same figures. All the results are summarized in Table I.

Figure 6.
Bathymetry
of configuration C4.

CONFIGURATION C4: SUBMERGED DISPLACED BREAKWATER

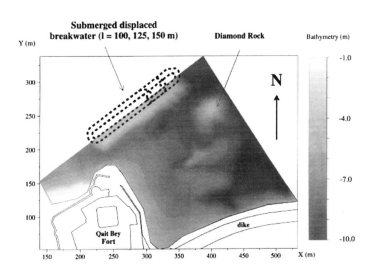

TABLE I. SUMMARY OF WAVE-AGITATION RESULTS

	NW WAVES	WNW WAVES	NE WAVES
CONFIGURATION C1	P1: 75% / 25% (FIG. 9) P2: 35% / 75%	P1: 75% / 20% P2: 20% / 75%	P1: 45% / 65% P2: 70% / 90%
CONFIGURATION C2	P1: 80% / 55% (FIG. 10) P2: 65% / 70%	P1: 80% / 30% P2: 35% / 75%	P1: 50% / 80% P2: 85% / 100%
CONFIGURATION C3 LENGTH = 100 M	P1: 30% / 25% (FIG. 11) P2: 25% / 50%	P1: 35% / 20% P2: 25% / 30%	P1: 50% / 80% P2: 80% / 100%
CONFIGURATION C4 LENGTH =100 M	P1: 75% / 25% (FIG. 12) P2 : 35% / 75%	P1: 45% / 20% P2: 25% / 50%	P1: 30% / 80% P2 : 85% / 100%

Notes: For each simulation, results are given in terms of relative significant wave height Hs/Hs$_0$ along profiles P1 and P2; the lefthand value, in each case, is for the first part of the profile, and the righthand value is for the second part. NW and WNW wave simulations were run using an incident Hs$_0$ of 4.0 m; NE wave simulations used an incident Hs$_0$ of 3.0 m.

CONFIGURATION C1: PRESENT SITUATION

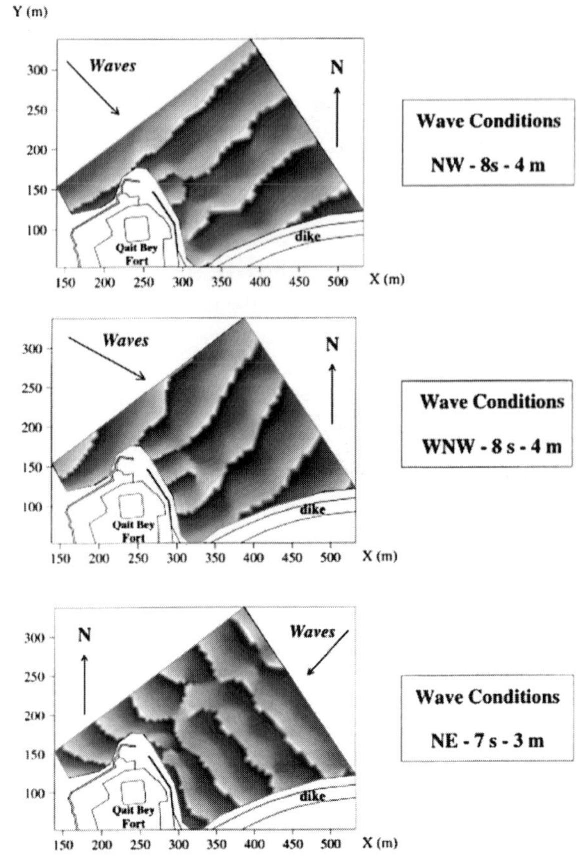

Figure 7a.
Wave refraction-diffraction patterns resulting from model configuration C1.

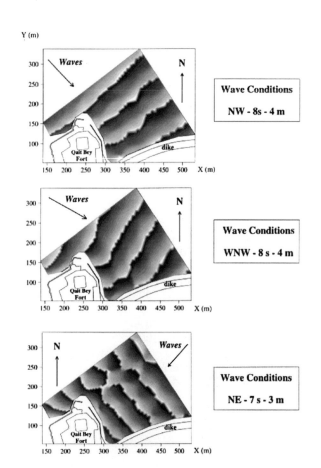

CONFIGURATION C2: SUBMERGED WALL REMOVED

Figure 7b.
Wave refraction-diffraction patterns resulting from model configuration C2.

CONFIGURATION C3:
EMERGED DISPLACED BREAKWATER

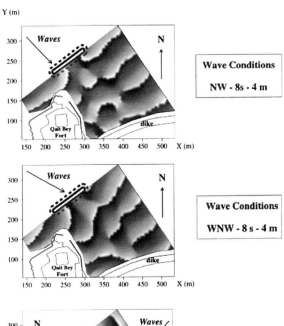

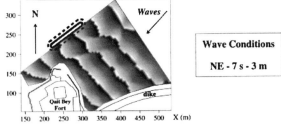

Figure 7c.
Wave refraction-diffraction patterns
resulting from model configuration C3
(breakwater length = 100 m).

CONFIGURATION C4:
SUBMERGED DISPLACED BREAKWATER

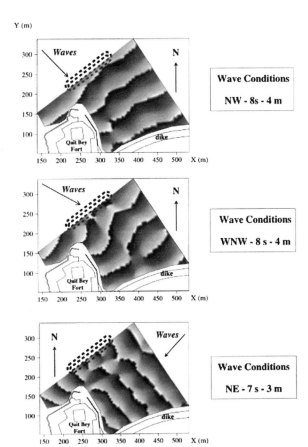

Figure 7d.
Wave refraction-diffraction patterns
resulting from model configuration C4
(breakwater length = 125 m; depth over
breakwater top = 3 m).

Analysis of wave-simulation results

WNW and NW waves (prevailing conditions): The results observed for incoming NW and WNW waves are similar, even if the last part of profile P1 is more protected against WNW waves than against NW waves. This is why we do not give herein the figures related to WNW wave conditions. In the configuration C1, the NW waves propagate almost parallel to the axis of the submerged wall. Strong wave breaking occurs over the top of this wall, as shown in Figure 12 (for example, $Q_b = 50\%$ roughly means that 50% of the waves break). This may generate a strong residual current, induced by breaking and driven along the corridor between the submerged wall and the fortress seawall. This may emphasize the undermining of the fortress's foundations through direct erosion and/or transport of bottom sediment material suspended by oscillatory wave currents.

Figure 8. Distribution of significant wave heights resulting from model configuration C1 (for NW waves only).

CONFIGURATION C1: PRESENT SITUATION

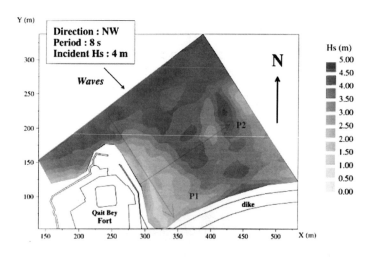

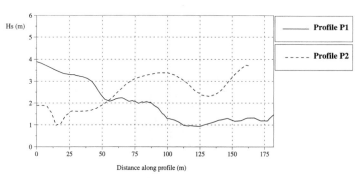

Conversely, when the submerged wall is removed (configuration C2), the degree of wave agitation obviously increases (Fig. 9) relative to configuration C1 (Fig. 8): the risk of sea-bed scouring may increase, because wave agitation and wave reflection are stronger, and wave overtopping is also emphasized, even if waves propagate along the fortress wall.

It is not possible in this preliminary study to quantify precisely which of the two previously mentioned processes is prevailing. But this shows that: (a) special attention has to be given to the protection of Qait Bey fortress, considering the damage observable on the site; and (b) the present situation may be dangerous for the foundation's stability.

The installation of an emerged breakwater along a SW–NE axis (configuration C3) notably decreases the level of wave agitation (Fig. 10). However, agitation behind such a detached breakwater depends on the length of the structure and is not zero, owing to diffraction.

The wave agitation behind the submerged displaced breakwater (configuration C4) is not reduced in the same range as for configuration C3, owing to wave transmission over the maritime structure (Fig. 11). It is interesting here to refer to experimental flume results obtained by Elkamhawy[7] for the transmission of waves through 2-dimensional submerged obstacles, to estimate the transmitted wave height for any other water depth over the breakwater. In our case, we observed a transmitted wave height of about 2.5 m, which is consistent with the experimental observations of Elkamhawy.[7] But here, the finite length of the breakwater induces 3-dimensional processes that slightly modify the expected results, according to Elkamhawy's experimental results. And again, the 'shadow' area (in terms of wave agitation) behind the detached breakwater depends on the length of the structure.

We observe no difference between C1 and C4 in terms of agitation for NW waves. This means that a smaller water depth over the top

[7] Elkamhawy, H. (1995). *Submerged Rubble-mound Breakwater. (PhD thesis) University of Windsor, Canada.*

of the breakwater would be necessary to improve the protection of the area of interest from wave agitation, if the present 2-layer concrete block wall were displaced as shown in Figure 6. If a criterion of wave agitation is imposed in the excavation area, it is possible, using[7], to estimate firstly the depth over the submerged wall required roughly to meet the adopted criterion, after which, a numerical simulation might be used to compute the wave agitation in the whole area, to estimate the horizontal wave energy distribution.

All computations for WNW and NW waves showed wave-breaking over Diamond Rock (see as an example Figure 12 for NW waves). During our second visit to Alexandria, a NW-wave climate was present over the area, with an estimated significant wave height of 2.5 to 3.0 m. Wave-breaking was clearly observable over Diamond Rock. This is directly comparable to the computational results shown in Figure 12.

NE waves: None of the proposed configurations offers satisfactory protection against NE waves. We can see the impact of Diamond Rock on wave propagation: it diffracts waves around the rocky point. For annual conditions, configurations C1 and C2 do not show any quantitative differences. If stronger incident wave heights occurred for the NE direction, the effect of the present submerged wall may be positive with respect to the risk of overtopping the fortress seawall; but again, the presence of the corridor may emphasize the risk of undermining the fortress seawall foundations.

Once criteria can be specified for prescribed priorities, the design of an emerged/submerged breakwater is possible; it would have to guarantee the stability of the structures against extreme events using relevant design methodology[8], but keeping in mind that the installation of such marine structures may have an impact on the sedimentological environment in a way not compatible with intended touristic or archaeological objectives.

---

[8] Feuillet, J., Coeffe, Y., Bernier, J. and Chaloin, B. (1987). Le dimensionnement des digues à talus. Collection EDF-DER, no.64. Éditions Eyrolles.

Sedimentological aspects

Generalities

Even if we are here concerned with a very limited area, sedimentological preoccupations require us to view the matter on a large scale, in time and in space. Alexandria was founded on a coastal barrier. Its coasts are formed by: a sandy shoreline from Sidi-Krir to El Agami; a mixed shore with rocky zones and sandy beaches in Alexandria Bay; and, on the eastern side of the Eastern Harbour, as far as Abu Qir; and Abu Qir Bay itself.

Information from the evolution of coastal morphology

A previous study of the site of Sidi-Krir[1] showed that the estimated mean longshore transport of sand is about 100,000 m³/yr from west to east. This seems to be in agreement

Figure 9. Distribution of significant wave heights resulting from model configuration C2 (for NW waves only).

CONFIGURATION **C2**: SUBMERGED WALL REMOVED

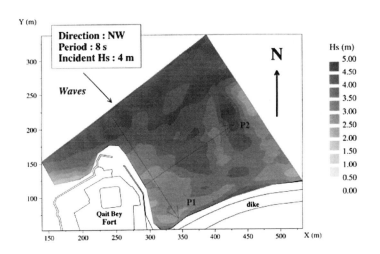

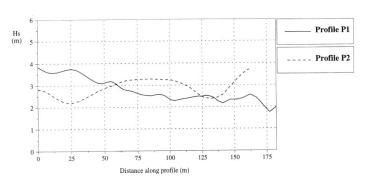

with the shape of the shoreline in the vicinity of the large rocky area of Abu Qir. Obviously, the large number of human activities along the coast over many centuries depicted in the maps available in the Centre d'Études Alexandrines does not allow clear conclusions about the natural trends in the large-scale sedimentological regime. It seems that recent activities linked to tourism in the western part of the Egyptian coast showed sand accretion on the western side and erosion on the eastern side of groynes. Some sandy beaches on the eastern side of the Eastern Harbour are subject to strong erosion. Some of them are periodically renourished with fine desert sand, which rapidly disappears under wave and current action.

This incomplete analysis of the large-scale sedimentological evolution of the Alexandrian coast suggests, however, the existence of significant longshore sand transport from west to east, which can be locally interrupted by the construction of obstacles.

Figure 10. Distribution of significant wave heights from model configuration C3 (breakwater length = 100 m; for NW waves only).

Local sedimentological data

Non-cohesive sediments: No precise and quantitative data on the sediments in the area of interest could be collected during our missions. The only information available comes from observations by archaeologists diving in the submarine excavations. It seems that the bottom in the area is rocky and partly covered with sand 20 cm to 50 cm thick. Farther offshore, the sand thickness could be greater. The sand in the excavation area seems to be coarse ($D_{50} \approx 0.5$ mm; that is, the mesh size through which 50%, by weight, of the sand grains pass). This is consistent with constant wave agitation which imposes resuspension of fine sediment which can be transported by currents and redeposited in calmer areas, the coarse sand staying in place. The French nautical instructions manual[9] for 1981 indicates that the Eastern Harbour of Alexandria is no longer frequented, being partly filled by high inner sand banks. This evolution is probably due to the dikes and the detached breakwater built to protect the Eastern Harbour.

Cohesive sediments: The site of interest is surrounded by a lot of industrial, agricultural, and domestic sewage outfalls: 3 in the Western Harbour (Mahmoudia Canal, East Noubaria Canal, and the Umoum outfall), and 3 domestic sewage outfalls in the western part of the Qait Bey fortress, in the Eastern Harbour, and along the eastern part of the Silsila promontory. Divers have pointed out the fact that, in certain wind conditions, the water turbidity in the archaeological area becomes much too high for them to pursue their excavation. Mud deposition is also observable in the Eastern Harbour. It is clear that such conditions would compromise visits by tourist divers.

CONFIGURATION C3: EMERGED DISPLACED BREAKWATER

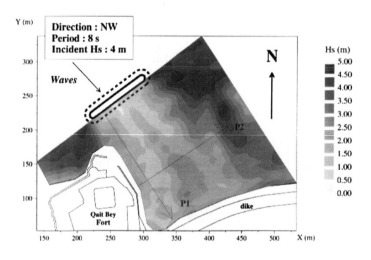

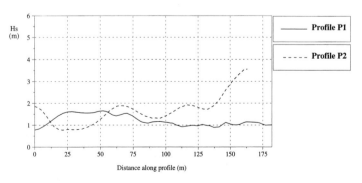

[9] *Service Hydrographique et Océanographique de la Marine. (1981). Instructions nautiques : Afrique - Côte Nord, entre la Mer Egée et le canal de Suez. Série D, vol. 6.*

Sedimentological risk

In the present case, it seems that:

(a) no significant non-cohesive (sand) sedimentation occurs in the archaeological area at present, owing to the frequently high level of wave agitation

(b) there may be a potential stock of sand seawards to be moved and displaced through cross-shore and along-shore transport if structures are displaced

(c) no precise quantitative data (grain-size distribution $\{D_{50}, D_{90}\}$, sand-layer thickness, etc.) are available

(d) cohesive sediments are often in suspension in the water column.

The protection solution consisting of a displaced emerged/submerged breakwater has to be carefully considered; here, we must focus on the possible use of such marine structures to increase sedimentation on the wave-protected side of the breakwater (formation of tombolos: sand accretions on the wave-protected side of a detached breakwater), to improve the nourishment of the beaches and the shore by sand, for instance. This potential effect would be completely opposite to that required for the creation of a submarine museum.

The rate of sand accretion in the lee of such a detached breakwater depends on the incident-wave characteristics, the distance from the shore, the water depth, and the sand's characteristics and availability. For instance, a small wave length brings less wave energy (i.e., less agitation) in the lee of the breakwater than a larger wave length for a given Hs value, and thus promotes sand accretion.

Numerical modelling of such processes is in progress, but requires a consistent linking between wave regime, wave-induced currents, and sediment-transport modelling. We performed such modelling within a recent European research programme dealing with tombolo formation behind a hypothetical detached breakwater on a sandy beach (D_{50} = 0.25 mm).[10]

For the estimation of long-term sedimentary impacts, laboratory studies on reduced scales are generally used to check and finalize the options that could be indicated by numerical modelling. Physical modelling of sedimentary impacts due to the installation of marine structures facilitates reproduction of the long-term morphological evolution to be expected when exposing the site to a representative wave climate. Such an approach has already been applied in our laboratory for instance to assess the sedimentary impacts around the new Olympic harbour in Barcelona (Spain).[11]

Figure 11. Distribution of significant wave heights resulting from model configuration C4 (breakwater length = 125 m; depth over breakwater top = 3 m; for NW waves only).

CONFIGURATION C4: SUBMERGED DISPLACED BREAKWATER

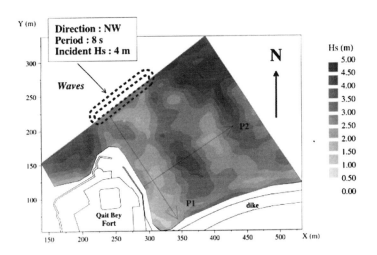

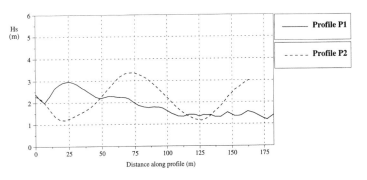

[10] Pechon, P. et al. (1997). Intercomparison of wave-driven current models. Coastal Engineering, 31:199–215.

[11] Pechon, P., Leymarie, J-C., Caillat, M. and Rabeau, J. (1991). Étude sédimentologique sur modèle réduit du Port Olympique de Barcelone. EDF-LNH Report, HE-42/91.33.

Conclusion

Localized numerical wave-agitation simulations in the vicinity of the Pharos excavation site in Alexandria (Egypt) have been carried out for annual wave-climate conditions. They show how WNW, NW and NE waves propagate towards the site. Depending on criteria that have not yet been specified and on the priorities to be fixed by Egyptian authorities, it is possible to assess the wave-agitation level in the case of emerged or submerged detached breakwaters.

Figure 12.
Distribution of
breaking rate
resulting from model
configuration C1
(for NW waves only).

A rapid investigation of the Qait Bey fortress area, reinforced by local information, has shown the necessity of looking carefully at the present protection system. The presence of a corridor between the submerged concrete wall and the fortress is favourable to high wave-driven currents during extreme events. The present submerged concrete blocks may therefore be unuseful, at best, or harmful, at worst.

Suspended materials from a large number of adjacent industrial and domestic outfalls in the vicinity of the archaeological site caused high water turbidity which can compromise the visit to the site by divers.

Local sedimentological data are not readily available. Nevertheless, previous experience at LNH suggests that the creation of a submarine museum, protected from wave agitation by a detached breakwater, could be considered, but with much caution. Morphological evolution observed along the Alexandrian coasts shows that the risk of sedimentation by sand or mud, associated with the installation of detached marine structures, is appreciable.

EDF-LNH has been asked questions that relate to a more global problem. A solution therefore has to take into account all the sources of complexity in the problem. A durable solution may be reached through a few temporary actions consistent with the priorities to be fixed.

No definitive solution for durable marine structures can be proposed at the moment without an extensive and integrated study, which must include:

(a) complete field-data collection; (particularly regarding sediments)
(b) complete diagnosis of the efficiency of the present Qait Bey fortress protection;
(c) refined numerical modelling of wave-induced currents and sediment transport; and
(d) validation of a physical model of the projected configurations.

CONFIGURATION C1: PRESENT SITUATION

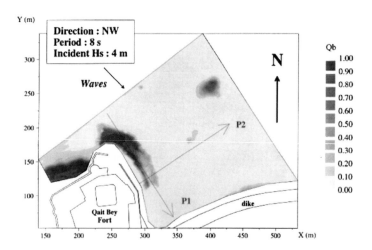

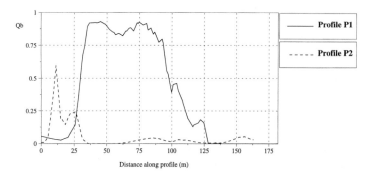

Coastal processes and proposed protection works along the Alexandrian coastline

ALFY MORCOS FANOS
Director, Coastal Research Institute, and
OMRAN EL SAYED FRIHY
Deputy Director, Coastal Research Institute

Introduction

The city of Alexandria is on the north-western border of the Nile delta coast. It lies between latitudes 31° 06' and 31° 20' N and between longitudes 29° 45' and 30° 04 E. Its coastline is about 42 km long, from El Agami in the west to Abu Qir in the east. Alexandria is the second largest city in Egypt and the principal harbour and trade centre of the country. Its coast is bordered by a highway (corniche) which is protected from the sea by a concrete sea wall. The corniche follows the coastline for a distance of 16 km, from Montazah to Ras El-Tin. On the landward side of the corniche is some of the most valuable property in Egypt. The corniche itself represents a significant investment and its cost is estimated now at £E200 million.

The city itself was founded on a narrow sandy coastal plain (Ridge No. II); a part of the corniche is built on rocks, as in Roshdi, and the rest, on the sandy plain, as in the El-Mandara area. The beaches are narrow, with a maximum width of about 50 m, to the east of the Eastern Harbour and wider, to the west. They are, however, suffering from erosion, with a shoreline retreat of 20 cm/yr.

Shoreline and sea-bed morphology

The shoreline is undulating and interrupted by rocky headlands, forming embayments and pocket beaches ranging from 300 to 1,600 m in length, except for El-Mamora (4,000 m), and of maximum width of 50 m (Fig. 1). Most Alexandrian coasts are rocky and have very little or no sandy beaches. The small rocky islets submerged in the nearshore zone off Alexandria serve as wave energy dissipaters. The predominant features of Alexandria's coastline, extending from El Agami to Abu Qir headland, are depicted in Figure 1. The Alexandrian beaches are moderately dissipative of wave energy; they are steeper than those on the rest of the Nile delta coast, having a slope of 1:30 and crescent-shaped sand bars associated with rip currents which are hazardous to swimmers. Some of the beaches are suffering from erosion. Nourishment has been carried out using desert sand with or without solid protection works such as groynes.

The nearshore zone contains outcrops of emerged and submerged rocky islets aligned more or less parallel to the shoreline and extending 300 m into the sea. These outcrops form rocky shoals in front of most of Alexandria's beaches and act as natural wave breakers. They reduce wave heights and change wave direction near the coastline. The nearshore bathymetry is complex, owing to these outcrops.

The Alexandria beach sediments are derived from the adjacent limestone ridges west of Alexandria and/or from local rocky limestone outcrops. They may also be

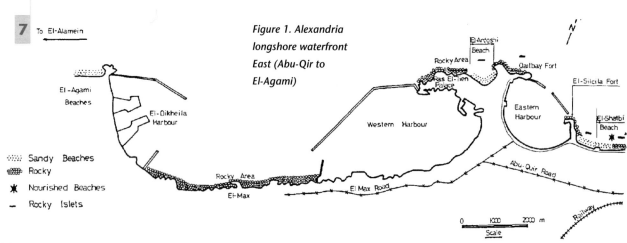

Figure 1. Alexandria
longshore waterfront
East (Abu-Qir to
El-Agami)

Sandy Beaches
Rocky
Nourished Beaches
Rocky Islets

TABLE I. MAIN FEATURES OF THE ALEXANDRIAN COAST

Region	Length (m)	Type	Beach width (m)	Altitude of corniche (m)	Status	Expected future protection works
El-Anfoshi	900 1 000	Sandy Rocky	40	–	• deposition area • submerged concrete blocks about 100 m offshore	–
Eastern Harbour	3 800	Rocky	–	(5.00)	• narrow beach at Scout Club (300 x 5 m) • protection by concrete blocks	–
El-Shatby	850 200	Sandy Rocky	40	(5.00)	• erosion area • nourished in 1988 (59 000 m³) maximum erosion is 0.7 m/yr	8-10 detached breakwaters in water depth of 2 to 4 m + 60 m groyne on the western side + 270 000 m³ nourishment sand
Sporting and Ibrahimiya	400 700	Sandy Rocky	3	(4.00)	• nearly stable • narrow eroded beaches	–
Cleopatra and Sidi Gaber	200 1 000	Sandy Rocky	10 –	(4.00) –	protection of the corniche by concrete blocks maximum erosion is 0.7 m/yr	4 to 6 detached breakwaters in water depth of 2.5 to 4 m + 60 m groyne on the eastern side + 180 000 m³ nourishment sand
Roshdi and Mostapha Pasha	850	Rocky	–	(6.50)→(4.00)	• erosion area • narrow pocket beaches	5 to 7 detached breakwaters in water depth of 2.5 to 5 m + 60 m and 40 m groynes on the western and eastern sides + 15 000 m³ nourishment sand
Saba Pacha and Stanley	200 1 250	Sandy Rocky	20 –	(4.00)→(8.00) –	• erosion area • nourished in 1987 (23 000 m³)	2 short detached breakwaters in water depth of 2.5 m
San Stefano and Gleem	1 000 150	Sandy Rocky	– 30	(3.75)	• deposition area • narrow sandy beach	5 or 6 detached breakwaters in water depth of 4 to 5 m + 40 m groyne to the west + 216 000 m³ nourishment sand

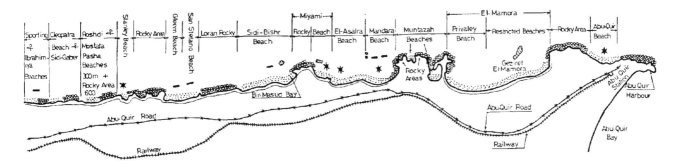

TABLE I. (Continued)

Region	Length (m)	Type	Beach width((m)	Altitude of corniche (m)	Status	Expected future protection works
Loran and El-Raml	1 200	Rocky	–	(5.00)→(350)	• protection of the corniche by concrete blocks	–
Sidi Bishr	1 700 250	Sandy Rocky	15 –	(4.00)	• nearly stable maximum accretion is 0.7 m/yr	–
Miyami	500 450	Sandy Rocky	30 –	(4.00) –	• erosion area • nourished in 1989 (19 000 m³) in 1995 (49 000 m³)	–
El-Asafra	1 100	Sandy	20	(5.00)	• erosion area • nourished in 1990 (48 000 m³)	–
El-Mandara	950	Sandy	25	(2.00)→(5.00)	• erosion area • nourished in 1988 (60 000 m³)	3 or 4 detached breakwaters + 4 m groyne to the west in water depth of 3 to 5 m + extension of 30 m to the existing eastern groyne + 9 000 m³ of nourishment sand
El-Montazah	900 1 500	Sandy Rocky	Variable –	(4.00)→(8.00)	• erosion area • Ayda and Venice beaches	–
El-Mamoura	3 500 350	Sandy Rocky	40 –	(2.75) –	• erosion area • maximum rate is 0.7 m/yr on western side • maximum accretion rate is 0.7 m/yr on eastern side	–
Abu Qir	1 000 2 000	Sandy Rocky	20 –	(1.60) –	• erosion area • nourished in 1987 (20 000 m³) in 1993 (15 000 m³)	–

Figure 2. Existing situation of Qait Bey Fort.

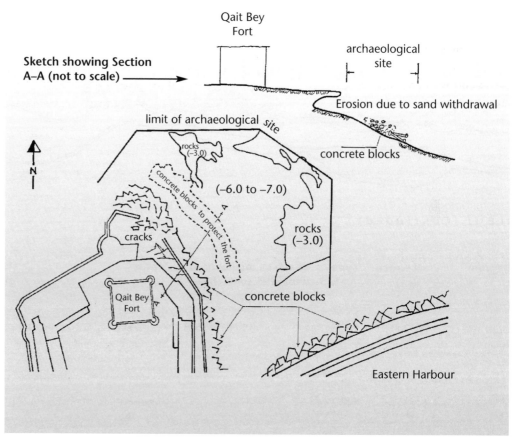

Figure 3. Proposed solution for saving the archaeological site and protecting Qait Bey Fort.

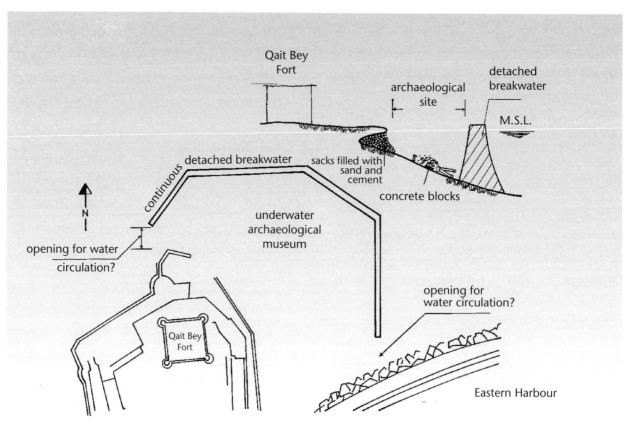

derived from the sediment discharge from El-Mahmoudia Canal and El-Umoum outfall. The sand-grain size range is from medium to coarse. Table I summarizes the main features of the Alexandrian coast. The predominant wave directions are mainly from the N–NW sector and this is responsible for the generation of a longshore current towards the east. In addition, an appreciable percentage of waves from the N–NE sector generates a reverse longshore current towards the west. The net sediment transport direction is towards the east.

Recommended actions

Given the lack of hydrodynamic data and underwater surveys and the objective of optimizing the planning and design of protective works, the following actions are recommended:

(a) Collection of data on waves, currents, sea-level variations, bottom characteristics (sandy or rocky), littoral drift rate, storm surges, etc.

(d) Conduct of bathymetric side-scan sonar and high-resolution seismic surveys to determine the depth contours and bed slopes, and to locate submerged and/or buried monuments (if any).

(c) Utilization of the existing emerged and submerged islands of Alexandria to achieve better protection for recreational activities.

(d) Avoidance of the use of vertical seawalls or any similar hard structures, because they will accelerate erosion and cause undermining of the bottom sand as well as overtopping and high uprush.

(e) Careful design of underwater museums to ensure preservation of archaeological finds and to encourage underwater tourism in Alexandria, as in the Red Sea. Figures 2 and 3 illustrate one possible solution for a problem facing Alexandria's underwater heritage.

(f) Prohibition of protective works in the Alexandria area until it has been established that there are no monuments buried in the sea floor.

(g) Beach nourishment to overcome erosion problems in Alexandria, if there are no

monuments in the area, so that unwanted side-effects will be avoided.

(h) Assessment of future consequences for submarine and onshore archaeological remains, based on a predictive model and realistic scenarios of sea-level change.

(i) Prohibition of the quarrying and removal of the natural carbonate ridges west of Alexandria that constitute a natural coastal-defence system (comprising also offshore islets and sandy beaches) and which could be effectively managed to protect the coastline and combat flooding and the consequences of sea-level rise.

Need for a coastal management plan
The Alexandria case

IBTEHAL Y. EL-BASTAWISSI
Department of Architecture
University of Alexandria

Introduction

Coastal resources are not as widely scattered, geographically, as other natural resources. They are concentrated in a rather narrow band where the continent meets the tidal sea, and they are used by a population scattered throughout the continental land mass. The pressure on these scarce coastal resources has grown with an increase in population, wealth, mobility, leisure time and recreation. This growing pressure has raised issues and problems, such as, who are to use the resources of the coastal zone, how they are to be used, and when is that use to take place. The answer is to work out a management system or systems to control the development of the coastal zone. Any management system is, ultimately, a system that blends economic theory, law and politics into a programme that is theoretically sound, legally workable, and at least palatable from a political point of view. Last of all, it considers the environment and hence the ecology of the coastal zone. Nowadays, society's priorities have been reversed and man has become aware that his survival and well-being depend on a system of sustainable coastal development. If one attempts to develop a system of management for the coastal zone that does not first take into account the basic ecology of this zone, the system is doomed to fail.[1] Leisure is a key issue that is becoming increasingly related to coastal resources. The pressure of participation in recreational activities in

coastal areas and potential use conflict have been key factors, which has prompted the attention now being given to the planning and management of the coast as a resource. A key aim is to balance the needs of recreation against other activities, such as economic development (e.g. commerce), natural resources (e.g. wildlife), cultural preservation (e.g. archaeological sites) and aesthetic requirements (e.g. visual preference).[2]

The main aims of this paper are: (a) to examine the coastal zone and man's interactions with it; (b) to discuss the urgency of establishing guidelines for a Coastal Zone Management Plan and Programme and of implementing it; (c) to review urban waterfront revitalization and to apply it to Alexandria; and (d) to make recommendations concerning the Alexandrian coastal zone.

To facilitate the matters discussed herein, it is desirable to define some of the principal terms and concepts used, as follows (items a–e are adapted from the US Coastal Zone Management Act of 1972) :

(a) The term *coastal zone* means the coastal waters (including the lands therein and thereunder) and the adjacent shorelands (including the waters therein and thereunder), strongly influenced by each other and in proximity to the shoreline, and includes islands, transitional and intertidal areas, salt marshes, wetlands and beaches.

(b) The term *coastal resources of national*

[1] Cooper, A. W. (1971). Ecological considerations. pp. 127–40, in: J. C. Hite and J. M. Stepp (eds.), Coastal Zone Resource Management. Praeger Publishers, New York.

[2] Johnson, D. and Seabrooke, B. (1996). Sustainable enjoyment: the need for leisure management at the coast. pp. 23–40, in: T. Goodhead and D. Johnson (eds.), Coastal Recreation Management. E. & F. N. Spon, London.

significance means any coastal wetlands, beach, dune, reef, estuary or fish and wildlife habitat, if any such area is determined by a coastal city to be of substantial biological or natural storm-protective value.

(c) The term *coastal waters* means those waters, adjacent to the shorelines, which contain a measurable quantity or percentage of sea water, including, but not limited to, sounds, bays, lagoons, bayous, ponds and estuaries.

(d) The term *estuary* means that part of a river or stream or other body of water having unimpaired connection with the open sea, where the sea water is measurably diluted with fresh water derived from land drainage.

(e) The term *water use* means use, activity or project conducted in or on waters within the coastal zone.

(f) The term *management plan* means a vehicle for recording systematically the characteristics of the site, acknowledging explicitly its most valuable aspects and specifying objectives for the site's management which will be achieved through the proposals and work programmes that are outlined in the plan.[3, 4]

(g) The term *coast,* from an environmental standpoint, is a popular destination for recreational activities. The natural beauty and landscape variety of the coast, its nature-conservation interest and its various natural resources for recreation, such as water, beaches and cliffs, make it a major attraction, and there have been growing pressures on its capacity. In most coastal areas, the aim should be to balance and reconcile these interests and contain the impact of these activities through appropriate management measures[2].

(h) The term *coastal management programme* is [intended to be] a co-ordinated process by which the government, with public and private input, designs and implements an agreed plan for the use and protection of coastal resources. The programme should rely on the government for leadership, with the input of local and national interests to supplement this leadership role. Coastal management is also designed to improve the technical and scientific framework within which coastal decision-making is based.[5]

The coastal zone and man's interactions with it

Any consideration of a coastal resources management system must take into account man's past and present interaction with the ecosystems of the coastal zone. From these past interactions, an effective initial model for a coastal zone management system can be developed. Man subjects coastal ecosystems to a number of direct stresses, or modifications, whose effects are immediately apparent. These involve activities ranging from building sites, through industrial and commercial activities, to sports and fishing.[1] For instance, beneficial use of sandy shores has included projects on navigation, recreation, waste disposal, power generation, food supply and others. Affluence, leisure time and transportation have made recreation a major shoreline activity, with mass accommodation and facilities for vacations or retirement in the vicinity of population centres and, at more remote locations.[6] Being the major shoreline activity, recreation, including its impact on nature conservation, has attracted the most attention. Johnson and Seabrooke[2] stated that

the impact of recreation on nature conservation can create short- or long-term damage and disturbance which can be either reversible or irreversible. English Nature (1991) recognizes disturbance as perhaps the

[3] Leay, M., Rowe, J. and Young, J. D. (1986). Management Plans: a Guide to Their Preparation and Use. *Countryside Commission, CCP 206, Cheltenham (UK).*

[4] Johnson, D. (1996). Coastal management plans. pp. 273–95, in: T. Goodhead and D. Johnson (eds.), Coastal Recreation Management. *E. & F. N. Spon, London.*

[5] Reimold, R. J. (1980). Effectiveness of assessments of coastal management. pp. 444–50, in: B. L. Edge (ed.), Coastal Zone '80: Proceedings of the Second Symposium on Coastal and Ocean Management. *Vol. I. American Society of Civil Engineers, New York.*

[6] O'Brien, M. P. and Johnson, J. W. (1980). Structures and sandy beaches. pp. 2718–40, in: B. L. Edge (ed.), Coastal Zone '80: Proceedings of the Second Symposium on Coastal and Ocean Management. *Vol IV. American Society of Civil Engineers, New York.*

major area of conflict, particularly in estuaries, affecting resident and migratory bird populations.

Dramatic examples of the consequences of the development of recreational facilities are also mentioned by Pickering[7], who stated that *facilities development, their location, design and management can affect the landscape quality, destroy habitats and disturb or increase the stress levels felt by the wildlife. The use of a site as a recreational area will inevitably lead to change in local ecosystems. Habitats will be destroyed and wildlife displaced to provide car parks and facilities. In terms of explicit provision, changes to the ecosystems will need to be made to withstand the intensity of use. It may be necessary to plant trees and shrubs able to withstand soil compaction and damage from vandalism.*

Moreover, the poor design of access routes can lead to a widening of the pathway or area affected by trampling, potentially to the point of creating a barrier to species movement.[7, 8]

Pickering[7], after Edington and Edington[9], highlighted the view on the environmental disturbance of the flora and fauna, that *flora and fauna typically have narrow tolerance levels in respect of the environmental conditions they require for survival and health. Aquatic animals, for example, are sensitive to salinity, water movement, temperature and plant formations. Plants not only form an important part of the food chain, but also provide essential shelter and support.*

To plan sustainable interaction between man and the coastal zone, a coastal management programme is needed that is specifically tailored to preserve, to protect, to enhance and to develop the use of the coastal renewable and non-renewable resources. The plan must be formulated to manage unique coastal resources prudently, giving equal consideration to economic and ecological goals, one of which should be to resolve conflicts that arise between natural-resource conservation and economic development. This resolution needs to be brought about in a timely manner to ensure the greatest possible long-term increase in public benefit for all user groups. For example, renewable resources, such as fisheries and forests, and non-

renewable resources, such as natural gas reserves, must be utilized in ways that best conserve their value for present and future generations, by recycling, for example. Other resources, including archaeological and historical sites, rare plants and animals, and freshwater wetlands, have special values which must be considered in wise planning for the coast, recognizing that some resources are suited for development, whereas others should be managed for maximum protection.[5]

The urgency of implementing a coastal zone management programme

In the light of the foregoing discussion, the US Coastal Zone Management Act of 1972, which provides definitions of terms relating to the coastal zone (see above), offers some points of resemblance to the case of the Alexandria region:

(a) There is a national interest in the effective management, beneficial use, protection and development of the coastal zone.

(b) The coastal zone is rich in a variety of natural, commercial, recreational, ecological, industrial and aesthetic resources of immediate and potential value to the present and future well-being of the country.

(c) The increasing and competing demands upon the lands and waters of coastal zones occasioned by population growth and economic development – including requirements for industry, commerce, residential development, recreation, extraction of mineral resources and fossil fuels, transportation and navigation, waste disposal, and harvesting of fish, shellfish and other

---

[7] Pickering, H. (1996). Limitation of coastal recreation. pp. 69–91, in: T. Goodhead and D. Johnson (eds.), Coastal Recreation Management. E. & F. N. Spon, London.

[8] Sidaway, R. (1993). Sport, recreation and nature conservation: developing good conservation practice. In: S. Glyptis (ed.), Leisure and the Environment: Essays in Honour of Professor J.A. Patmore. Belhaven Press, London.

[9] Edington, J. M. and Edington, M. A. (1986). Ecology, Recreation and Tourism. Cambridge University Press, Cambridge.

living marine resources – have resulted in the loss of living marine resources, wildlife, nutrient-rich areas, permanent and adverse changes to ecological systems, decreasing open space for public use, and shoreline problems.
(d) The habitat areas of the coastal zone, and the living marine resources and wildlife therein, are ecologically fragile and consequently extremely vulnerable to destruction by man's alterations.
(e) Important ecological, cultural, historical and aesthetic values in the coastal zone, which are essential to the wellbeing of all citizens, are being irretrievably damaged or lost.
(f) New and expanding demands for food, energy, minerals, defence needs, recreation, waste disposal, transportation and industry are placing stress on coastal areas and are creating the need for resolution of serious conflicts among important and competing uses and values in coastal and sea waters.
(g) Special natural and scenic characteristics are being damaged by ill-planned development that threatens these values.
(h) In the light of competing demands and the urgent need to protect and to give high priority to natural systems in the coastal zone, present governmental and local institutional arrangements for planning and regulating land and water uses in such areas are inadequate.
(i) Land uses in the coastal zone and the uses of adjacent lands which drain into the coastal zone, may significantly affect the quality of coastal waters and habitats, and efforts to control coastal water pollution from land-use activities must be improved.
(j) Because global warming may result in a substantial sea level rise with serious adverse effects in the coastal zone, coastal cities must anticipate and plan for such an occurrence.
(k) Because of their proximity to and reliance upon the sea and its resources, the coastal cities have substantial and significant interests in the protection, management and development of the resources of the exclusive economic zone that can only be served by the active participation of coastal cities in all governmental programmes affecting such resources and, wherever appropriate, by the development of sea resource plans as part of their governmentally approved coastal zone management programmes.

Guidelines for the implementation of a coastal zone management programme

Any system of management devised for the the coastal zone must, as a first consideration, reflect the ecological processes that occur in that zone. Clearly, any management system must also take into account political and social constraints, but, when concessions are made, they must be made in favour of natural processes, not in favour of man-oriented processes. This is the only safe path to be taken if the coastal zone resources that are prized so much and that are so necessary to sustainable welfare of the country are to be protected.[1]

The US Coastal Zone Management Act of 1972 offers a set of guidelines that may be included in the national policy and used as a basis for implementing a coastal zone management system. These guidelines are:
(a) To preserve, protect, develop and, where possible, to restore or enhance the resources of the country's coastal zone for present and future generations.
(b) To encourage and assist the cities to effectively exercise their responsibilities in the coastal zone through the development and implementation of management programmes to achieve wise use of the land and water resources of the coastal zone, giving full consideration to ecological, cultural, historical and aesthetic values, as well as the need for compatible economic development. Such programmes should at least provide for:
• the protection of natural resources, including wetlands, estuaries, beaches, dunes, coral reefs, fish, wildlife and their habitat, within the coastal zone;
• the management of coastal development to minimize the loss of life and property caused by improper development in areas prone to floods, storm surges, geological hazards and erosion, and in areas likely to be affected by or vulnerable to sea-level rise, land subsidence and salt-water intrusion, and by the destruction of natural protective features such as beaches, dunes and wetlands;
• the management of coastal development to improve, safeguard and restore the quality of coastal waters, and to protect natural

resources and existing uses of those waters;
• priority consideration of coastal-dependent uses and orderly processes for siting major facilities related to national defence, energy generation, fishery development, recreation, ports and transportation, and the location, to the maximum extent practicable, of new commercial and industrial developments in or adjacent to areas where such development already exists;
• public access to the coasts for recreational purposes;
• assistance in the redevelopment of deteriorating urban waterfronts and ports, and sensitive preservation and restoration of historical, cultural and aesthetic coastal features;
• the co-ordination and simplification of procedures, to ensure expeditious governmental decision-making for the management of coastal resources;
• continued consultation and co-ordination with the affected governmental agencies;
• the creation of opportunities for public and local-government participation in coastal management decision-making;
• assistance to support comprehensive planning, conservation and management for living marine resources, including planning for the siting of pollution control and aquaculture facilities within the coastal zone, and improved co-ordination between local and national coastal zone management agencies and wildlife agencies; and
• the study and development of plans for addressing the adverse effect upon the coastal zone of land subsidence and of sea-level rise.
(c) To encourage the preparation of special area management plans which provide for increased specificity in protecting significant natural resources, reasonable coastal-dependent economic growth, improved protection of life and property in hazardous areas, including those areas likely to be affected by land subsidence and sea-level rise, and improved predictability in governmental decision-making.
(d) To encourage the participation and co-operation of the public and of local government.
(e) To encourage co-ordination and co-operation with and among the appropriate

governmental and local agencies, and international organizations where appropriate, in the collection, analysis, synthesis and dissemination of coastal management information, research results, and technical assistance to support governmental regulation of land-use practices affecting the coastal and sea resources of the country.

Development of a coastal zone management plan

The concept of Coastal Zone Management (CZM) has developed, as discussed previously, from the struggle to find a mechanism to balance the demands on the coastal resources, promote their sustainable use and manage individual activities. It is now recognized that coastal areas need to be managed in an integrated way. Each activity should be considered as a part of the whole and not managed independently of other activities in the same area. All of them must co-exist with other maritime activities. The need to work in harmony with the numerous agencies involved with the coast is therefore an important element of the job of coastal managers.[2] This approach was articulated at the World Coast 2000 Conference[10]:
A national CZM programme should facilitate integrated decision-making through a continuous and evolutionary process for co-operation and co-ordination among sectors, integrating national and local interests in the management of activities concerning the environment and development [through] education, public awareness and an equitable process for the participation of all stakeholders.
Decisions on which is the best use of a given unit of the coastal zone must be made with full input from scientists, ecologists, geologists, economists, anthropologists, planners and architects.[1] Therefore, the preparation of coastal management plans requires a systematic approach.[4] To fulfil

[10] World Coast 2000. (1993). Preparing to Meet the Coastal Challenges of the 21st Century. Conference Statement, Noordwijk, The Netherlands, 5 November 1993.

this requirement, Kennedy[11] identified five preparatory stages in developing a coastal management plan. They are:

Stage 1: Identifying the real management issues. This involves information-gathering to give a picture of the management situation prior to formulating the management plan. This stage may result in the production of a preparatory document, or interim or issues report, to serve as a consultation document, helping to shape and build support for the plan.

Stage 2: Planning for what is desired as an outcome and how to achieve it; in effect, the work programme for the management planning.

Stage 3: Agreeing on the management structure for the plan is essential with any project where there are multiple responsibilities. An accepted format is the formation of a steering group or working party consisting of the primary decision-makers. The government advises local authorities to take the lead in preparing coastal management plans.

Stage 4: Doing the work (i.e., analysis of information, formulation of objectives and production of a detailed action programme).

Stage 5: Presenting the plan firstly as a draft for consultation, to allow for comment and public/user reaction, and then as a finalized document.

These stages serve only as guidelines because it would be inappropriate to set out a universal list of contents applicable to every coastal management plan. Each plan is specific to its site, managing agencies and subject focus. Johnson[4] also added:

However, while detailed content will vary from location to location, many of the component parts are common to all such documents.

He supported this view by giving a brief summary of a typical management plan format set out by Leay, Rowe and Young.[3] Their headings are as follows:

Aims

Statement of intent reflecting strategic policies and the balance of interests.

Survey

Background information and baseline data that are both regional and site specific. This section usually includes a description of the site and a detailed audit of the site's key features.

Analysis:

Resolution of conflicting management proposals together with consideration of opportunities and constraints, and an assessment of their importance.

Objectives:

Specific, measurable and precise targets, which can be priced and time-tabled, outlining courses of action.

Prescription:

An overview of the work required to meet the management objectives together with resource requirements.

Implementation:

A detailed action programme explaining how management objectives will be achieved and work executed.

Monitoring and review:

A record and assessment of action taken and proposals for reviewing the plan.

Finally, Johnson recommended that, while the preparatory stages are important and largely determine the management plan's content, the result should be a working document rather than merely a paper exercise.

Principles for an effective coastal management programme

An effective coastal management programme must be founded on principles that can be repeated in time and space. It must not rely solely on any individual, public official, or conservation leader, but must be founded on a series of goals and objectives established for the wise use of the coast. For instance, the programme may emphasize significant natural resources such as dunes, beaches and wetlands, or point to the increasing need for accessibility to the coastal areas for recreational uses; at the same time, assurance of the protection and restoration or enhancement of the cultural and natural

---

[11] Kennedy, K. (1994). Producing management plans for major estuaries: the need for a systematic approach. Case study: the Thames Estuary. Conference on Management Techniques in the Coastal Zone, *University of Portsmouth, 24–25 October 1994.*

resources is needed. Such a programme may also document the need for increased co-operation in intergovernmental co-ordination so as to bring about greater predictability in public decision-making. An analysis of how effective the programme has been in reaching these goals is required.

Standards and criteria adopted through laws and applicable rules and regulations should provide guidelines on evaluation and assessment. Guidelines should include, for example, a review of the public interests, the water-dependent nature of the proposed activity, whether the proposed change is essential for safe navigation and/or public health, and address the public recreational benefits. In addition, an effective coastal management programme should provide free technical assistance to the applicant to assist in following the guidelines of the coastal regulation programme. Reimold[5] provided planners with a set of important components of an effective coastal management programme. These components are summed up in nine headings; a tenth heading is also added, as follows:

Understanding the value of dunes, beaches and offshore bars: An important component of a coastal management programme is the ability to manage the dunes, beaches and offshore bars. These areas are fragile products of shoreline evolution and are quite easily disturbed. Exposed to the full effect of waves, tides, currents and winds, the visible beach undergoes changes in width in response to changing conditions; high, steep storm waves cut into the beach and move sand offshore, whereas low swells move it back and rebuild the beach. For this reason, beaches are generally narrower towards the end of winter in most locations during the stormy season than in the late summer.[6]

The offshore sandbars and shoals are the shore's first line of defence against destructive energy generated by winds, tides and storms, and consequently protect the onshore portions of the system by serving as a sand reservoir for the beaches. These sea beaches frequently provide an unparalleled natural recreational resource which has become vitally linked to the economy of the

coastal zone. Wise conservation of this sand-sharing system is of vital concern to all citizens to maintain their health, safety and welfare. Appropriate conservation regulations for this dynamic sand-sharing system ensures that all structures and activities on the offshore sandbars, shoals, beaches and dunes do not adversely affect the functioning and the value of the sand-sharing system.

The role of scientists in establishing an effective coastal zone programme: Another component of an effective programme in coastal management is the utilization of the most recent advances in science and technology as a foundation upon which to base coastal legislation. This involves close networking with scientists of many disciplines so as to ensure that recent discoveries of science are integrated into wise resource management. An effective coastal management programme will be one that reviews existing laws and rules and regulations relative to coastal resource and land use, and that makes recommendations in the light of recent findings. In this instance, the scientists and government officials cannot work in a vacuum. Care must be taken to ensure that the discoveries of science are interpreted for use by the layman and the legislator alike.

Managing the conflict between natural resource conservation and economic development: The need to reconcile conflicting uses should be supported by increased environmental awareness. Worldwide, there is an increased willingness to accept the economic costs of measures to protect the environment (see [2], for example). The coastal resource manager therefore aims to manage the coast, not only because it is all too easily destroyed by a range of human activities but also for its own sake. (For further details refer to the section on the coastal zone and man's interactions with it, discussed above.)

Encouraging the optimum location of private and public development projects: Another important component of assessing the effectiveness of coastal management is to determine whether or not the programme encourages the location of private and public development projects in the most suitable areas so that adverse impacts upon natural resources are minimized. The programme must effectively control the quality and kinds of development that takes place in the coastal zone. This can be best accomplished through zoning. These zoning decisions must be made by weighing ecological values against the values associated with other uses.[1]

Maintaining and/or improving water quality: Another component of wise coastal management is the maintenance or improvement of the quality of coastal waters. Maintenance and, where possible, improvement of coastal waters are essential to public health as well as to the improvement of the tourist industry. Great care must be taken to ensure that industrial waste and port activities, as well as urban growth, do not adversely degrade coastal water quality.

A range of substances that exert a variety of polluting effects enter coastal waters via a number of sources. These include landborne sources – discharges via rivers, streams, drains, pipes and direct run-off; shipborne and marine industrial sources – accidental, deliberate or operational; regulated dumping of material at sea (radioactive waste, sewage sludge etc.); environmental sources, such as atmospheric deposition. Sewage should only be discharged into the sea after it has been screened and comminuted; it should also be discharged through long sea-outfalls, not through short ones.[12] Water quality is a critical consideration in water sports, being not only important for immersion and wet sports but also for sports directly exploiting the resource, such as gamefishing and wildfowling. Surfers and divers are regarded as being more at risk than swimmers, owing to their longer periods of exposure.[7]

Boat users and marina operators should, in theory, be in favour of sensible environmental controls, since water and environmental quality are important to maintaining the quality of their recreational enjoyment. Marina operators need to preserve business, therefore water quality is of primary environmental concern. A number of marina development projects are also in coastal areas of outstanding natural beauty and ecological importance. It is therefore also appropriate for marina sites to operate in an environmentally aware manner, whereby these ecosystems can be protected.[13]

Ensuring public access to the coastal water: Another way of assessing the effectiveness of the coastal management programme is to determine whether it has had an impact on public accessibility to coastal waters and beaches. As the coastal area grows and more people use the coast, additional regulation of public access is essential, although the public should continue to have access to the coastal waters.

Identifying, preserving, and rehabilitating historic sites: Historic sites, structures and relics, whether man-made or natural, are essential cultural resources which must be preserved. The effectiveness of a coastal-management programme can be assessed by its ability to identify, preserve and rehabilitate important historic sites.

Designing a balanced/sustainable use of the coast: In designing a balanced use of the coast, it is essential that local governments not unreasonably restrict or exclude facilities from being sited in the coastal zone when they cannot be easily sited elsewhere, as long as this allows for safety zones and does not come into conflict with other human activities. Facilities of regional and national benefit include power plants, transmission lines, public port development, regional airports, sewage treatment plants, regional solid-waste disposal facilities, and energy-resource exploration and production facilities.

Recreational water activities provide obvious examples of a critical use of the coast. Growth in the number of people participating in water sports, changes in lifestyle,

[12] Lewey, S. (1996). Water quality and pollution. pp. 93–114, in: T. Goodhead and D. Johnson (eds.), Coastal Recreation Management. E. & F. N. Spon, London.
[13] Harris, I., Hill, Z., Hill, R., Pourzanjani, M. and Savill, T. (1996). Legislation or self-regulation. pp. 297–320, in: T. Goodhead and D. Johnson (eds.), Coastal Recreation Management. E. & F. N. Spon, London.

technology and disposable incomes all add to the complexity of the equation, making this the most dynamic of activities to be managed.[14] The location and spatial distribution of activities is fundamentally important. The recreation manager should be able to identify, systematically and objectively, the potential uses of any site, the likely duration of those uses, and the capacity of the site to accommodate recreational pressures. All managers are charged with responsibility for maintaining or enhancing the worth of the resources to which they have access. Such values can easily be swept aside as managers strive to maximize use values, and the collective failure of managers and planners to take proper account of 'existence' values leads, inevitably, to long-term deterioration of the natural environment and to resource management that is manifestly unsustainable in the long run.[2]

Co-ordination between the different levels of authority: Another important component of a coastal management programme should be the involvement of the public, as well as local authorities, in decision-making on coastal resources. It is essential that there be co-ordination between the government and local authorities in all resource planning for the coast. Such co-ordination recognizes the importance of considering development and conservation needs in deciding the future use of all coastal resources.

Public participation: Public participation is a key component of the success of any coastal management programme. In the case of a management programme that contains as one of its major elements restrictions on land use, there must be strong acceptance by the general public or the programme will fail. Cooper[1] noted that

traditionally, coastal people have been unwilling to accept limitations on the use of their lands and waters, and one may expect that many of them will approach any programme of zoning with the same jaundiced view. Therefore, the reasons for the programme, the ecological bases for the land-use restrictions that are proposed, must be

very carefully explained and justified. One must be optimistic that, with a careful job of explanation, wide public acceptance of the needed restrictions can be achieved.

Johnson and Seabrooke[2] supported this view, noting that

the way in which sites are perceived varies according to the nature and context of the use which it supports and the degree of imagination and sensitivity of the users. Visitors who are new to a site or visit infrequently may need to be informed about the site and how best to use it. Managers should not assume that all visitors will use a site in the planned manner when this is in any way unclear.

On the other hand, Harris et al.[13] noted that

there is, however, a reticence towards introducing formal environmental management techniques among some coastal recreational managers for the following reasons. Firstly, it is felt that there is no economic advantage. Secondly, managers do not consider that their operations are causing environmental damage. Thirdly, an environmental approach is difficult to put into practice since most coastal recreation currently operates in an environmental management policy vacuum where few statutory guidelines exist.

Therefore, the introduction of an appropriate environmental programme to protect the coastal ecosystem depends heavily on the participation of all involved individuals in the community.

Reimold, of the Georgia Department of Natural Resources, highlights the importance of having an effective coastal management programme.[5] His comments included the following:

The effective coastal management programme must produce a manageable impact on the government's ability to assure that its coast is wisely utilized for a balanced concern between economic and ecological factors. Careful consideration of the above components of effectiveness assessment in coastal management should enable the planner, the manager, the environmental specialist, and the economist to all better understand the effective means of coastal management.

Urban waterfront revitalization

This section is based mainly on the work of T.R. Hudspeth.[15] It is likely that urban waterfronts will continue to be the sites of intense pressures for re-development. Intensive use of waterfronts is still expected, owing to the growth in the number of people participating in water sports and to changes in lifestyle, technology and disposable incomes.[14, 2] This growth is usually related to achieving optimal use of waterfront resources. Therefore, a coastal zone management programme should comprehend problems and relevant solutions.

Historical background

Human settlements have been associated with water throughout history. The uses of water include drinking, carrying away human wastes, farming, fishing, industrial processing, transporting raw materials and finished products for trade and commerce, power production, and aesthetic and recreational activities. For these reasons, many cities are located near rivers, lakes, bays, oceans and seas.

A very long time ago, man settled at river mouths or at harbours protecting him from stormy seas and tides. In time, these settlements became active sea ports through which came materials, goods and people from around the world. Commercial well-being of citizens was tied to the fisheries, ship-building yards and brisk coastal shipping trade. Systems of canals built to form links between larger navigable waterways helped to promote the prosperity of these cities. The development of urban areas and the predominance of certain cities over others depended largely on their combination of transportation systems; those places that combined railroads and port or river access became dominant. The waterfronts were the centre of activity of these urban areas and development took place along the water's edge. There were large wooden docks, behind which were warehouses, shops, offices, bars, restaurants and hotels.

The history of Alexandria's waterfront development is not far from this description. Alexander the Great must have been struck by the excellent position offered by the village of Rhakotis, protected by the island of Pharos, for the establishment of a harbour for intercourse with the rest of the world. The plans for the future city were traced by the architect Dinocrates and work began at once. Two harbours were formed: The Eastern Harbour (Magnus Portus) which was considered the more important of the two by the ancient Alexandrians, and Port Eunostos (the modern Western Harbour). Consequently, Alexandria provided an excellent, safe and large port, connected by a navigable canal to Lake Mariout, and in easy communication with the Red Sea, realized all the conditions favourable to becoming the centre of universal commerce[16], and its waterfronts became full of activity and life.

Waterfront decline

Great changes in the use of urban waterfronts have resulted from four changes during the present century:

Steadily decreasing waterborne passenger travel: Tourists are largely carried by planes to different destinations all over the world. Travelling by ship has become a luxury. Given the limited vacation periods, people prefer to travel by air to take advantage of rapidity. Every year, over 775 million people, worldwide, fly on commercial aircraft. Commercial flight has become so common that having to travel without flying as an option would be inconceivable to many people.[17] Railroads and highways affected passenger activity at seaports negatively.

[14] Ratcliffe, T. (1992). Responsibility for watersports management and development. Ocean and Coastal Management, 18:259–68.
[15] Hudspeth, T. R. (1980). Urban waterfront revitalization employing visual preference as a strategy for managing visual resources and facilitating public participation. pp. 33-50, in: B. L. Edge (ed.), Coastal Zone '80: Proceedings of the Second Symposium on Coastal and Ocean Management. Vol. I. American Society of Civil Engineers, New York.

Technological changes in marine transportation and cargo handling: The phenomenal growth in size of bulk petroleum carriers has created a need for new and specialized terminals which cannot – and need not – be located at traditional urban waterfront sites. The largest crude oil carriers are so large that they cannot enter many ports. Increasingly, offshore terminals are being constructed which connect with onshore refineries and oil-tank 'farms' via submarine pipelines. The petrochemical complexes and oil-tank 'farms' are located far from waterfront areas; Sidi Krir, situated on the outskirts of Alexandria, has many offshore terminals to serve the refineries. The fear of oil spills has also contributed to this trend.

The movement, storage and processing of hazardous bulk liquids (e.g. liquefied energy gases and toxic chemicals) should be placed in concentrated locations away from urban waterfronts, since the public has become more aware of the effects on human health of accidental releases of combustible, radioactive or toxic agents, and has questioned the compatibility of such activity with heavily populated areas.

The most significant change in cargo handling and shipping is the shift from break-bulk operations to containerization, which allows goods to move more efficiently. With containerization, goods may be shipped directly from a manufacturing plant to a port and then to point of distribution without breaking bulk, or packing and unpacking the cargo. The container revolution has created major land-use changes in waterfront areas. Container-ship terminals require fewer berths and less frontage on shipping channels than the old ports, but considerably greater acreage for back-up facilities. They are highly land-intensive operations. This is the case of the new port of Dekheila which is 20 km from Alexandria. The old port was not able to provide the acreage needed for container terminals. Consequently, newer container facilities are generally developed in areas remote from traditional urban waterfronts where requirements for back-up space, less expensive land, deeper and wider shipping channels, and access to good highways and rail transportation can be met. So traditional

finger piers and much of the break-bulk cargo-vessel system are being rendered obsolete as a smaller number of specialized container ports receive most of the cargo-shipping business.

Changes in land transportation modes: Since the late 19th century, coastal shipping of goods has yielded considerably to rail and, later, truck transport. With the increasing dependence on such transport, many industrial concerns shifted their operations away from the waterfront to rail lines and major highway interchanges, so as to be able to move their goods more efficiently. The city began to expand farther from the waterfront which was no longer the hub of activity.

Since the development of the agricultural and desert highways, transportation of goods by truck is used heavily. This tendency caused a decline in the use of waterways leading to Cairo and Upper Egypt. From Alexandria's maritime port, a bridge is under construction to provide direct connection to the agricultural and desert highways crossing the Nile Delta , the desert, Cairo and on to Upper Egypt.

Changing economic role of the central city: Many local businesses traditionally located on urban waterfronts have succumbed to centralized mass production. Changing space requirements in manufacturing and mass-production technologies have led to the shift of this activity to the suburbs. In many places, the economic role of the central city has shifted from manufacturing to highly specialized services, thus eroding the traditional link between urban industry and shipping. Consequently, the importance of waterfronts in contemporary industrial operations has declined.

A large number of port areas next to the central business districts of large cities no longer meet the requirements of modern shipping and transportation technology. For instance, Alexandria Iron and Steel, Alexandria Petroleum, and Egyptian Oil [companies] were all constructed near the new maritime port of Dekheila, to meet these modern requirements.

These four changes have rendered the traditional uses of urban waterfronts functionally or economically obsolete, and have resulted in a decline in urban waterfronts and in the loss of their position as the economic, commercial and industrial centres of cities. They have forced cities to focus their attention inland and turn their backs on the place where they were born: their waterfronts.

Rediscovery of waterfronts

Coastal cities are, nevertheless, beginning to realize that their waterfronts are an asset. They are being eyed as potential sources of new income, depending on the needs, on the nature of the waterfront, or on the citizens themselves. For example, the Eastern Harbour is now viewed as a potential tourist attraction after the discovery of the submerged land and ancient ruins.

As many coastal cities have sought to improve their image as good places to live, work and play in, and visit, they have re-examined their waterfronts, have recognized that they are special and important places, and have made an effort to revitalize them. Alexandria has thought of revitalizing its Mahmoudeya riverfront. It succeeded in removing the slums along its banks and is trying to clear the water stream. This project has not yet been completed, but it hopes to demonstrate the multiple uses and advantages of re-developing this riverfront.

Urban planners have re-discovered these areas (e.g., the Eastern Harbour, the Mahmoudia Canal), where the natural amenities of water and coast are combined with a rich cultural heritage, recreation and commerce, and they have recognized that these are exciting and unique places. They have also suggested that the most obvious re-uses are quality housing and recreation, including marinas, aquariums, restaurants, theatres, promenades, etc.; and if the location is close enough to the downtown area, it might also be attractive for prestigious commercial buildings.[15, 18]

Preservation and conservation of historical heritage resources

Citing Whiteman *et al*. and Hudspeth[15, 18], *City waterfronts areas are old sections, often full of history. In renewing them, cities are finding precious relics of their beginnings and earliest days. In many cases, preservation and restoration of such historic riches are part of waterfront renewal programmes.*

Restoring historic homes, adapting older buildings to new, economically viable uses, and recreating traditional cultural events in these areas of picturesque natural settings, distinctive architecture, colourful heritage and rich history add to the amenity value of urban waterfronts for residents and to their attraction for tourists and other visitors.

Citing the Institut Européen d'Archéologie Sous-Marine[19],

[Unfortunately] *some areas* [in Alexandria's Eastern Harbour] *are covered by modern structures, most probably hiding antique remains. This primarily concerns the areas covered by the modern piers and breakwaters, as well as the Cape Silsileh structural complex.*

Conservation of natural heritage resources

Revitalizing urban areas, instead of new development construction, helps to conserve the natural environment by preventing urban sprawl and the filling of valuable yet fragile ecosystems. Unfortunately, the northern coast development – a new developing tourist urban area – is an example of urban sprawl. This is obvious in the establishment of many tourist villages overlooking the open sea while eliminating the possibility of a safe swim. Some projects were pushed to install breakwaters to overcome this problem, forgetting that they are severely disturbing the ecosystem of the area.

[16] Breccia, E. V. (1922). Alexandrea ad AEgyptum: a Guide to the Ancient and Modern Town, and to its Graeco-Roman Museum. *Istituto Italiano d'Arti Grafiche, Bergamo.*
[17] McCool, A. C. (1995). In-flight Catering Management. *Wiley, New York.*
[18] Whitman, I. L., David, R. M. and Goldstone, S. E. (1964). Renewal of waterfront areas. Journal of Housing, *June, pp. 236–55.*
[19] Institut Européen d'Archéologie Sous-Marine (1996). Mission 1996: Alexandria East Port.

Guidelines for effective waterfront revitalization as an element of a total coastal management programme

Urban waterfronts constitute a limited resource. There is fierce competition for waterfront space among industrial, commercial, residential, recreational, defence, transportation, and other land-use interests. Some are incompatible and result in conflicts – as between heavy industry, petrochemical or energy storage facilities or marine transportation terminals and residences in the same neighborhood. Because water is common property, the disposition of shoreland is often considered to be a public-interest issue, but public interest is often in conflict with private property rights, and with a developer's expectations of an appropriate economic return. Coastal management programmes must include guidelines on setting priorities for waterfront use within particular areas of the coastal zone. The following are suggested:

(a) Increase public understanding of the opportunities for, and environmental, social, and economic benefits of, urban waterfront revitalization.

(b) Improve environmental planning and design by adopting criteria for the development of an information clearing house for:
• enhancing the special and unique qualities, the sense of place, of each waterfront;
• providing the full range of water-dependent recreational activities;
• considering the particular needs of low-income people, minorities, the elderly, the handicapped and the young, in the provision of recreational opportunities and mixed uses;
• optimizing public access (physical and visual) opportunities; and
• reducing access barriers caused by railways and highways.

(c) Technical assistance, such as techniques for gaining the support of citizens and the business sector.

(d) Encourage private sector support of public access goals.

Visual preference in urban waterfront environments

The use of visual preference offers considerable promise as a strategy for managing the visual resources of urban waterfront environments and in facilitating public participation in urban waterfront revitalization.

A significant part of the increased environmental awareness deals with aesthetics, the visual landscape and scenic resources. Visual resource management has developed to assist planners by providing technology to address challenges in landscape planning. The assessment systems and technology employed in this field are derived from a variety of academic and professional disciplines (e.g. psychology, architecture, landscape architecture, geography, economics, engineering, natural sciences, natural resource management), through interdisciplinary approaches, and make use of descriptive, computerized, quantitative, psychometric and special scientific approaches.

There are two major types of systems employed in visual resource management:
(a) *Expert professional judgment systems:* They use professional planning and design norms to evaluate landscape qualities; in such an approach, variables are selected arbitrarily, and the scoring values are therefore arbitrary.
(b) *Public preference or empirical systems:* They evaluate peoples' preferences for various landscape characteristics.

For either system, numbers are assigned to each factor or variable, and the scores are then determined. To elicit responses, actual on-site visits, black and white photographs, colour slides, videotapes, line drawings, art pictures, and tachistoscopic [extremely brief exposure to the eye] projections are used.

A specific type of empirical assessment system is the visual environmental preference assessment, or, simply, visual preference, which requires participants to rate how much they like what black and white photographs show, using a Likert scale.

Visual preference offers an effective tool for obtaining peoples' perceptions of and preferences for urban waterfront projects, and is a necessary prelude to building consensus and mustering support for such projects. Asking people to share their visual images encourages them to participate and to provide feedback to planners and agency members sponsoring redevelopment efforts. Visual preference assessments can provide useful information to such people on all aspects of planning and decision-making.

Seabrooke and Miles[20] and Johnson and Seabrooke[2] proposed three factors to be considered in the evaluation of a natural environmental site. These factors, which are related to location, site attraction and carrying capacity, will influence people's perceptions and preferences with respect to urban waterfront projects. They are:

Location factors: The relationship between the location of a site and its accessibility to the people for whom it is intended to be attractive is fundamental to any resource evaluation. The distance that day trippers will casually cover from home by car should be considered.

Site attraction: The most positive influence on the value of a site in recreational use is its ability to attract visitors. For water-based recreation, the site may:
• offer special physical water conditions (sheltered, safe/exposed, exhilarating);
• be where facilities, such as marinas or clubhouses, exist;
• be near to competition areas; and
• be naturally beautiful, as are some harbours or beaches.

The attractiveness of a site may be categorized by the site's distinctiveness, available quality, quality of management, and price. Matching the physical characteristics of the site with specific activities is a routine stage in evaluation.

Carrying capacity: Management needs to balance the attraction of visitors against the likelihood of their causing an unacceptable deterioration which could have a resultant knock-on effect from the recreational experience to the likelihood of a return visit. However, when people are involved in the evaluation of urban waterfront projects, planners should take into account the perceptual and social carrying capacity. Sites can be said to have a perceptual or social carrying capacity which relates to people's perceptions of other users and the extent to which this affects their enjoyment[21, 7], affecting the quality of their leisure experience. The type, numbers and speed of craft and the behaviour of their occupants in

relation to the attributes of the leisure experience sought by an individual will determine that individual's perception of the density of occupation and the carrying capacity of the site.[22, 7] Individuals seeking quiet enjoyment may similarly have the quality of their leisure experience affected by the shore-side by-products of water-side recreation, as, for example, noise generated by radios, dogs and even children.

Urban waterfront revitalization may be a valid enterprise for all cities on the coasts of sea, rivers, lakes, bays and oceans that have rediscovered their long waterfronts. But the form the revitalization takes should be different – as different as each city's history. The particular combination of tools and techniques used should reflect the needs, interests, resources, and constraints of each city; and visual preference serves as a promising strategy for determining what these are.[15]

Conclusion and recommendations

Alexandria's coastal zone has undergone great pressure for participation in recreational activities, especially in the summer. This pressure has prompted attention to the implementation of an effective system for managing its resources. The recent discovery of submerged ruins in the Eastern Harbour has also encouraged coastal planners to give full consideration to its cultural and historical values.

The following recommendations are made:
(a) Technical and financial assistance should be provided for the sustainable re-development of deteriorating urban waterfronts and for the sensitive preservation and restoration of historic, cultural and aesthetic coastal features.

[20] Seabrooke, W. and Miles, C. (1992). Recreation Land Management. E. & F. N. Spon, London.
[21] Curry, N. (1994). Countryside Recreation: Access and Land-use Planning. E & F. N. Spon, London.
[22] Ashton, P. G. and Chubb, M. (1972). A preliminary study for evaluating the capacity of waters for recreational boating. Water Resources Bulletin, 8:571–7.

(b) In the light of various proposals on the exploitation of the Eastern Harbour area, including the submerged relics of our ancient civilization, management of sustainable coastal development should aim to improve, safeguard and restore the quality of coastal waters, and to protect the natural, cultural and historical resources and existing uses of these waters.

(c) Land use in this coastal zone and the use of adjacent lands which drain into the coastal zone is significantly affecting the quality of the coastal waters. Therefore efforts to control water pollution from land-use activities must be improved.

(d) The co-ordination of, and co-operation among, different governmental agencies involved in planning, development and environment should be developed fully and applied also to international organizations involved. Such co-ordination and co-operation are concerned with collection, analysis, synthesis and dissemination of coastal management information, research results and technical assistance. Such an action will help to support governmental regulation of land-use practices affecting the coastal and marine resources.

(e) Coastal planners and developers should consider public participation as a key component in the success of any coastal management programme, especially when it comes to restrictions on land use, since wide public acceptance of the needed restrictions are only likely to be achieved if a careful job of explanation has been done.

(f) The rediscovery or revitalization of waterfronts, as in the case of the Eastern Harbour of Alexandria, and its potential sources of new income should be considered along with the conflict that may occur with the natural environment and coastal resources. Any relevant compromises that have to be made should be in favour of natural processes, not in favour of human activities. Any coastal land-use decisions should be made with full input from ecologists, as well as from local government officials, development authorities, economists and planners.

(g) Any re-development of the Eastern Harbour area should ensure that the public continues to have access to the coastal waters. Existing uses of these waters, such as commercial or sport fishery, should be protected.

(h) Implementing systems for evaluating people's preference towards proposed urban waterfront revitalization offers a useful tool for ensuring public support for such projects through participation and the provision of feedback to planners and agencies that are sponsoring re-development.

(i) Social or perceptual carrying capacity should be determined to improve the tourist's recreational experience and increase the potential for a return visit.

(j) The form of urban waterfront revitalization in Alexandria should be tailored to its history, needs, interests, resources and constraints. Revitalization of the Eastern Harbour waterfront should be developed in the light of the recent discovery of submerged antiquities.

In the same boat and learning the ropes
An Alexandria/Boston comparison

VICTOR T. MASTONE
Massachusetts Board of Underwater
Archaeological Resources

Introduction

I have included the metaphorical phrases 'in the same boat' and 'learning the ropes' to describe the theme of my presentation. Whether we are managing submerged cultural resources, here or anywhere on the globe, there are common issues and problems which place us 'in the same boat'. And as with learning the management of a ship's sails, the management of submerged heritage resources is very much a process of 'learning the ropes'.

Why compare Alexandria with any other place, such as Boston? While local circumstances are unique, there are issues that have a wider application beyond this city and the Mediterranean region. Through even the most casual observations, we readily see the region's [maritime] heritage in the form of monuments, palaces, fortifications, religious and domestic architecture, and harbour facilities. The same is true for the Boston Harbour region with its ship captains' homes, lighthouses, public buildings, fortifications, wharves and boatyards. While many of these terrestrial resources reflect the seaward nature of this heritage, a maritime legacy can be found in the submerged reaches of both regions as prehistoric sites, historical and modern shipwrecks, sunken buildings, disposal areas, and even aircraft. Both cities and both harbours offer an opportunity for the

interpretation of history side by side with the contemporary.

The heritage resources lying at the bottom of Boston Harbour may not have the same World Heritage values as those in Alexandria. However, the circumstances determining the potential to identify and exploit these resources are quite similar. More specifically, the Boston Harbour/Massachusetts experience has a number of parallels that provide a good basis for comparison. It is a major tourist destination. The Boston Harbour Islands was recently designated a National Recreation Area. In the 19th century, the coastal communities around Boston were developed as summer residences for the affluent. Boston Harbour is heavily polluted and the clean-up effort involves a sewage treatment project with an ocean outfall. The reconstruction and relocation of Boston's main transportation link requires extensive development in an historic area unearthing heritage resources.

Submerged cultural resources represent a non-renewable scientific resource: statements left by time to be preserved through their documentation for public study and benefit. The study of harbours offers the opportunity to examine the sweep of history rather than a point in time (time capsule) of synchronic resources, such as shipwrecks.

Rapid advances in technology, particularly for marine exploration, are revolutionizing capabilities to discover and exploit resources. The pace of their application to the discovery and recovery of submerged cultural resources has effectively shattered the access barrier. Access was a major limiting factor in the exploitation of these resources. In some respect, these technological advances have outstripped the institutional ability to ensure the appropriate management of the resource. The exploitation of submerged cultural resources is not a new phenomenon. Marine salvage has a long tradition developed from the need to protect lives and property and to maintain the highways of commerce and communication. Until recently, there was no need to accommodate or consider alternative natural and cultural uses of these resources. The recognition of these resources as habitat and heritage resources led to the need to create a new management regime governing their use. Frameworks and linkages must be established with agencies, other disciplines and individuals outside the traditional preservation community. These would recognize and accommodate a wide range of appropriate uses for these non-renewable resources. By viewing submerged heritage as a multiple-use resource, we assume these resources provide multiple benefits and values. To optimize the allocation of the benefits, there is a need for collaboration among the interested parties, the stakeholders, in designing and institutionalizing the management regime.

The management of heritage resources, whether terrestrial or submerged, involves a sequence of: (a) inventory (discovering and recording the resources present); (b) evaluation (determining their scientific and public importance); (c) planning (determining how they could be most appropriately used); (d) protection (safeguarding the resource); and (e) utilization (authorizing or otherwise accommodating the proper use). This regime could serve to integrate heritage concerns into the goals of all stakeholders.

Stakeholders

A wide variety of interest groups, stakeholders, are concerned, actually or potentially, with submerged cultural resources (such as historic shipwrecks), including:
Preservation – historians, conservators, archaeologists, history preservationists
Diving – diving clubs, diving instructors, sport divers, diving-boat operators, diving shops, diving certification organizations

Marine sciences – marine scientists, marine biologists, natural resource specialists, technology developers
Fishing – commercial fishermen, recreational fishermen, boaters, chartered fishing-boat operators, marina operators
Regulatory agents – governmental managers, law-enforcement officers
Information – journalists/writers, educators
Commercial interests – salvage companies, technological services

While these categories represent the major interest groups, they cannot be viewed as mutually exclusive. The type and extent of exploitation varies among them. There is overlap, competition and conflict; some types can be described as symbiotic, and others, parasitic. Additionally, the use, or rather exploitation, of these resources can be characterized as destructive or non-destructive. The appropriate management regime would demonstrate conceptually, then practically, that stakeholders can work together and that they add value.

There are several ways to view the potential benefits and values of submerged cultural resources. They include: commercial advantage (traditional salvage); recreational value; ecological/habitat (cost of replication) value; educational value; and historical/archaeological value. However, it might be more appropriate to redefine value in terms of the effects of exploitation due to the activities of the stakeholders. Value can be more simply defined in several broad areas:
Commercial value – financial (profit)
Intellectual value – historical/archaeological
Public value – multiple concerns
Other value – to be defined
In this way, one might be able to incorporate these values and their associated issues directly into the management regime.

Commercial value

Commercial value can be defined as the income derived from the direct sale of objects themselves and/or the income derived from the sale of ancillary materials such as reproductions, print media, books, video/movie rights and royalties, etc. However, commercial value may be viewed more broadly as a mechanism by which a project's sponsor raises capital (investors) to undertake the venture. This is becoming increasingly evident with respect to the development and application of advanced technology.

In addition, commercial value may be viewed as a subset of recreational value. That is the income derived from charters and equipment sale and rental. There is the indirect cost (income) derived from SCUBA certification programmes and related diving literature. This could be expanded to consider encompassing the entire range of economic impacts related to the expenditure patterns of divers: food and lodging costs, travel costs, etc. Numerous accommodations and good transportation attract more people who in turn visit resources. The impact on resources can be viewed in relation to the ability of support facilities to improve and/or increase access to resources.

Public value

Through structural deterioration and plant/animal colonization, submerged cultural resources are transformed from their original function into habitats. In the case of shipwrecks, their value to the stream of commerce no longer manifests itself in the cargoes carried or the functioning of the vessel, but rather in its ability to function as a habitat and thereby support the food web. In economic terms, it might be viewed as ecological/habitat value as derived from the cost of replication. Ancient sites would achieve not only biological value, but also historical and/or archaeological value.

As with commercial value, the diverse recreational activities, particularly related to diving, fishing and heritage tourism, can have a significant effect on the resource. Since benefit is derived, these activities can be assigned to public value.

Intellectual value

Intellectual value, or more simply archaeological value, is defined as the information derived from the objects and their context. The issue of re-study, including access to the information, objects or previous analyses, powers the strong ethical arguments against commercial exploitation. Removal of archaeological materials, be they tools, pottery or dwellings, can diminish or even destroy the value of the site for future study. Often, sites are best preserved intact and *in situ*. Moreover, in the case of historic shipwrecks, there is an intellectual value which may or may not have a fiscally assignable value.

The changing view of multiple-use values assignable to submerged cultural resources means that these resources could possess historical value, and that there exists competing interest in these resources. Access to these resources for recreation must be guaranteed. Management responsibility for these resources is vested in governments. Therefore, governments must develop management policies that accommodate a wide range of appropriate uses for these non-renewable resources.

In Boston Harbour (as well as elsewhere in the United States), a mechanism for accommodation and collaboration exists across various governmental management structures. Heritage interests are integrated into an individual agency in the form of specific agency personnel. Certain agencies are charged with a heritage mission, and their staff members have a role to advocate heritage issues in organizations whose missions are not heritage-oriented, such as those concerned mainly with economic development or construction. Fortunately, this development took place over the past several decades in a benign budgetary and regulatory climate; today, with tight budgetary constraints and a different government philosophy, this regulatory infrastructure would not exist. By eliminating the adversarial role, stakeholder and non-stakeholder interests can be reconciled.

Established in 1973, the Massachusetts Board of Underwater Archaeological Resources is the trustee of the State's underwater heritage. The Board works to protect the State's proprietary, scientific and historical interest in these resources. It maintains a balance between these diverse and sometimes conflicting constituencies and the interests of the State. The Massachusetts programme is viewed as a model management scheme.

The nine-member State Board is administered by the Executive Office of Environmental Affairs. The Executive Office is responsible for the protection and enhancement of the Commonwealth's [State of Massachusetts] natural resources; one of the agency's diverse missions is to enhance public access to historic and scenic resources. The Board membership is composed of: four statutory appointments – the State Archaeologist, the State Archivist, the Commissioner of Waterways, and the Director of Mineral Resources; and five gubernatorial appointments – one representative of the Massachusetts Historical Commission, one marine archaeologist, one law-enforcement specialist, and two representatives of the diving community. The statutory composition of the Board is an early recognition of the need to bring the major constituencies and critical technical knowledge into the management scheme. The Board's staff undertakes a programme of public outreach, project review, technical assistance, resource identification, inventory and assessment.

Those granted permits by the Board work with the Board to maximize the cultural value of the site, while enjoying the Board's protection of their proprietary interest in the site. Board permittees are required to provide all necessary resources to complete their projects and demonstrate their financial ability to carry out their plans. Depending on the nature of the resource and the proposed activities, permittees are required to have a project staff (research team) which could include a project archaeologist and a project conservator. Work is undertaken in conformity with an approved research design/work plan.

The Board currently has issued twelve active permits. Permittees range from individual sport divers to commercial

ventures to museums. An applicant must provide demonstrable proof (documentary evidence alone is insufficient) to be granted a permit. The Board grants two types of permit: reconnaissance and excavation. Permits are granted for a period of one year and are renewable. The majority of the permits are issued as reconnaissance permits which can be best characterized by non-disruptive research activities aimed at site identification and delimitation; excavation is prohibited and recovery is limited to surface finds. Excavation permits are required when any destructive activities are to be undertaken, ranging from test excavations to mitigation. Permit areas (not to exceed one nautical mile square) are located across the state's coastal and inland waters.

To deal with certain types of artefact discoveries, the Board's regulations provide an exemption from the permit process for isolated finds, exempted sites, and underwater archaeological preserves. The Board maintains a list of such sites. The intention in creating an exempted site list is to preserve shipwrecks for the continued enjoyment of the recreational diving community. Recreational diving on exempted sites does not require a permit from the Board. However, any major disruption of these sites is prohibited. The recreational diving community is encouraged to work with the Board to protect these sites for the continued enjoyment of all.

The Board may designate underwater archaeological preserves to provide special protection to those underwater archaeological resources of substantial historical value. Access to underwater archaeological preserves for recreational, historical and scientific purposes shall be guaranteed. It will serve to encourage the public enjoyment, use and appreciation of the resource.

The various stakeholders must collaborate with archaeologists and cultural-resource managers. There is a need to identify and characterize impacts, clarify issues of professional responsibility and standards, and improve cross-disciplinary understanding and awareness of the diverse concerns associated with these resources. The following examples from the Boston experience illustrate adversarial and collaborative aspects of the management regime.

Outfall and power-supply cable sitings

The construction of the sewage-treatment facility serving 2.6 million people includes the installation of several miles of new buried submarine power cables and an outfall effluent disposal site nine miles seawards from the city. Remote sensing surveys were undertaken to collect data for engineering and archaeological purposes. Unfortunately, these efforts were not co-ordinated at the research-design level. While the data suited engineering purposes, they were inadequate for archaeological interpretation. Additional survey work was required to meet archaeological needs; the work was essentially done twice (increased cost and time lost), owing to a lack of co-ordination.

Artificial-reef placement

As part of project mitigation (Spectacle Island, see below), proponents are required to replicate habitats lost to construction. It was determined that an artificial reef would be created to replace lost habitat. Research, including remote sensing and visual inspection, was undertaken to ensure that the new habitat did not adversely affect submerged cultural resources, as well as to assess the viability of the site from a habitat perspective. In this case, data collection and evaluation were co-ordinated to meet engineering, archaeological and biological needs, with results satisfactory to all parties.

Tea-party tea-chest search

The Boston Tea Party has become a symbolic event in the history of the American War of Independence from England. Today, a replica ship exists with daily re-enactments of the event. In some respects, it is a cultural icon. There is one known tea chest in existence. If another could be discovered archaeologically, it would have both intellectual and commercial value. With much orchestrated

press coverage, an applicant attempted to pressure the State into sanctioning recovery efforts. Poor historical research was undertaken and evidence completely inconsistent with the resource sought was offered as proof of the existence of the resource. The fact that the actual event site was several city blocks away, under landfill and a building, was initially ignored by the applicant. A permit was not granted. In the end, the press felt manipulated. The project could not be successful because it was couched in adversarial terms of public perspective versus the professional perspective. It did not capitalize on available data or collaborative relationships. The project's proponent failed to read his Boston Strabo.

British evacuation project

In an effort to capitalize on another event in the history of the American Revolution, the evacuation and abandonment of Boston by British troops, an application was filed with the Board. The location, Long Wharf, exists as an historic resource today. Sufficient proof was presented to grant a permit. When positive results were not immediately achieved and press coverage waned, the permittee sharply curtailed research activities. The city ordered the fieldwork to be stopped, when it was revealed that these activities were stirring up pollutants. Better background research and alternative field methods might have achieved a different result. As with the Tea Chest Search, this project failed because it was couched in adversarial terms of public perspective versus the professional perspective.

Spectacle Island expansion

As part of the massive highway project and sewer-tunnel project, a fill disposal site was needed. It was determined that Spectacle Island in Boston Harbour would be greatly enlarged. Extensive geological coring and boring samples were collected to support this undertaking. The data were re-analysed to produce a geomorphological history of the island and its surroundings. This analysis assisted the interpretation of the island's archaeological sites and the evolution of the harbour. It resulted in the creation of a web site depicting the island's natural and cultural history – essentially an on-line exhibit. The enlarged island will become a new recreation area. This project demonstrates that collaboration adds value to all components and for all the stakeholders.

Clearly, successful collaboration must involve the use and distribution of data. As we see when stakeholders do not co-ordinate, or take adversarial roles, the results are unsatisfactory for all parties.

The Massachusetts programme has attempted to bring the various stakeholders together to manage jointly the submerged heritage properties in state waters. The approach balances traditional uses with contemporary views of the value of these resources. There is an attempt to accommodate conflicting commercial and historical values of these resources. The newly created underwater archaeological preserves will provide a non-destructive recreational outlet, encourage scientific research and elevate the public's awareness of the State's submerged heritage. The Massachusetts programme depends heavily on active involvement of the public, whether as Board members, permittees or casual visitors to the State's resources, to identify, evaluate and protect these non-renewable resources. In conclusion, Alexandria, with its World Heritage resources and concerned public, is in a unique position to provide a showcase for successful collaboration.

Urban design and eco-tourism: The Alexandria Comprehensive Master Plan

MOHSEN ZAHRAN
Professor of Urban Planning
University of Alexandria
Chairman of the Alexandria Planning
Commission

Introduction

The city of Alexandria was founded by
Alexander the Great and planned by
Denocratis in 332 BC. Stretched out linearly
for 25 km between the Mediterranean Sea
and Lake Mariout, it is considered one of the
oldest living metropolises in the world.
Today, it is the second largest city in Egypt
and in Africa, and is recognized as a major
port in the Mediterranean, as well as being a
principal industrial and tourist centre.
Alexandria is the primary centre of
commercial, business and cultural activity in
lower Egypt, and is recognized nationally as
the capital of the Western Delta's economic
region which comprises three important
governorates. As such, this great metropolis
has attracted continual waves of immigrants,
allowing strong vertical and horizontal
mobility, thus influencing the pattern and
tempo of urbanization and the state of the
city's environmental health.

Population

The present population of greater Alexandria
borders on four million people, increasing at
a rate of about 3.8% per annum. This is high
in comparison with 2.5% in neighbouring
governorates. During the crowded, hot
summer months, tourism in this famous
seaside resort may add to the city as many as
2.2 million tourists from all over Egypt, as
well as from some other Arab countries. This
seasonal influx drastically increases the
population to approximately five million
residents, overtaxing its roads, traffic,
utilities and services.

The overall population density was about
975 persons per square kilometre in 1986,
compared to 856 persons per square
kilometre in 1976 and 672 persons per
square kilometre in 1966. The most crowded
district, locally and nationally, is the El-
Gomrock district, near the port, with a
density of 133,000 persons per square
kilometre.

Housing and health

The housing situation in Alexandria is a
major source of health and environmental
problems. These are due to the following
factors:
(a) Informal housing is commonplace.
(b) Shantytowns and squatter settlements are
mushrooming in the southern and western
districts.
(c) The deterioration of housing stock,
especially in the old quarters, is alarming.
(d) There is a major shortage of housing
stock generally.
(e) There is a widening gap between housing
supply and demand, particularly for housing
the lower income groups.
(f) Rent and land values, as well as
condominium prices, are spiralling beyond
the affordability of the majority of the
resident population.

(g) There is a shortage of building materials.

(h) There is a continuing increase in construction materials and labour costs, which reflects on housing costs.

(i) Housing patterns and design seem to be orthodox and too regimented, owing mostly to restrictive building and housing laws and rent controls.

In addition, despite the continuing tide of migration, the average household size in Alexandria is 4.9 people as compared to 5.2 nationally (1976). The occupancy ratio was recorded in 1976 as 1.9 persons per room, as compared to 1.8 nationally. The total number of dwelling units was 400,000 units.

Water supply and sewage

Alexandria seems to have a better standard and availability of utilities than other governorates in Egypt. Yet, 10% of households are still not connected to the electricity grid, and more than 20% of households do not have a private drinking-water tap, although 98% of dwelling units have access to the public water supply. This is a very bright picture, of course, when compared to the waste-water network which only served 40% of the city up to 1983 and will serve about 70% by the end of this year, after the implementation of a major waste-water project, in which major improvements (new treatment plants) and overhauling are being implemented. The city of Alexandria is served by a combined sanitary and drainage system which is more than seventy years old. However, the present utility capacity cannot cope with the continuing urban development.

Air, water and noise pollution and industrial waste

Pollution in an expanding metropolis, as in Alexandria, is a common phenomenon. Air pollution from car exhaust is omnipresent, now that car ownership has more than

quadrupled during the last decade, although the north winds, when prevailing, seem to dissipate it. Gas and dust emissions from factories to the east, as well as from seasonal sand-bearing winds in the west, require measures to control health and environmental hazards caused by alarming pollution levels. Gases produced by industrial and waste-water effluents in Lake Mariout cause unpleasant and noxious odours that engulf the Cairo–Alexandria Desert Expressway on approaching the city from the south. This, of course, adds to the water pollution of the Lake itself, endangering sea life and hampering fishing. Waste-water effluent is still dumped into the Mediterranean Sea, although there are legal measures and protocols to control water pollution. Owing to the high cost of anti-pollution devices, efforts to control industrial pollution are hampered, and there is laxity in the enforcement of the relevant regulations.

Noise and visual pollution, as well as congestion, are also beyond normal acceptable levels, and they too require more drastic and stern intervention to reduce the number of violations by individuals and by private/public sector companies.

Solid-waste management

The collection and disposal of solid waste lacks proper management. Such waste is a primary source of health and visual hazards. The urban pattern does not allow either for collection points or for easy truck access. Lack of commitment and improper conduct by the citizenry and the waste collectors contribute to continually growing piles of refuse everywhere. City refuse dumps are located farther and farther away from local districts, which overtax the limited fleet capacity to collect solid waste from all districts. Donkey-drawn garbage carts are still playing an important role in collection, but this practice does not complement collection policy or strategy. There is a limited refuse-treatment capacity which needs to be doubled in various districts.

Social services

The circulation and transport networks are generally adequate in new areas. Narrow streets and alleys in inner-city districts, as well as in marginal and slum areas, hamper the flow of traffic and cause congestion. They also hamper the access of fire and emergency vehicles. Although twenty-two new classrooms are built daily, the number and facilities of public schools are in great shortage, making it necessary for some schools to work in two or even three daily shifts. Schoolyards have been generally taken over for building new classrooms, depriving pupils of the needed athletic and sport facilities. Overcrowded classrooms (reaching sixty pupils per classroom in some districts) hamper learning and overburden teachers. Naturally, such overcrowding and lack of facilities contribute to intolerable hazards and threats to public safety, public health, educational standards and learning.

Green space and recreational facilities

The size and percentage of green areas throughout the city have been dwindling during the last few decades. It has fallen to 1/3 acre per 1,000 inhabitants with very few additions in existing districts, despite the quadrupling of the total population. Other than the recent establishment of the International Garden (Fig. 1), which constitutes the real addition of 150 acres during this century, new communities are being provided with adequate open space and sport facilities, but drastic addition and improvement of recreational areas are needed in crowded districts and in slum areas.

The Alexandria 2005 Comprehensive Master Plan

Alexandria has a distinctive character that derives fundamentally from its ribbon-like development along the Mediterranean coast of Egypt. The city's development has centered principally on its importance as a port and trading centre, and more recently on its value as a major coastal tourist resort and industrial centre. The importance of these activities to the present local economy is indicated below:
(a) The port of Alexandria handles 80% of Egypt's shipping.
(b) Alexandria attracts 2.2 million tourists each year.
(c) Alexandria's manufacturing industry constitutes 38% of Egypt's industrial activity.
Until recently the scale of unanticipated growth had not threatened Alexandria's unique character and historical heritage. But now there is an urgent need to house the growing population (expected to reach 7.75 million by the year 2005) and to improve the deteriorating condition of many existing houses. This situation has been made worse by the inflation of land values and building costs. In addition, there is a need to protect irreplaceable agricultural land from sprawling urban development, to manage industrial expansion and to reduce the serious erosion of Alexandria's beaches. There is therefore an urgent need to adopt a sound comprehensive master plan for systematic development. The key factors of such a structural plan are outlined as follows:
(d) The growth in population.
(e) Deteriorating housing conditions.
(f) Increasing land values and construction costs.
(g) Preservation of the historical heritage.
(h) Protection of agricultural land.
(i) Management of industrial expansion.
(j) Control of environmental pollution and beach erosion.

The Comprehensive Master Plan strategy

(a) The Comprehensive Master Plan is intended not only to deal with the problems of Alexandria's expansion, but also to be compatible with the plans for the new city of Amriah (to the west) and the recommendations of the North Coast Tourist Development Plan.

(b) The fundamental concern of the Alexandria Comprehensive Master Plan is how best to deal with the anticipated growth in population of approximately two million people above the present population of about four million inhabitants and yet maintain favourable environmental conditions. The intention is to develop an extensive expansion area to the west of the city. This decision was taken so as to preserve the valuable agricultural land located south-east of the city.

(c) The Plan attempts to preserve the unique coastal character of Alexandria as an important tourist centre, and is especially concerned with the preservation of Alexandria's unique historical heritage.

(d) The expansion zone from east to west surrounds Lake Mariout which will thus provide two more extensive waterfronts for urban development and will increase the recreational and commercial opportunities for the city.

(e) The southern limit for Alexandria's expansion is to be defined by a 'green belt'. This buffer zone will protect the agricultural land and restrict industrial expansion. The green belt will also act as the southern boundary of the western expansion zone.

(f) A broad zone, running south from the new port of Dekheila, has been designated for existing and proposed industry. Such a zone will reduce the inherent conflict between industrial and residential areas.

(g) The Plan establishes a comprehensive circulation network to link the city from east to west, and provides a number of axes along which the city can be approached and tied to regional circulation networks.

(h) The Plan capitalizes on the development of the city's archaeological and touristic resources and further develops facilities and amenities to enhance and promote these major assets.

(i) The Plan proposes major programmes of housing development, serving a variety of population groups, especially the low and limited-income groups.

(j) The Plan bans or controls water pollution of waterfront beaches and recreational lakes. It proposes the use of primary-treated waste water as a major resource in land reclamation with a view to increasing agrarian production and employment opportunities.

(k) To overcome the present lack of adequate open and recreational space, the Plan proposes a hierarchical system of playgrounds, parks and exposition facilities to be planned city-wide.

(l) Downtown Alexandria is to be revitalized through urban-renewal projects in inner-city districts, in addition to the provision of an efficient urban transport system.

(m) The city is sub-divided into various zones of definite building heights and floor area ratios, depending on location, character and intensity of activity.

(n) The Plan defines city limits within a green belt beyond which no urbanization is to be allowed.

(o) The Plan is a continuing process that should be periodically monitored, reviewed and updated, taking into account the material and human resources which are always in flux.

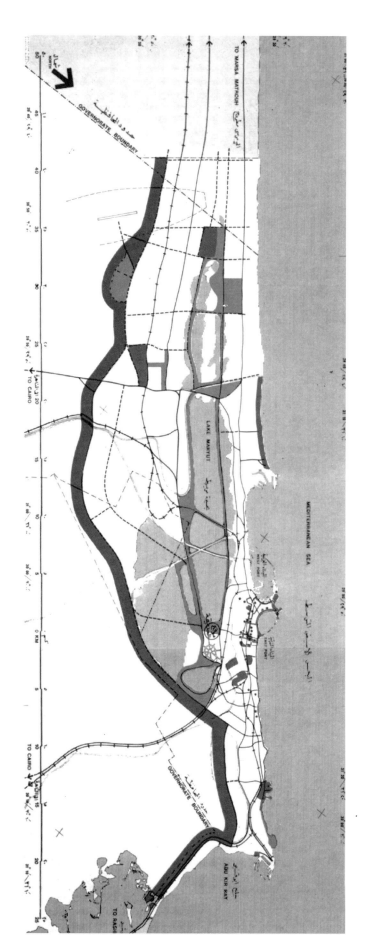

Figure 1.
Map of Alexandria showing the disposition of green spaces, including the International Garden. At lower edge, thick dark line represents the green belt, and generally delimits the City of Alexandria. The grey shading represents proposed (particularly around Lake Mariout) and existing recreation areas; several tourist landmarks and trails are concentrated around the area of the East, and to a lesser extent, the West Ports.

International Workshop on Submarine Archaeology and Coastal Management
Recommendations

The Declaration of Alexandria

The significance of Alexandria in history has made the threat on its land and marine archaeological sites a matter of urgent concern to Egypt and the world.

The recommendations below dealing with the erosion under the Qait Bey fortress and long term preservation and management of the cultural assets of Alexandria have been made by the scientific community attending the International Workshop on "Submarine Archaeology and Coastal Management". With the cooperation of the world community, we believe that Egypt will be able to succeed in the above goals; and preserve the cultural heritage of the City of Alexandria as part of the heritage of us all.

10 April 1997,

Alexandria, Egypt

Recommendations

To the National Authorities, including:
Egyptian Environmental Affairs Agency
Ministry of Culture (Supreme Council of Antiquities)
Ministry of Public Works and Water Resources (Coastal Research Institute) and (Coastal Protection Authority)
Ministry of Tourism
Ministry of Education
Ministry of Transport
Ministry of Defense
Governorate of Alexandria

Recognizing the necessity of a strategic framework for future management of underwater and onshore cultural heritage and the need for urgent action to protect and preserve the Qait Bey/Pharos area, *the workshop recommends*:

I. Qait Bey/Pharos area Pilot Project

1. An assessment be made of the present condition of the Qait Bey Citadel and the threat of erosion to this Citadel. For this assessment, a request to UNESCO be considered, to solicit its assistance in identifying and dispatching competent international experts in engineering and coastal processes. The nature of such an intervention should take into consideration the need to protect and preserve the integrity of both the submerged Lighthouse site and the Citadel.

2. Concurrently, a targeted program to collect key environmental data be implemented immediately in order to rapidly identify (4–6 months time) temporary remedial actions. These temporary actions are to stabilize the erosion threatening the Citadel without compromising the integrity of the underwater archaeological site until such time as a lasting solution can be found.

3. No remedial action, including the further placing of cement blocks, should take place until completion of the assessment of the situation of the Citadel and the proposal of temporary solutions after collection, analysis and interpretation of key environmental data, nor without consultation of all appropriate agencies and experts.

4. In addition, the competent archaeological experts be requested to complete to the extent possible, the surveying and mapping of the underwater archaeological site of the Lighthouse.

5. The aforementioned data collection program be extended and if necessary expanded in order to provide the environmental information required to identify and implement a long-term and lasting solution which to the greatest extent possible maintains the integrity of both cultural heritage sites.

6. An ad hoc Task Force, possibly coordinated by UNESCO, be established whose membership should include the relevant decision-making bodies such as the Egyptian Environmental Affairs Agency, the Supreme Council of Antiquities, the Coastal Protection Authority, the Ministry of Transport (marine transport), the Coastal Research Institute, the University of Alexandria and the Governorate of Alexandria and other relevant bodies, along with experts in submarine archaeology and coastal processes. This cross-sectoral Task Force will be responsible for setting an overall strategy for implementing and monitoring this pilot project.

II. Long term management plan:

1. A strategic framework be drafted for the conservation and integrated management of the coastal heritage (cultural and natural) to be incorporated into the coastal management plan of the Egyptian Environmental Affairs Agency.

2. The placement of concrete blocks inside or outside the Eastern Harbour, and any increased use or activity in the Eastern Harbour and Qait Bey be stopped until the proposed survey

recommended in para. 3 has been completed, and urgent action be taken to stop the discharge of sewage into the Eastern Harbour.

3. To survey the archaeological sites and the geomorphological and hydrodynamic processes environmental conditions and state of pollution of the coast of Greater Alexandria; and that experts and agencies transmit to the Department of Underwater Archaeology of the Supreme Council of Antiquities all information on the coastal heritage (cultural and natural) of Alexandria.

4. On the basis of the survey, to set the priorities for the critical problems faced and to direct the continuing monitoring of the area.

5. The existing laws be studied to ensure that the special problems of the underwater archaeological sites of Alexandria are appropriately dealt with and in particular:
a) The Supreme Council of Antiquities be included as one of the responsible agencies concerned with the protection of the water environment (Law No. 4 on the Environment, Art. 1.38);
b) The possibility of establishing a special legal status for the underwater archaeological sites of Alexandria be studied as well as the possibility of inscription on the World Heritage List.

6. The potential economic value of the archaeological sites of Alexandria for tourists and visitors be studied, e.g. by way of museums, archaeological parks (on-land or underwater).

7. A small group be established to follow up the recommendations of this workshop, to prepare project proposals and investigate funding possibilities.

Addendum

The workshop further recognized
the importance of the following issues:

• The University of Alexandria should consider developing specialized courses for graduate and under-graduate students on submarine archaeology and related disciplines; it should also consider open education for the public at large.

• The need to promote awareness of public at large including youth through media coverage and dissemination of information, on the value and the significance of the coastal (natural and cultural) heritage of humanity.

• Participants attending this workshop expressed the wish, to convene an international conference on Underwater Archaeology and Coastal Management in 1999.

• The participants wish to express their thanks to national organizations and to UNESCO and other international organizations for sponsoring and financing the workshop.

• The participants also wish to express their appreciation to the Egyptian Navy and to the international community for their cooperation which led to the remarkable archaeological discoveries at Qait Bey and the Eastern Harbour.

Contributors

FATMA ABOU SHOUK
Environment Department,
60 Horria Street,
Alexandria Governorate,
Alexandria,
Egypt.
fax: (20-3) 484 7192

OSSAMA M. T. ABOUL DAHAB
Oceanography Department,
Faculty of Science,
Alexandria University,
Moharram Bey,
Alexandria,
Egypt.
fax: (20-3) 491 1794

DENIS AELBRECHT
Laboratoire National
d'Hydraulique,
Direction des Études et
Recherches, EDF,
6, quai Watier,
B.P. 49,
78401 Chatou Cedex,
France.
fax: (33-1) 30 87 80 86
e-mail: denis.aelbrecht@edf.fr

NICOLA BONACASA
Director,
Archaeological Institute,
Palermo University,
Facoltà di Lettere,
Viale delle Scienze,
90128 Palermo,
Italy.
fax: (39-091) 6560268 / 6421494
e-mail: bonacasa@ipalet.unipa.it

H. ARNOLD CARR
American Underwater Search
and Survey, Ltd.,
Box 768,
Cataumet, MA 02534-0768,
USA.
fax: (1-508) 564-6600
e-mail: a.carrauss@aol.com

NEAL W. DRISCOLL
Clark Laboratory,
Woods Hole Oceanographic
Institution,
Woods Hole, MA 02543,
USA.

MOSTAFA EL-ABBADI
Archaeology Department,
Faculty of Arts,
University of Alexandria,
Alexandria,
Egypt.
or
27, Abdel Hamid Badawi St,
Azarita, Alexandria,
Egypt
fax: (20-3) 483 3088
　　　(20-3) 483 3136 (Faculty)

IBTEHAL Y. EL-BASTAWISSI
Department of Architecture,
Faculty of Engineering,
University of Alexandria,
Alexandria,
Egypt.
fax: (20-3) 586 2107
e-mail: aielawi@aast.egnet.net

FAROUK EL-BAZ
Director,
Center for Remote Sensing,
Boston University,
725 Commonwealth Avenue,
Boston, MA 02215-1401,
USA.
fax: (1-617) 353 3200
e-mail: farouk@bu.edu

AHMED ABDEL HAMID EL-GINDY
Oceanography Department,
Faculty of Science,
Alexandria University,
Alexandria,
Egypt.

OMRAN EL SAYED FRIHY
Coastal Research Institute,
15 El-Pharaana St., El-Shallalat,
21514 Alexandria,
Egypt.
fax: (20-3) 484 4614

JEAN-YVES EMPEREUR
Directeur, Centre National de la
Recherche Scientifique,
Centre d'Études Alexandrines,
50, Rue Soliman Yousri,
21131 Alexandria,
Egypt.
fax: (20-3) 484 6245
e-mail: jye@cea.com.eg

ENRICO FELICI
Associazione Italiana
Archeologi Subacquei
(A.I.A. Sub.),
via Tripolitania, 195,
00199 Roma,
Italy.
fax: (39-06) 86208038

HONOR FROST
31 Welbeck Street,
London W1M 7PG,
England.

FRANCK GODDIO
Institut européen d'archéologie
sous-marine (IEASM),
41-43, rue de Cronstadt,
75015 Paris,
France.
fax: (33-1) 45 49 18 03

NICOLAS GRIMAL
Former Director,
Institut français d'archéologie
orientale,
37, rue el-Cheikh Aly Youssef,
B.P. 11562 Qasr el-Ayni,
11441 Cairo,
Egypt.
fax: (20-2) 354 4635
e-mail: ngrimal@ifao.egnet.net

HALA HALIM
97 Abdel Salam Aref St.,
Glym, Alexandria,
Egypt.
fax: (20-3) 545 7611
e-mail: hhalim@humnet.ucla.edu
(Hala Youssef Halim)

YOUSSEF HALIM
Oceanography Department,
Faculty of Science,
Alexandria University,
Alexandria Governorate,
Alexandria 21511,
Egypt.
fax: (20-3) 545 7611
e-mail: asclub@soficom.com.eg

MOSTAFA HASSAN MOSTAFA
Vice President,
Graduate Studies and Research,
University of Alexandria,
Alexandria,
Egypt.
fax: (20-3) 595 2715

DIMITRIS KAZIANIS
Department of Underwater
Antiquities,
30, Kallisperi str.,
117 42 Athens,
Greece.
fax: (30-1) 92 35 707 / 92 21 888

VICTOR T. MASTONE
Director,
Board of Underwater
Archaeological Resources,
Executive Office of
Environmental Affairs,
Suite 2000,
100 Cambridge Street,
Boston, MA 02202,
USA.
fax: (1-617) 727 2754
e-mail:
victor.mastone@state.ma.us

J.-M. MENON
Laboratoire National
d'Hydraulique,
Direction des Études et
Recherches,
Électricité de France (EDF),
6, Quai Watier, BP 49,
78401 Chatou Cedex,
France.
fax: (33-1) 30 87 80 86
e-mail: jean-michel.menon@edf.fr

SELIM A. MORCOS
28204 Kenton Lane,
Santa Clarita, CA 91350,
USA.
fax: (1-661) 296-1034
e-mail: selimmorx@aol.com

ALFY MORCOS FANOS
Director,
Coastal Research Institute,
15 El-Pharaana St.,
El-Shallalat,
21514 Alexandria,
Egypt.
fax: (20-3) 484 4614

DOUGLAS NAKASHIMA
Coastal Regions and Small
Islands Unit (CSI),
UNESCO,
1, rue Miollis,
75732 Paris Cedex 15,
France.
fax: (33-1) 45 68 58 08
e-mail: d.nakashima@unesco.org

VINCENT NÉGRI
21 rue René Leynaud,
69001 Lyon,
France.
fax: (33-4) 72 00 44 57
e-mail: negri@culture.fr

IVÁN NEGUERUELA
Director,
Museo Nacional de Arqueología
Marítima y Centro Nacional de
Investigaciones
Arqueológicas Submarinas,
Ministerio de Educación y
Cultura, Dique de Navidad,
Apdo. de Correos 72,
30280 Cartagena,
Spain.
fax: (34-9) 68 52 96 92

ERIC PELTIER
Électricité de France (EDF),
Direction des Études et
Recherches,
Les Renardières,
77818 Moret-sur-Loing Cedex,
France.
fax: (33-1) 60 73 75 69
e-mail: eric.peltier@edf.fr

LYNDEL V. PROTT
Chief,
International Standards Section,
Cultural Heritage Division,
UNESCO,
1, rue Miollis,
75732 Paris Cedex 15,
France.
e-mail: l.prott@unesco.org

ANGELIKI SIMOSSI
Department of Underwater
Antiquities,
30, Kallisperi str.,
117 42 Athens,
Greece.
fax: (30-1) 92 35 707 / 92 21 888

VINCENZO SOMMELLA
ES s.r.l. - Progetti e Sistemi,
Via Zoe Fontana 220,
Tecnocitta ed. B1,
00131 Roma,
Italy.
fax: (39-06) 419 1713
e-mail: v.sommella@es-it.com

NILS TONGRING
Woods Hole Oceanographic
Institution,
Marine Policy Centre,
Woods Hole, MA 02543,
USA.
fax: (1-508) 457 2184
e-mail: ntongring@whoi.edu

HARRY E. TZALAS
Hellenic Institute for the
Preservation of Nautical
Tradition,
94 Skra, Kallithea,
Athens 17673,
Greece.
fax: (30-1) 95 64 388
e-mail: hmarine@hol.gr

HOWARD WELLMAN
Director of Conservation,
Institute of Nautical Archaeology
(INA),
P.O. Box 432, El-Ibrahimia,
Alexandria,
Egypt.
fax: (20-3) 546 6872
e-mail: ina_misr@acs.auc.eun.eg
or
106000.3617@compuserve.comp

MOHSEN ZAHRAN
Project Director,
Bibliotheca Alexandrina,
The Executive Secretariat,
Shallalat Bldg.,
116. El Horreya Av.,
P.O. Box 138, El Mansheya,
Bab Sharqi, Alexandria,
Egypt.
fax: (20-3) 483 6001
e-mail: mzahran@bibalex.gov.eg
      zahranba@frcu.eun.eg